中国文化双语用书

中国文化概论
（汉英对照）

Introduction to Chinese Culture

主　编　彭爱民
副主编　李　虹　高　涛　张桂群
　　　　李　俊　罗　彬　张桂香

暨南大學出版社
JINAN UNIVERSITY PRESS

中国·广州

图书在版编目（CIP）数据

中国文化概论：汉英对照/彭爱民主编. —广州：暨南大学出版社，2014.9
（2021.7 重印）
ISBN 978 – 7 – 5668 – 1153 – 0

Ⅰ.①中… Ⅱ.①彭… Ⅲ.①中华文化—汉、英 Ⅳ.①K203

中国版本图书馆 CIP 数据核字（2014）第 212711 号

中国文化概论：汉英对照
ZHONGGUO WENHUA GAILUN：HANYING DUIZHAO
主　编：彭爱民

···

出 版 人：张晋升
策划编辑：古碧卡
责任编辑：林丽旋
责任校对：王嘉涵
责任印制：周一丹　郑玉婷

出版发行：暨南大学出版社（510630）
电　　话：总编室（8620）85221601
　　　　　营销部（8620）85225284　85228291　85228292　85226712
传　　真：（8620）85221583（办公室）　85223774（营销部）
网　　址：http://www.jnupress.com
排　　版：广州市科普电脑印务部
印　　刷：佛山市浩文彩色印刷有限公司
开　　本：787mm×1092mm　1/16
印　　张：15
字　　数：371 千
版　　次：2014 年 9 月第 1 版
印　　次：2021 年 7 月第 4 次
定　　价：43.00 元

前　言

随着中国经济发展突飞猛进、经济实力不断提高，中国文化也越来越受外国人重视，"中国文化热"在世界各地不断升温。向全世界推介中国文化，让外国更加深刻了解中国文化，体会华夏文明的魅力，是新时代赋予我们外语工作者的光荣使命。

很多年前，编者就有了编写中英文双语教材的想法。经过多年的观察和酝酿，机会来了，本人终于有幸面向全学院开设"中国文化概论"这门公选课。然而，编教材难，编中英文教材更难。本教材是编者在三年的亲身教学基础上，牺牲自己的周末时间和寒暑假时间编写而成，经历了从编撰到编译的艰难过程。

本教材详尽论述了中国文化的基本精神、类型和主要特征，中国历史文化、传统文化、宗教文化、文学文化、饮食文化、医药文化、茶与酒文化、服饰文化、建筑文化、旅游文化、武术文化、节日文化，四大发明和万里长城，全书共十五章。

本教材的完成，不只是主编一人的心血，在此要特别感谢广东第二师范学院教务处的立项资助，感谢广东第二师范学院外语系同仁的鼓励与帮助，感谢暨南大学出版社领导对本教材出版的支持与帮助，感谢各位副主编付出的各种努力，同时还要感谢家人的支持与配合。

本教材适用于高等院校英语专业选修课和非英语专业公选课，也适用于出国留学人员和外国友人茶余饭后阅读。

由于编写人手和编写时间有限，书中难免有瑕疵，敬请各位读者指正。

本教材配有中英文教学用PPT，需要的老师可联系：allanpeng2004@163.com。

编者

2014 年 6 月于广州客村

目　录

第一章　中国文化的基本精神

Chapter 1　The Basic Spirit of Chinese Culture

经过几千年的发展，中国文化逐渐演变并形成了自己独特的精神，即中国文化的基本精神。中国文化的基本精神，是中华民族特定的价值体系、思维方式、社会心理、伦理观念、道德情操和审美情趣等精神特质的基本风貌的反映，是指长期受到人们推崇的思想观念或固有传统，成为人们生活和行动的最高原则。中国文化基本精神的优秀成分，构成中华民族的精神，成为推动中华民族不断前进的内在动力。

After thousands of years' development, Chinese culture has evolved and gradually formed its own unique spirit, namely, the basic spirit of Chinese culture, which is the reflection of basic styles and features of the ethos of a specific value system, ways of thinking, social psychology, ethics, moral sentiment and aesthetic taste of the Chinese nation, which refers to the ideas or inherent tradition people praise highly and has become the highest guiding principle for people's life and action. The outstanding ingredients of the basic spirit of Chinese culture have constituted the spirit of the Chinese nation and become the power to promote the progress of the Chinese nation.

中国文化的基本精神实质上是一种民族精神，是中华民族发展的精神动力和精神支柱，是民族文化的主导思想，是一种非常卓越的思想，它渗透于民族文化的优秀传统之中。

很多学者都定义过、研究过中国文化的基本精神，并对此产生了很多不同的看法。

在《论中国文化的基本精神》一文中，作者张岱年认为，中国文化长期发展的思想基础，可以叫做中国文化的基本精神。其主要内容包括：①刚健有为；②和与中；③崇德利用；④天人协调。

The basic spirit of Chinese culture is a kind of national spirit, the spiritual motive force and the spiritual support in the development of the Chinese nation, the dominant idea of national culture and the great thoughts penetrating the fine tradition of national culture.

On the basic spirit of Chinese culture, many scholars have ever defined it, studied it but viewed it differently.

In the article *On the Basic Spirit of Chinese Culture*, Zhang Dainian thinks that the ideological basis for the long-term development of Chinese culture can be called the basic spirit of Chinese culture which includes：①being energetic；②being harmonious and moderate；③advocating virtues；④being coordinative between nature and human.

《论中国文化二题》一文的作者许思园认为，"中国文化之根本精神为融和与自由"。

《对中国传统文化的再评价》一文的作者杨宪邦认为，以自给自足的自然经济为基础的、以家族为本位的、以血缘关系为纽带的宗法等级伦理纲常，是贯穿中国古代社会的主要线索、本质和核心，这就是中国古代传统文化的基本精神。

《略论中国民族精神》一文的作者刘纲纪认为，中国民族精神包括理性精神、自由精神、求实精神和应变精神四个方面。

《文化社会学》一文的作者司马云杰认为，中国传统文化的基本精神可以概括为"尊祖宗、重人伦、崇道德、尚礼仪"。

这些定义的背后，无疑都包含着"进取"、"融和"及"人本"思想。

In the article *On Two Questions About Chinese Culture*, Xu Siyuan thinks that "The fundamental spirit of Chinese culture is harmony and freedom".

In the article *Re-evaluation of Traditional Chinese Culture*, Yang Xianbang thinks that ethical laws, taking self-sufficient natural economy as the basis, family as the basic unit, blood relationship as the link of patriarchal clan system, are the main clue, the essence and the core of ancient Chinese society, which forms the basic spirit of traditional culture in ancient China.

In the article *On Chinese National Spirit*, Liu Gangji thinks that Chinese national spirit includes the rational spirit, the spirit of freedom, matter-of-fact attitude and strain spirit.

In the article *Cultural Sociology*, Sima Yunjie thinks that the basic spirit of Chinese traditional culture can be summarized as "respecting ancestors, stressing on ethics, advocating morality and etiquette".

In these expressions, there is no doubt that the thoughts of "persistence" and "harmony" and "human-oriented-ness" should be included.

第一节　自强不息的进取精神和"和而不同"的宽容精神

Section 1　Persistent Enterprising Spirit and Tolerance of "Harmony in Diversity"

自强不息的进取精神是中华文化的基本精神之一。"自强不息"一词最早出现在距今两千多年以前的《易经》中，它说，"天行健，君子以自强不息"，意思是天道运行刚劲雄健，与此相应，君子应力求进步，发愤图强，积极进取，永不停歇。这是自强不息的进取精神的真实写照。它说明自然界是不断地向前运行和发展的，君子应以此为榜样，自强不息，努力向上，以便与自然界的发展规律协调一致。

Persistent enterprising spirit is one of the basic spirits of Chinese culture. The word "persistency" first appeared in the *Book of Changes* more than two thousand years ago in which it said: "Gentlemen should be persistent and self-reliant before success", which means that natural law is powerful, accordingly, a gentleman should strive for progress, be positively enterprising and persistent and never give up. This is a real portraiture of persistent enterprising spirit which shows that the nature is constantly running forward and that a gentleman should be based on this model, be self-reliant and work hard in order to coordinate with the developing law of nature.

中国长期的统一与中华文化中自强不息的进取精神是分不开的。中国文化中自强不息的进取精神，增强了民族的凝聚力和向心力，在两千多年的历史发展长河中，一直鼓舞着人们奋发向上，不断学习，不断前进。无数仁人志士，为了维护国家统一和民族团结，坚持与内部的邪恶势力和外来入侵势力作不屈不挠的斗争。诸如"剑外忽传收蓟（jì）北，初闻涕泪满衣裳。却看妻子愁何在，漫卷诗书喜欲狂。白日放歌须纵酒，青春作伴好还乡。即从巴峡穿巫峡，便下襄阳向洛阳"（杜甫：《闻官军收河南河北》）式的激动；"出师未捷身先死，长使英雄泪满襟"（杜甫：《蜀相》）；"遗民忍死望恢复，几处今宵垂泪痕"（陆游：《关山月》）式的感慨都是以高度的自信自尊而表现出来的自强不息精神。"大禹治水"妇孺皆知，大禹三过家门而不入的精神成为中华民族自强不息的典范。自强不息的进取精神是中华民族特有的精神气质，成为激励中华儿女不断开拓进取的永恒的精神力量。正是这种自强不息的进取精神，培育了中华民族的自立精神和反抗压迫精神，以及中华一体、国家一统的精神。中华文化这种自强不息的精神，鼓舞着中华民族不断进取，也推动了中华民族的发展。

The long-term unity of China is partly due to the persistent enterprising spirit of the Chinese culture which has enhanced the centripetal and cohesive force of the nation, which has been inspiring people to exert themselves, to constantly learn and move forward in the long history of more than two thousand years. Myriad people with lofty ideals have adhered to struggle indomitably with internal evil forces and external invasion and oppression forces in order to maintain the unity of the state and the national unification. This may be reflected in some poems, such as "In Jianmen when I heard government troops had recovered Jibei, my tears streamed down on my clothes. Looking back at my wife and children, I found they did not look worried any more. I felt on the top of the world as I put away all the books. In the daytime I sang happily in a loud voice and indulged in drinking. With the beautiful spring scenery all around I'll return to my long-awaited hometown. I will set off right now, passing through Ba gorge, Wu gorge and Xiangyang area to the former capital city of Luoyang." (By Du Fu) "But he did not win after sending armed forces to suppress the State of Wei and died of illness in the army. For a long time heroes have shed tears for this." (Also by Du Fu) "The submerged people are looking forward to the restoration of the state, many of them are in tears tonight!" (By Lu You) in which unyielding and persistent spirit with self-confidence and self-esteem is embodied. The story *King Yu Tamed the Flood* is widely known in which King Yu's spirit was reflected as a model of the Chinese nation. Persistent enterprising spirit is the characteristic of the Chinese nation and has become the eternal spirit of Chinese people constantly forging ahead. It is the persistent enterprising spirit that has nurtured the spirit of self-reliance and resistance against oppression and the spirit of national integration and unification. It is the persistent enterprising spirit that has been inspiring and promoting the continuous development of the Chinese nation.

"和而不同"中的"和"，指不同事物之间的搭配、融合、平衡，以达到最为圆满程度的一种状态。例如音乐，五音的高低疾缓臻于完美，就称为"和"；又如饮食，五味的多寡浓淡搭配得宜，也称为"和"；又如身体，阴阳之气平衡饱满，也称为"和"。

"和而不同"是一种宽容的态度。"和而不同"一语出自《论语》，"君子和而不同，小人同而不和"。戚戚小人的外同而内不和，决定了他们只能以"小"称之。而坦荡的君子内在要求的一致性成就了他们的"君兰"美名。他们以其包容的态度理性地接纳各门各派的观点、精神思想，奠定了中华民族五千年的思想文化根基；以更大的胸怀迎接外来文化，吸取其长处，成就了博大精深的中华文化。

In "harmony in diversity", "harmony" refers to the collocation, integration and balance between different things to be in best status. Such as the high-low and fast-slow tune of the music, the thick-light taste of the diet, the yin-yang balance of the *qi* in the body can be called "harmony".

"Harmony in diversity" is an attitude of tolerance which comes from *Analects* of Confucius, "The gentlemen aim at harmony but not at uniformity. The mean men aim at uniformity but not at harmony." The mean men with harmony outside but uniformity inside can only be called "mean" while the inherent requirement of the consistency of the gentlemen has helped themselves to win the reputation of "orchid", with whose attitude of tolerance they rationally accept various views and thoughts, which have laid the ideological and cultural foundation for the Chinese nation; they greet foreign culture warmly, absorbing its merits and integrating it into the extensive and profound Chinese culture.

"和而不同"的包容精神，既是一种君子之风，也是协调君臣关系、君民关系的准则，同时还适用于处理国家、民族以及各种文化之间的相互关系。早在《尚书·尧典》中就有"克明俊德，以柔九族。九族既睦，平章百姓。百姓昭明，协和万邦。黎民于变时雍"的记载，主张用"和"的方式对待族群和邦国。"协和万邦"，需要承认差异性并互相包容，其中所体现出来的原则，正是"和而不同"。包容和智慧无处不在。大地以其宽阔的背脊支撑万物，成就大自然的绚丽多姿；海洋以其伟岸的胸怀接纳百川，成就大海的博大稳重；天空以其无垠的胸襟包容云朵，成就了蓝天的自由与宽广。在历史的长河中，"和而不同"的包容精神内化成为中华文化的基本精神，赋予了中华文化海纳百川的气魄。无论是儒、道思想的互融互补，还是佛教文化与中国本土文化相激相荡而最终成为中华文化的组成部分，或者对我们的思想带来强烈冲击的西方文化仍然能够被中华文化加以化解并有效吸收与融会贯通，都体现了中华文化的包容精神。今天，

"和而不同"仍是各种文化交流的基本原则。正如汤一介先生所言："如果我们希望中国文化得到更好的发展，如果我们希望中国文化今后能对人类文明有所贡献，就必须以'和而不同'的态度对待其他民族、国家、地域的文化，充分吸收他们的优秀文化成果，更新自己的传统文化，以创造适应现代社会生活的新文化。"

The tolerance of "harmony in diversity" refers not only to the demeanor of the gentlemen but to the norms of coordinating monarch-subject and monarch-common people relationships. It may be also used for dealing with the co-relationship among states, nations and cultures. There were related records in the book *Minister—Stories About Emperor Yao*. "Examining past events in ancient times, we get to know that Emperor Yao is named Fangxun, who serves for common people respectfully and encourages frugality, who is moderate and tolerant and does well in governance. He is honest and diligent, and gives room to better men so that he is very popular among the common people. He carries on virtues and unites family members closely, perceiving political affairs of other peoples and coordinating the relationship among the governors. Thus, the common people unite themselves closely together." He advocates harmony to treat the ethnic groups and neighbor states. To coordinate the relationship among the governors, one needs to acknowledge differences and mutual tolerance, which reflects the principle of "harmony in diversity". Tolerance is ubiquitous, wisdom everywhere. The earth nourishes everything on its broad plateaus and ridges and makes the nature colorful; the oceans take in the waters in its grand bosom and makes the sea vast and stable; the blue sky embraces the clouds and makes itself free and broad. In the long history, the tolerance of "harmony in diversity" has internalized the basic spirit of the Chinese culture and endowed Chinese culture with the spirit of all rivers running into sea. The mutual complement and integration of Confucianism and Taoism, the collision and fusion of Buddhism and local culture has eventually formed a part of Chinese culture. The western culture bringing strong impact on our thoughts can still be resolved and taken in into Chinese culture. All of these have embodied the spirit of Chinese culture. Today, "harmony in diversity" is still the basic principle of all the cultural exchanges. As Mr. Tang Yijie puts it: "If we want to make a better development of Chinese culture, if we want our culture to make a contribution to human civilization, we must take the attitude of 'harmony in diversity' towards the culture of other ethnic groups, nations and regions, fully absorbing their achievements in culture, updating the traditional culture of our own so as to create a new culture adapting to the modern social life."

第二节　"以人为本"的人本主义精神

Section 2　"Human-oriented" Humanistic Spirit

人文主义或人本主义即"以人为本"的学说，也是中国文化的基本精神之一。在中国传统文化价值体系中，人居于中心地位，人为万物之灵和宇宙万物的中心，天地之间人为贵。

以人为本，就是肯定人的个体价值；强调人性尊严，注重人性的完善，肯定人在天地间的崇高地位和伟大作用；高扬个体在道德自省自律与道德实践上的主体性和自觉性；重视人的道德修养，主张人们通过自身的修养和学习，成为高尚的人，成为有理想的人。人本思想的确立有助于人们合理地对待人与神的关系，增强人的主体意识，以抵制宗教神学。

Humanism refers to the theory of "human-oriented-ness". It is one of the basic spirits of Chinese culture. In the value system of Chinese traditional culture, human is at the center position, for human is the lord of creation, the intelligent part of the universe and the most important on the earth.

Human-oriented-ness affirms the individual value, emphasizing on human dignity, paying attention to the perfection of human nature, confirming human's high position and great effect in the world, chanting the praises of individual's subjectivity and consciousness in the moral introspection, self-discipline and moral practice, attaching great importance to the moral accomplishment, advocating people to be noble with lofty ideals through training and learning. The establishment of humanistic thought is helpful for people to properly treat the relationship between man and god, to strengthen the subject consciousness and to avoid the religious theology.

孔子将人的生命放在第一位，一贯反对以神为本，坚持以人为本的人文主义立场。以人为本是相对于宗教家以神为本而言的。孔子虽然承认天命，却怀疑鬼神。他说："务民之义，敬鬼神而远之，可谓知矣。"[1]（《雍也》）认为生命最重要，而不必求助于鬼神。孔子认为应更重视生的问题，而不必考虑死后的问题。《论语》记载："季路问事鬼神，子曰：'未能事人，焉能事鬼？'曰：'敢问死！'曰：'未知生，焉知死？'"[1]（《先进》）孔子更不赞成祈祷，《论语》记载："子疾病，子路请祷。子曰：'有诸？'子路对曰：'有之。诔曰：祷尔于上下神祇。'子曰：'丘之祷久矣。'"[1]（《述而》）孔子对于鬼神采取存疑的态度，既不否定，也不肯定，但认为应该努力解决现实生活中的问题，而不必向鬼神祈祷。孔子的这种思想观点是非常深刻的。这种思想其实是倡导"人事为本，天道为末"（用天道指引人道）。在自然万物之间，人为贵，而不像佛家所一概之以"众生"。

Confucius puts human life in the first place, opposing to god-oriented-ness, adhering to the humanistic position of human-oriented-ness which is relative to the case of religious-based god-oriented-ness. Confucius, who acknowledges the mandate of heaven, suspects of ghosts and gods. He said: "Those who try to do something for the people, revering ghosts and gods but being far away from them, can be called the wise." [1](On Harmony) He thinks that life is the most important in the world and people do not have to resort to ghosts and gods. He also believes that we should pay more attention to life rather than considering problems after death. It is recorded in

The Analects：Ji Lu asked Confucius how to serve the ghosts and gods. Confucius answered："No one can serve men, how can he serve the demons?" Ji Lu asked："What's the story about death?" Confucius said："We still don't know anything about life, how can we know death?" [1] Confucius is not in favor of prayer. It is recorded in *The Analects*："One day, Confucius was seriously ill. Zi Lu requested to pray to ghosts and gods. Confucius said：'Is it workable?' Zi Lu said：'Yes. It's said in *Lei*：'I'll pray to god for you.' Confucius said：'If it were workable, I would have prayed for a long time.'"[1] Confucius suspects of ghosts and gods, but neither does he deny them, nor is he sure for them. He thinks we should try to solve the problems in real life, rather than praying to ghosts and gods. His view on ghosts and gods is profound which is actually to advocate that "human events are rather important than natural law". Human beings are the most important in nature, but not all living creatures as Buddhists suggested.

历史上所有战争的本质都是利益的争夺。物质的富有和军力的强悍只会加剧占有欲的膨胀，并不能提升文化。对内统治的"人本"和对外掠夺的"物本"不但不能使世界和平，反而会导致同归于尽式的仇杀。相反，"己所不欲，勿施于人"的理念，宽容和"善性"是使人类"融合"的能量。把"憎恨"与"报复"转变为"慈悲"与"报恩"，把"独霸"转变为"共享"的人文主义智慧也许是长治久安的良方。

The nature of all the wars in history is to fight for benefits. Affluent materials and tough military strength can only exacerbate the expansion of the possessiveness but cannot ascend culture. The internal rule of so-called "human-oriented-ness" and external plunder of "material-oriented-ness" cannot make world peaceful but lead to mutually revengeful murder. Instead, the concept of "Do not do to others what you do not want others do to you", tolerance and "goodness" can make human kind "convergent". The humanistic wisdom of changing "hate" and "revenge" into "compassion" and "gratitude", and "dominance" into "share" may be a way out for the long-term stability.

从历史发展的主流来看，中国文化在过去几千年的发展中，人本主义占据着显赫和重要的地位。文艺复兴时高举的人本主义火炬，驱逐了欧洲政教合一制度下神本主义统一的黑暗，给人类带来了资产阶级文化的曙光，其影响是巨大的、深远的。

人本主义在中国社会的发展过程中有其独特的意义和巨大的贡献。然而，仅有人本主义思想是不足以造就理想社会的；仅强调道德是不足以使社会稳定有序地发展的，还需要民主法制来维护社会的公平与秩序，还需要科学技术的发展来提高劳动生产率，满足社会需求以保证人文质量。极具包容力的中国文化还需要学习和借鉴西方在对内政治方面的民主法制文化，逐步充实和发展中国文化中人本主义和民主的内涵。现代文明的大鼎，还需要人文道德、民主法制和现代科技这三足方可鼎立。

From the perspective of the mainstream of history, humanism occupies a prominent and important position in the past several thousand years of development of Chinese culture. The humanism torch in Renaissance expelled the darkness of European system of unification of the state and the church, and brought the dawn of the bourgeois culture and enormous and far-reaching influence to human kind.

Humanism has its unique significance and great contribution in the development of Chinese society. However, it is not enough to create the ideal society with humanistic thoughts; it is not enough to make the society stable and orderly develop only by emphasizing morality. Democracy and legal system are needed to safeguard social fairness and order; the development of science and technology is also needed to improve the labor productivity to meet the needs of society and to ensure the quality of the humanities. Highly tolerant Chinese culture is also needed to learn more about western democratic legislative system, to gradually enrich and develop the connotation of humanism and democracy of Chinese culture. Thus, the big "pot" of modern civilization can be set up by the support of the humanity morality, democratic legislative system and modern science and technology.

[1]（魏）何晏. 论语注疏. 北京：中华书局，1980.

口述题

1. 中国文化的基本精神是什么？
2. 对于"以人为本"的人本主义精神，你有什么看法？

Questions

1. What is the basic spirit of Chinese culture?
2. What do you think of the humanistic spirit of "people-oriented"?

学习网站

1. 中华文化大学（http://zhwhdx.ustc.edu.cn/zhwhdx/）
2. China HIGHLIGHTS（https://www.chinahighlights.com/travelguide/culture/）

第二章　中国文化的类型和主要特征

Chapter 2　Types and Main Features of Chinese Culture

第一节　中国文化的类型

Section 1　Types of Chinese Culture

从文化的内容和社会功能等方面来看，人类文化的类型可分为三种：以人与他人为核心的中国伦理政治型文化；以人与自然为核心的古希腊科学型文化；以人与自身关系为核心的印度宗教型文化。从精神角度来看可以将人类文化分为三类：意欲型的西方文化；调和持中型的中国文化；反身向后型的印度文化。（梁漱溟《东西文化及其哲学》）

任何一种文化类型的产生都离不开特定的自然条件和社会历史条件，即在特定自然地理环境下的物质生产方式和社会组织结构。从地理环境看，中国处于一种半封闭状态的大陆性自然环境，与西方地中海沿岸国家的地理环境大不相同；从物质生产方式看，封建性质的小农经济在中国有几千年的历史，中国文化扎根于农业社会的基础之上，这与中亚和西亚地区的游牧民族以及工商业比较发达的海洋民族有很大区别；从社会组织结构看，在中国漫长的历史中宗法制度成为维系社会秩序的重要纽带，专制制度在中国延续了两千年，这在世界文化史上也是极为罕见的。

Human culture can be divided into three types from the angle of its content and social function, i. e., Chinese ethics-politics-oriented culture with human being and others as the core; ancient Greek science-oriented culture with human and nature as the core; Indian-religion-oriented culture with human and itself as the core. Human culture can also be divided into three categories from the angle of spirit, i. e., intention-oriented western culture; compromise-oriented Chinese culture; reversing-backward-oriented Indian culture. (Liang Shuming, *Culture and Philosophy in China and Western Countries*)

The form of any type of culture is inseparable from the specific natural and historical conditions, namely, material production mode and social structure under specific geographical environment. From the angle of geographical environment, China belongs to semi-closed continental one, which is quite different from that of Mediterranean countries. From the angle of material production mode, the feudal small-scale farming economy in China has a history of several thousand years. Chinese culture is rooted on the basis of agricultural society, which is quite different from those of the nomads in central and western Asian area and those of marine nations with highly developed industry and commerce. From the angle of social structure, patriarchal clan system has become an important link to maintain social order in the long history of China, making autocratic monarchy last for two thousand years in China, which is extremely rare in the history of world culture.

伦理政治型的中国传统文化不仅在人们的意识形态方面有着久远的影响，而且还深刻地影响着传统社会心理和人们的行为规范，如孝亲敬祖、尊师崇古、修己务实、不佞鬼神、乐天安命等。正因为如此，斯宾格勒才把道德灵魂当作中国文化的基本象征符号。黑格尔说："中国文化完全建立在一种道德的结合上，国家的特性便是客观的家庭孝道。"如果把西方的文化视为"智性文化"，那么中国文化则可以称为"德性文化"。这种说法有一定的道理。但是，中国传统文化重"德"而不轻"智"，是一种德智统一、以德摄智的文化。

中国文化的伦理型特征，主要源于中国古代社会宗法制度的完善及其影响。与独特的宗法制度相联系的血亲意识，即所谓"六亲"（父子、兄弟、夫妇）、"九族"（父族四、母族三、妻族二）的观念构成社会意识的轴心，而且其形态愈益精密化。经过历代统治者及其士人的加工改造，宗法制度下的血亲意识有的转化为法律条文（如"不孝"成为犯法的"首恶"），更主要的是形成宗法式的伦理道德，长久地左右着人们的社会心理和行为规范。在社会心理方面，中国人向来对血缘关系格外注重。与此相联系，中国人往往怀有浓烈的"孝亲"情感，这种情感不仅表现为对死去的先祖的祭奠，更表现为对活着的长辈的绝对孝顺，所谓"百善孝为先"。孝道被视为一切道德规范的核心和母体，忠君、敬长、尊上等，都是孝道的延伸。正是由于整个社会的"孝亲"意识，才使得绝大多数炎黄子孙不致成为"六亲不认"的宗教狂徒。从这个意义上说，纲常伦理观念如同一具庞大严密的"思想滤清器"，阻挡、淡化了宗教精神对国民意识的渗透。

Ethics-politics-oriented Chinese traditional culture has not only influenced the ideology for a long time, but also profoundly influenced the traditional social psychology and the behavior of people, such as showing filial piety to ancestors and parents, paying respect to masters and elders, self-cultivating and being practical, not trusting in ghosts and spirits, etc. Thus, philosopher Spengler took moral spirit as the basic symbol of the Chinese culture. Philosopher Hegel said: "Chinese culture is completely based on the combination of moralities. The feature of the nation is filial piety." If the western culture is taken as "intellectual culture", Chinese culture may be called "moral culture". There is some truth in the saying. Chinese traditional culture stresses much on "morality" but never neglects "intelligence". It is a culture of unification of "morality" and "intelligence" and a culture of taking in intelligence from morality.

The ethical characteristic of Chinese culture mainly comes from the improvement of the social patriarchal clan system in ancient China and its influence. The consanguinity consciousness associated with distinctive patriarchal clan system, i. e., the concept of so-called "six kins" (father and son, brothers and couples) and "nine clans" (four father family members, three mother family members, two wife family members) forms the axis of social consciousness, and its form is becoming more and more complicated. After the improvement of rulers and scholars in all ages, some blood consciousness under the patriarchal clan system has changed into the legal codes, (such as "un-filial piety" has become "arch-criminal") and formed patriarchal ethics which controls people's social psychology and behaviour. In the aspect of social psychology, Chinese people have been paying much attention to blood lineage. Likewise, Chinese people tend to have a strong emotion of "filial piety" which is shown through holding grand memorial ceremonies for the deceased ancestors and owing absolute filial piety to the living elders. That is the so-called "Of all virtues filial piety is the most important". Filial piety is regarded as the core of all ethics. Being loyal to the king, respecting the elders and honoring the superiors, etc., are the extension of filial piety. It is due to "filial piety" consciousness of the whole society that most of the Chinese people will not become religious fanatics who repudiate all of the relatives. In this sense, the concept of ethics is like a "mind-filter" which blocks and plays down the penetration of the religious spirit into the national consciousness.

在古希腊和古罗马，人们关注的重心不是人际伦常关系，而是大自然和人类思维的奥秘，主体与客体二分、心灵与物质对立的观念深入人心，宇宙理论、形而上学得到较充分的发展。以柏拉图为代表的古希腊哲学体系三分为思辨哲学、自然哲学和精神哲学，此后直到近代，西方以"求真"为目标的学术范式一脉相承，宇宙论、认识论与道德论各自独立发展，虽有联系，但从未混淆不清；中国则不同，人伦效法自然，"人法地，地法天，天法道，道法自然"（《老子》第二十五章）。自然亦被人伦化，天人之间攀上了血亲关系，君王即"天子"，从而形成了天人合一、主客混融的局面。中国古代的知识论从未与道德伦理学说明晰地区分开来，为学的目标主要固在于求"真"——探索自然奥秘，但更在于求"善"——追求道德觉悟。外在的自然界既未被当作独立的认知对象与人伦相分离，以外物为研究对象的科学便遭到冷遇和压抑，自然科学、分析哲学因此难以获得充分的发展。伦理学却滋生扩张，甚至成为众多学科门类的出发点和归结点；政治学成为道德评判，政事被归结为善恶之别、正邪之争、君子小人之辨；文学强调教化功能，成为"载道"的工具；史学往往不以存史为基本任务，而以"寓褒贬，别善恶"为宗旨；教育更以德育居首，所谓"首孝悌，次见闻"（《三字经》），"行有余力则以学文"（《论语·学而篇》），知识的传授倒退居其次；至于哲学，在中国文化体系中则往往与伦理学相混融，主要是一种道德哲学。这一点在儒学中体现得尤为鲜明。宗法社会特定的伦理型文化，自有其正面的积极效用。

In ancient Greece and Rome, what people concern is not ethical interpersonal relationship but the secrets of nature and human thinking. The idea of the dichotomy of subject and object and the opposition of spirit and material are commonly accepted. Universe theory and metaphysics are fully developed. Ancient Greek philosophy represented by Plato is divided into speculative philosophy, natural philosophy and spiritual philosophy. Till modern times, the academic norm of setting "pursuit of truth" as the goal comes down in one continuous line. Cosmology, epistemology and ethics develop independently, co-related but never confused; in China, on the other hand, human beings are the potential of all things, " Human beings are a manifestation of the earth; the earth, a manifestation of the physical universe; the physical universe, a manifestation of Infinity; Infinity, the potential of all things." (Chapter 25, *Lao Zi*). Nature can also be ethical, which formed the kinship between universe and human beings. The king is "son of universe", thus forms the case of the syncretism between universe and human beings and the fusion of subject and object. Ancient Chinese theory of knowledge has never had a clear distinction with ethics. The chief goal of learning is to pursue the "truth" —to explore the mystery in nature, and furthermore to pursue the "kindness" —to seek ethical consciousness. External nature is not regarded as independent cognitive object and separated with ethics. Science taking external content as the research object was confronted with snub and depress, which makes natural science and analytic philosophy difficult to be fully developed. Ethics is breeding for expansion and has even become the starting and ending point of many disciplines. Politics has become moral judgments. The political events are ascribed to judge the difference between good and evil, to battle the struggle between the vital energy and the pathogenic factor, to debate between a gentleman and a base man. Literature emphasizes the function of enlightenment and has become the tool of spreading "Taoism". Historiography tends not to preserve historical records as basic tasks, but to "imply judgement and differentiate good from evil" as the objective. Moral education is put in the first place. That is so-called "Begin love, and then see and hear". (*Three Character Primer*), "When all this is done and there is time for other things, they should use it for the study of the classics." (*The Analects*: *About Learning*). That imparts knowledge back in the second place. As for philosophy, it is often mixed with ethics in the Chinese culture system and mainly a kind of moral philosophy which is obviously embodied in Confucianism. The specific ethical culture in patriarchal society has its positive utility.

在中国文化系统里，强调在道德面前人人平等，如孟子说"人皆可以为尧舜"，王阳明说"满街都是圣人"，都是肯定凡夫俗子也可以通过道德修养达到最高境界。伦理型文化对包括君主在内的统治者也可以形成道德制约和严格要求。自周朝开始，帝王死后有谥号，群臣根据其德行政绩加一概括语。这种人格评判式的道德制约，在缺乏分权制的古代中国，所发挥的社会调节功能不可低估。伦理型文化在特定历史条件下，还能鼓舞人们自觉维护正义，忠于国家民族，抵御外来侵略，保持高风亮节。千百年来，无数"舍生取义"、"杀身成仁"的志士仁人，都从传统道德伦理思想中汲取营养，立德、立功，彪炳千秋。伦理型文化也有其消极的一面。它将伦理关系凝固化、绝对化，以致在某种程度上又成为人身压迫、精神虐杀的理论之源。

In Chinese culture system, everyone is equal before morality. Mencius once said "Everyone can be a sage" and Wang Yangming also said "There are saints everywhere", which implies that common people can reach highest level through moral cultivation. Ethical culture may form moral restriction and strict requirements for rulers including monarchs. Since Zhou Dynasty, emperors after death may be granted posthumous title. A commendatory or derogatory summary may be added after the title according to their virtue achievements. The moral constraints on personality playing a function of social regulation should not be underestimated in the absence of a decentralized system in ancient China. Ethical culture in the specific historical conditions can also inspire people to consciously maintain justice, to be loyal to the nation, to resist foreign aggression and to keep noble moral principle. For thousands of years, countless people with lofty ideals who died for justice or for achieving virtue have drawn nutrition from traditional moral and ethical thought and made contributions and achieved great virtue which was handed down one generation after another. Ethical culture has its negative side, too. Sometimes it made ethical relations too absolute, which makes it the theoretical source of oppression and mental cruelty to some extent.

第二节 中国文化的主要特征

Section 2　Main Features of Chinese Culture

归纳起来，中国文化有以下七个方面的特征：

1. 强大的生命力和凝聚力

英国历史学家汤因比认为，在近 6 000 年的人类历史上，出现过 26 个文明形态，但在全世界只有中国的文化体系是长期延续发展而从未中断过的。中国文化的强大生命力，表现在它的同化力、融合力、延续力和凝聚力等诸多方面。所谓同化力，是指外域文化进入中国后，大都逐步中国化，融入中国文化而成为其中一部分，如佛教文化的传入和中国化。所谓融合力，是指中国文化并非单纯的汉民族文化或黄河流域的文化，而是在汉民族文化的基础上善于有机地吸收中国境内各民族及不同地域的文化，也有同化的意义。中国文化的同化力和融合力，是其无与伦比的生命延续力的内在基础。中国文化的强大生命力还表现在它具有历久弥坚的凝聚力。这种凝聚力具体表现在文化心理的自我认同感和超地域、超国界的文化群体归属感。

To sum up, the features of Chinese culture lie in the following seven aspects:

1. The strong vitality and cohesion

British historian Toynbee thought that in nearly 6,000 years of human history, there have been 26 patterns of civilization, but among them only China has got long-term un-interrupted culture in the cultural system. The powerful vitality of Chinese culture lies in its assimilatory power, fusion power, great vitality and cohesion. Assimilatory power refers to foreign cultures gradually integrating into the Chinese culture and becoming part of it, such as the introduction of Buddhism culture and its Chinization. Fusion power implies that Chinese culture is not a pure Han ethnic group culture or the culture of the Yellow River, but basing itself on the Han ethnic group culture absorbing the cultures of all ethnic groups in various regions in China. The assimilatory power and fusion of Chinese culture is the basis of its unparalleled vitality. The powerful vitality of Chinese culture is also shown in its enduring cohesion, which is specifically embodied in itself ratification and supra-territorial and transnational perception of affiliation of the cultural group.

2．重实际求稳定的农业文化心态

在以农业生产为生存根基的中国，农业生产的节奏早已与国民生活的节奏相通。传统节日均来源于农事，是由农业节气演化而成的，并不像其他民族，节日多来源于宗教。农本商末、重农抑商的观念在中国式的农业社会可谓根深蒂固。

务实精神是"一分耕耘，一分收获"的农耕生活导致的一种群体价值趋向。作为农耕民族的中国人，从小农业的简单再生产过程中形成的思维定式和运思方法是注意切实领会，并不追求精密严谨的思辨体系，被西方人称赞为"最善于处理实际事务"的民族。

"安土乐天"的生活情趣，更是直接从农业文明中生发出来的国民精神，包含着循环与恒久意识的变易观念，与农业文明存在着深刻的联系。中国人受到农业生产由播种、生长到收获这一循环状况以及四时、四季周而复始现象的启示，产生一种循环论的思维方式。农业社会中的人们满足于维持简单再生产，缺乏扩大社会再生产的能力，因而社会运行缓慢迟滞。在这样的生活环境中，很容易滋生永恒意识，认为世界是悠久的、静定的，袭故蹈常，好常恶变。

2. The mentality of being practical and maintaining stability of agricultural culture

China takes agricultural production as its base of survival. Its pace of agricultural production has already been in line with that of the national life. Its traditional festivals deriving from farming are evolved from agricultural throttle but not from religions like other nations. The concept of "agriculture the first but trade the last and encouraging agriculture rather than trade" is deeply rooted in Chinese agricultural society.

The pragmatic spirit is a group value tendency which "no pains, no gains" of farming life leads to. The farming Chinese are praised as "the people best at dealing with practical things" by westerners. Their mind-set and operational method formed in the process of simple reproduction of agriculture is to pay attention to practical grasp but not to pursue precise and exact theoretical system.

Setting down in the local place to enjoy the life is also the national spirit directly coming from the agricultural civilization which contains circulation and constant awareness of original ideas, which has a deep connection with agricultural civilization. The Chinese were enlightened from the phenomenon of seeding, growing and harvesting in agricultural production and four seasons in circles and formed a way of thinking in theory of cycle. People of agricultural society are content to maintain a simple reproduction but lack of the ability to expand social reproduction, which leads to slow the development of society. In such a social environment, it is easy to breed constant awareness, which believes the world is eternal, static, going on in the same old way and invariable.

3．以家族为本位的宗法集体主义文化

中国古代历史的发展脉络，不是以奴隶制的国家代替氏族血缘纽带联系起来的宗法社会，而是由家族走向国家，以血缘纽带维系奴隶制度，形成"家国一体"的格局。氏族社会的解体在我国完成得很不充分，因而氏族社会的宗法制度及其意识形态的残余被大量积

淀下来。几千年来，全社会并未长期存在如同古代印度和欧洲中世纪那样森严的等级制度，社会组织主要是在父子、君臣、夫妇、长幼之间的宗法原则指导下建立起来的。宗法制度在中国根深蒂固，不仅由于氏族社会解体极不充分，还由于此后自然经济长期延续，"鸡犬之声相闻，民至老死不相往来"的村社构成中国社会的细胞群，而这些村社中又包含家庭宗族与邻里乡党两大网络，由家庭而家族，再集合为宗族，组成社会，进而构成国家。这种社会结构给宗法制度、宗法思想的迁延、流播提供了丰厚的土壤。两千多年来，中华民族始终以宗法氏族社会传说的圣人——尧舜为圣人，以宗法氏族社会的"大同世界"为理想的社会境界，社会组织结构长久地笼罩在父系家长制的阴影之下，父是家君，君是国父，家国一体，宗法关系渗透到社会生活的最深层。以家族为本位的社会关系的基本单元是"宗族"。在宗法观念下，个人是被重重包围在群体之中的，因此，每个人首先要考虑的，是自己的责任和义务，如父慈、子孝、兄友、弟恭之类，个人的权利则显得不那么重要。这就是所谓的"人道亲亲"。《礼记·大传》中解释"人道亲亲"说："亲亲故尊祖，尊祖故敬宗，敬宗故收族"。从"亲亲"的观念出发，可以引申出对君臣、夫妻、长幼、朋友等关系的一整套处理原则，都是以义务观念为核心的。《大学》提出"知止"的范畴，具体表现在"为人臣止于敬"，"为人子止于孝"，"为人父止于慈"等，这都是义务的概念。正是由于传统文化重家族而轻个人、重群体而轻个体，因而总是强调个人在群体中的义务和责任，而忽略了个人在社会中的权利，也就使得"人皆可以为尧舜"这样的道德平等意识仅仅成为一种理想，而与"权利"相联系的"法制"观念在这样的系统之内无用武之地，这正体现了传统文化的二元性。

3. Family-centered patriarchal collectivist culture

Ancient Chinese history does not develop through replacing the patriarchal society linked by the clan blood ties with slavery countries, but develop from the family to the country with blood ties to maintain slavery, which forms the pattern of co-construction of family and state. The destruction of the clan society in our country was incomplete. Therefore, patriarchal system in clan society and the remains of ideology accumulated in great number. For thousands of years, there did not long exist guarded hierarchy in China as ancient Indian and medieval Europe. Social organization was mainly set up under the guidance of the principles of patriarchal clan between father and son, monarch and subjects, husband and wife, the old and the young. The patriarchal clan system is deeply rooted in China, not only because the destruction of the clan society was incomplete, but because the natural economy lasted on for a long time since then. Villages completely isolated from each other and all their lives have formed the group units of Chinese society. The villages include two networks of neighborhoods and family clans in which families composed into clans, clans into patriarchal clans, patriarchal clans into communities and communities into a country. This kind of social structure provides the patriarchal clan system and the spread of the patriarchal ideology with rich soil. For more than two thousand years, the Chinese nation has always been in a social state which took Emperor Yao and Emperor Shun as saints in the legend of patriarchal clans, which took world of universal harmony of the clans as an ideal. Social structure has been under the shadow of patriarchal paternalism for long. Father is the

King of a family while the King is the Father of a nation, which forms the co-construction of family and state. The patriarchal relationship has gone into the deepest social life. The basic unit of social relationship taking family as its standard is "clan". Under the patriarchal concept, the individual is surrounded among various groups. So what everyone should consider first is their own responsibility and obligation, such as the loving father, the filial son, the friendly elder brother and the obedient younger brother. The rights of the individual seemed less important. This is the so-called "getting close to a man who deserves to be closed up". In *The Book of Rites*, it said getting close might result in respecting grandparents, which might also result in honoring ancestors, which would end up with the unity of the whole nation. Starting from the concept of "getting close", we may extend a set of principles coping with the relationship between monarchs and subjects, husband and wife, the old and the young, and friends, which set obligations as the core. *The Great Learning* put forth the category of "knowing how to do", such as "subjects should know how to respect the monarchs; sons and daughters should know how to show filial piety to parents; fathers should know how to be kind to children", which belong to the concept of obligations. It is due to traditional culture paying more attention to family but less to single personage, more to groups but less to individuals that individual's obligations and responsibilities are always stressed but his rights in society are ignored, which makes the moral equality awareness of "everybody can be Emperor Yao and Emperor Shun" be a dream while "legality" related to "rights" lack scope for its skills. This shows the duality of traditional culture.

4. 尊君重民相反相成的政治文化

长期运作于传统中国的农业自然经济，是一种商品交换欠发达、彼此孤立的经济。在这种土壤中生长起来的极度分散的社会，需要高高在上的集权统治加以整合，以抵御外敌和自然灾害，而人格化的统合力量则来自专制君主。因此，"国不堪贰"的尊君传统乃是农业宗法社会的必然产物。

中国农业社会需要并养育了一个君主集权政体，而这种君主集权政体一经形成，又成为超乎社会之上的异己力量，一方面，它剥夺了人民群众的一切权力，将军、政、财、文大权全部集中到朝廷以至皇帝个人手中；另一方面，农业宗法社会的正常运转，又要依赖以农民为主体的民众的安居乐业，如此方能为朝廷提供租税赋役，保障社会所需的基本生活资料，社稷家国方得以保全，否则便有覆灭崩溃之虞。因此，"敬德保民"、"民为邦本"的思想传统也是农业宗法社会的必然产物。"民为邦本"、"使民以时"、"民贵君轻"等民本思想是中国古代农业社会的一种传统政治思想，反对"杀鸡取卵"、"竭泽而渔"的"仁政"、"王道"学说由此派生出来。民本主义同君主专制主义的关系是双重的，"尊君"和"重民"相反而又相成，共同构成了中国传统政治文化的一体两翼。一方面，以"爱民"、"重民"、"恤民"为旗帜的民本思想与专制主义的极端形态——"残民"、"贱民"、"虐民"的暴政和绝对君权论是对立的，历来抨击暴政的人几乎无一例外地提倡民本思想。另一方面，民本主义又和君主专制主义的一般形态相互补充，构成所谓"明君论"。这种明君"重民"、"惜民"，民众则将安定温饱生活的希望寄托于明君。民本主义与主权在民的民主主义是不可同日而语的。民本主义严格划分"治人者"与"治于人者"，它是从治人者的长治久安出发，才注意民众的力量和人心向背。中国历代封建统治者及其知识分子，一方面强调"国以民为本"，另一方面又强调"民以君为主"，在他们看来，"尊君"和"重民"是统一的。

4. Political culture of honoring the emperor and valuing the people and being both opposite and complementary to each other

The long-term agricultural and natural economy in China is a kind of economy being isolated with each other with underdeveloped economic exchange. The highly dispersed society growing up in the soil needs the authoritarian rule to integrate in order to defend against enemies and natural disasters while personal identity strength comes from autocratic monarchy. As a result, the tradition of honoring the emperor with "a nation not bearing the existence of the two cases" is the inevitable outcome of the patriarchal society of agriculture.

Chinese agricultural society needs and has brought up a centralized monarchy regime, and once it forms, it is known as the alien force beyond the society, it deprived all the power of the people. The power over generals, politics, finance and culture is concentrated into the hands of the court or the emperor himself. On the other hand, the normal operation of patriarchal society of agriculture has to rely on to farmers' living and working in peace and contentment in order to offer tax service to the court, to guarantee the basic means of livelihood the society needs. Thus the state will be kept safe and sound, otherwise it will be in danger of collapse. Therefore, "advocating morality and protecting people" and "the people are the foundation of the state" is also the inevitable outcome of the patriarchal society of agriculture. The people-oriented thoughts such as "the people are the foundation of the state"; "use manual labor by avoiding farming season"; "the people are more important than the ruler" are traditional political thoughts of Chinese ancient agricultural society. The theories of "benevolent policy and government" opposing to "killing the goose that lays the golden eggs" and "draining the pond to get all the fish" are derived from that. "Honoring the emperor" and "valuing the people" are both opposite and complementary, which co-constitute one body with two wings of Chinese traditional political culture. On the one hand, the people-based thought with loving the people, valuing the people and sympathizing the people is opposite to the extreme form of absolutism—the tyranny of slaughtering the people, damaging the people and maltreating the people and absolute monarchy. Those who have been advocating people-oriented thoughts have attacked the tyranny without exception. The general forms of feudal-despotism and absolute monarchy, on the other hand, complement each other, constituting the so-called "theory of enlightened ruler". The enlightened rulers "value the people" and "cherish the people". People would place their hope of stable life with just enough food and clothing on the rulers. People-oriented doctrine and democracy of sovereignty in people's hand can't be mentioned in the same breath. People-oriented doctrine strictly differentiated "rulers" and "the ruled", which starts from the stability of the rulers who pay much attention to the power of the people and their will only at this time. All the Chinese feudal rulers and intellectuals, on the one hand, emphasized "people-based nation"; on the other hand, they emphasized "the people should give priority to the ruler". In their view, "honoring the ruler" and "valuing the people" are unified.

5. 摆脱神学独断的生活信念

同世界上任何民族一样，在中国的远古时期，也产生过原始的宗教以及对天命鬼神的绝对崇拜。直到殷商，仍然尊神重巫。西周时，中国人的宗教观念产生了重要变化，开始"疑"天及"敬德保民"。从宗法中产生道德，道德便成为维系整个社会的根本纽带。宗法道德观念的确立，使神学独断的观念被削弱以至被摆脱了。这是中国传统文化与西方文化、印度文化等相区别的一个突出之处。

中国文化显示出它理性的一面。儒家孟子认为道德之善，来源于人的本性，把对道德问题的讨论引向人的主观修养一途，摆脱了有神论的道德观。荀子则认为，礼义道德来源于后天环境对人性的陶冶和改造。道家则认为道法自然，否定了有人格、有意志的神。

在世界各国历史上，都有对人类产生、人类文明的看法。例如，基督教文化认为"创造"一词只属于上帝，而世界的文明来源于上帝的智慧。而在中华民族的观念中，文明是圣人创造的，不是依赖于神，而是依赖于人。与此相对应，中国人对黄帝的崇拜远远超出了对伏羲氏与神农氏的崇拜。这似乎隐喻了这样的文化内涵：中国人更注重精神文明，形成中国文化的人文色彩。由于中国传统文化自先秦就具有摆脱神学独断的特点，所以在中国历史上，未出现过像欧洲中世纪基督教神学思想统治一切那样的"黑暗时代"。中国传统的民间宗教信仰，有极大的实用性。在民间"烧香拜佛"这样的口头语中，"佛"的含义既可能是释迦牟尼、观音菩萨，也可以是太上老君、城隍土地、妈祖娘娘……这与西方文化中宗教的唯一神、严格排他性迥然不同。

5. The life belief cast off the arbitrary of the theology

As with any nation in the world, in ancient times of China, the original religion has ever come into being and heaven and ghosts have ever been absolutely worshipped. Up to Shang Dynasty, gods and witches were still highly valued. In Western Zhou Dynasty, the Chinese had significant changes in religious concepts. They started to "suspect" heaven and "advocating morality and protecting people". Morality was generated from the patriarchal clan system and became the link to hold the whole society together. The establishment of patriarchal ethics made the theological arbitrary concept weaken to be got rid of. This is an obvious difference among Chinese traditional culture, western culture and Indian culture, etc.

Chinese culture has shown its rationality. Mencius thought that the kindness came from human nature. He put on the discussion of moral issues to the way of people's subjective cultivation, which has got rid of the moral concept of theism. Xuncius argued that etiquette morality came from the environment edifying and transforming human nature. Taoists thought Tao modeled itself after nature, denying the personality and the will of god.

Every country in the world has its own view on human generation and human civilization. Christian culture, for example, thought that the word "creation" belonged only to God, and the world civilization came from the wisdom of God. But in the minds of the Chinese, civilization was created by saints, which depended on people but not on gods. Accordingly, the Chinese worshipping to the emperor is far beyond the worship to Fuxi and the Emperor Shennong, which seems to be a metaphor for the culture connotation that the Chinese people pay more attention to spiritual civilization, which forms the humanities of Chinese culture. Chinese traditional culture has the characteristics of being free from arbitrary theology since the pre-Qin period, so Chinese history has never seen "the dark ages" like European medieval Christian theology thoughts ruling over everything. The traditional Chinese folk religion has great practicality. In spoken language as "burning incense and pray", "Buddha" may refer to Sakyamuni, the founder of Buddhism, the Goddess of Mercy, Lord Lao Zi, town and village gods, Mazu empress, etc., which is quite different from the only god and strict religious exclusivity in western culture.

6. 重人伦轻自然的学术倾向

中国文化以"人"为核心,表现在哲学、史学、教育、文学、科学、艺术等各个领域,乐以成德,文以载道,追求人的完善,追求人的理想,追求人与自然的和谐,表现出鲜明的重人文、重人伦的特色。《论语》中有关自然知识的材料共 54 条,涉及天文、物理、化学、动植物、农业、手工业等方面的现象,不可谓不丰富,但究其内容都是利用自然知识来说明政治、道德方面的主张,而不以自然本身为研究目的。"仁者乐山,智者乐水。"

6. The academic tendency of valuing human relations but devaluing nature

Chinese culture takes human as its core, which is shown in philosophy, history, education, literature, science, art and other fields. Being pleased to cultivating character and morals and writing for conveying truth, pursuing the improvement of the people, pursuing ideals, pursuing the harmony of man and nature, which shows the distinctive characteristic of valuing humanity and ethics. In *The Analects* of Confucius, there are 54 items of natural knowledge material, involving astronomy, physics, chemistry, animals and plants, agriculture, handicraft industry and so on, but its content is to use natural knowledge to illustrate the propositions of politics and ethics, but not for the purpose of the study of nature itself. "The benevolent like mountains while the wise like waters".

7. 经学优先并笼罩一切文化领域

中国伦理型文化还有一个突出的外在形式上的特点,就是它的经学传统。所谓经学传统,是指中国文化长期以儒家经学为主流,有着一以贯之的传统,形成了独自的特色。这对中国文化的发展产生了深远的影响:①是儒家思想对中国文化各个方面的广泛渗透;②在经学的影响下,科学未能充分独立;③经学对中国宗教的发展,也产生着一定影响,从而制约了宗教的发展和影响的扩大。

7. The priority of the study of Confucian classics and its hangover on every cultural aspect

Chinese ethical culture has another highlighted characteristic of the external form, i. e., its study of Confucian classics tradition, which refers to that Chinese culture has long taken Confucian classics as the mainstream and has a tradition of consistency, which has formed the characteristic of its own. This had a profound impact on the development of Chinese culture: ①It is the Confucianism that penetrated into Chinese culture in a broad range; ②under the influence of Confucian classics, science has failed to be fully independent; ③the study of Confucian classics has certain influence on the development of Chinese religions. It has restricted the development of religion and the expansion of the influence.

口述题

1. 根据书中所述，中华文化有哪些主要特征？
2. 中国文化中的伦理型文化对当时的人们有什么影响？

Questions

1. According to the book, what are the main characteristics of Chinese culture?
2. What influence did the Chinese ethical culture have on the people at that time?

学习网站

1. ANCIENT HISTORY（https://www.ancient.eu/china/）
2. 中国优秀传统文化百科知识库（http://ctwh.cnki.net/index.html?encode=cnki）

第三章 中国历史文化

Chapter 3　Chinese Historic Culture

第一节　中国古代历史文化

Section 1　Chinese Ancient Historic Culture

中国是世界上四大文明古国之一，有大约 3 600 年的历史记录。勤劳、勇敢、智慧的中国各族人民共同创造了伟大的文明，中国人民为全人类作出了巨大的贡献。

中国古代历史通常是指 1840 年鸦片战争爆发以前的历史。它可以分为几个时期：先秦时期，秦汉王朝时期，三国两晋和南北朝时期，隋唐时期，五国时期，北宋和南宋时期，元朝时期，明朝时期和 1840 年之前的清朝时期。这些历史时期可称为中国的黄金时期。中国古代历史根据不同时期的性质分类，则可分为原始社会时期，奴隶社会时期和封建社会时期。中国古代历史的核心是封建时期，其主要走向是：秦朝实现了古代中国的大统一，汉朝实现全面繁荣，唐代达到鼎盛时期，宋朝成为最富有的朝代，明代后期中国封建社会逐渐走向衰落，到清代中国封建王朝灭亡。

Representing one of the earliest four civilizations in the world, China has a recorded history of about 3,600 years. During this time the industrious, courageous and intelligent Chinese people of all nationalities created a great civilization collectively. They made great contributions to all of mankind.

Chinese ancient history usually refers to the history before the year 1840 when the Opium War broke out. It can be divided into several periods: history of pre-Qin Dynasty, history of Qin-Han Dynasty, history of Three Kingdoms Period, Double Jin dynasties and Southern and Northern Dynasties, history of Sui and Tang dynasties, history of Five-Kingdom Period, history of Northern Song and Southern Song dynasties, history of Yuan Dynasty, history of Ming Dynasty and history of Qing Dynasty before the year 1840. These periods are the golden ages of China. Classified according to the nature of different periods, China ancient history covers Primitive Period, Slavery Period, and Feudalistic Period. The core of China ancient history is feudalistic period, which is strongly featured with ancient China's first unification in Qin Dynasty, first all-sided flourish in Han Dynasty, the peak time in Tang Dynasty, the richest time in Song Dynasty, the feudalistic China's declining period beginning at Ming Dynasty and the absolute devastation of Chinese feudalistic period in Qing Dynasty.

中国各个朝代和现当代政府情况列表

历代			历时	首都	建立者	历史见证物
史前时期			170 万年前到公元前 21 世纪			
夏朝			前 2070—前 1600	夏县	启	青铜器
商朝			前 1600—前 1046	商丘	汤	青铜器
周朝	西周		前 1046—前 771	西安	周武王	诸子百家
	东周	春秋时期	前 770—前 476	洛阳	周平王	诸子百家
		战国时期	前 475—前 221			
秦朝			前 221—前 206	咸阳	秦始皇	秦始皇兵马俑，长城
汉朝	西汉		前 206—25	西安	刘邦	丝绸之路
	东汉		25—220	洛阳	刘秀	
三国	魏		220—265	洛阳	曹丕	
	蜀汉		221—263	成都	刘备	
	吴		222—280	南京	孙权	
晋朝	西晋		265—317	洛阳	司马炎	古墓壁画
	东晋		317—420	南京	司马睿	
南北朝			420—589	洛阳，南京		千佛洞（莫高窟）
隋朝			581—618	西安	杨坚	大运河
唐朝			618—907	西安	李渊	文学
五代十国			907—960	开封等		
宋朝	北宋		960—1127	开封	赵匡胤	宋词
	南宋		1127—1279	杭州	赵构	
辽朝			907—1125	赤峰	耶律阿保机	
大理王朝			937—1254	大理		大理古镇
西夏王朝			1038—1227	银川		石头雕刻
金朝			1115—1234	北京	完颜阿骨打	
元朝			1206—1368	北京	成吉思汗	戏曲
明朝			1368—1644	南京	朱元璋	长城，紫禁城
清朝			1616—1911	北京	努尔哈赤	颐和园，紫禁城
中华民国			1912—1949	南京		
中华人民共和国			1949 年 10 月 1 日成立	北京		

List of Chinese Dynasties and Modern Governments

Each Period			Period of Time	Capital	Founder	Historical Relics
Prehistoric Times			1. 7 million years ago – the 21st century BC			
Xia Dynasty			2070 BC – 1600 BC	Xia County	Qi	Bronzeware
Shang Dynasty			1600 BC – 1046 BC	Shangqiu	Tang	Bronzeware
Zhou Dynasty	Western Zhou		1046 BC – 771 BC	Xi'an	King Wu of Zhou	
	Eastern Zhou	Spring and Autumn Period	770 BC – 476 BC	Luoyang	King Ping of Zhou	Hundred Schools of Thought
		Warring States Period	475 BC – 221 BC			
Qin Dynasty			221 BC – 206 BC	Xianyang	Qin Shi Huang	Terracotta Army, the Great Wall
Han Dynasty	Western Han		206 BC – 25 AD	Xi'an	Liu Bang	The Silk Road
	Eastern Han		25 – 220	Luoyang	Liu Xiu	
Three Kingdoms	Wei		220 – 265	Luoyang	Cao Pi	
	Shuhan		221 – 263	Chengdu	Liu Bei	
	Wu		222 – 280	Nanjing	Sun Quan	
Jin Dynasty	Western Jin		265 – 317	Luoyang	Simayan	Tomb Fresco
	Eastern Jin		317 – 420	Nanjing	Simarui	
Southern and Northern Dynasties			420 – 589	Luoyang, Nanjing		Sacred Grottos
Sui Dynasty			581 – 618	Xi'an	Yangjian	The Grand Canal
Tang Dynasty			618 – 907	Xi'an	Liyuan	Literature
Five Dynasties and Ten Kingdoms			907 – 960	Kaifeng, etc.		

(Continued)

Each Period		Period of Time	Capital	Founder	Historical Relics
Song Dynasty	Northern Song	960 – 1127	Kaifeng	Zhao Kuangyin	Song Ci
	Southern Song	1127 – 1279	Hangzhou	Zhao Gou	
Liao Dynasty		907 – 1125	Chifeng	Yelv Abaoji	
Dali Kingdom		937 – 1254	Dali		Dali Ancient Town
Western Xia Dynasty		1038 – 1227	Yinchuan		Rock Carvings
Jin Dynasty		1115 – 1234	Beijing	Wanyan Aguda	
Yuan Dynasty		1206 – 1368	Beijing	Genghis Khan	Drama
Ming Dynasty		1368 – 1644	Nanjing	Zhu Yuanzhang	The Great Wall, the Forbidden City
Qing Dynasty		1616 – 1911	Beijing	Nurhaci	Summer Palace, the Forbidden City
Republic of China		1912 – 1949	Nanjing		
People's Republic of China		Oct. 1, 1949	Beijing		

传说时期

开天辟地——盘古

盘古创造天地之前，天地之间一片混沌。造物主盘古在一片混沌诞生之后，经过一万八千年，天与地开始分离。轻的、闪亮的物质升起来成了天，而重的、灰暗的物质沉下来，形成地。盘古则在天地之间，头顶着天，脚踏着地。他每天变化九次，比天和地更神圣。每天天上涨三米多高，地增三米多厚，而盘古也随之长三米多高。如此持续了一万八千年，天变得极高，地变得极厚，盘古也变得极其高大。后来三个重要人物伏羲、神农、黄帝诞生了。

Legendary Period

The Creation of the World—Pan Gu

Before the Creation, heaven and earth were in chaos. Pan Gu, the Creator was born in it. After about eighteen thousand years, the heaven began to be separated from the earth. The light and shining matters rose up and formed the heaven, whereas the heavy and dark matters sank down and formed the earth. Pan Gu was in between. With his head touching the heaven and his feet standing on the earth, he changed himself nine times a day, holier than both the heaven and the earth. Every day the heaven rose more than three meters high, the earth also thickened itself over three meters thick, while Pan Gu also grew over three meters tall. The case went on for eighteen thousand years and the heaven became extremely high, the earth extremely thick, and Pan Gu extremely big and tall. Then the three august figures Fuxi, Shennong, and Yellow Emperor were born.

伏羲

人们认为伏羲是第一个真正的统治者。他教人们如何设计工具、点火和煮食，如何驯养动物和照管家禽。他还设计了神秘的八卦，用来占卜。

Fuxi

Fuxi was considered the first real ruler. He taught people how to devise tools, kindle fire and cook food, how to domesticate animals and tend flocks. He also devised the mysterious Eight Trigrams which were used for divination.

炎帝神农

他发明了耕种，第一次把草药用于医疗。传说炎帝神农有一根神奇的鞭子。他用鞭子抽打各种草药，便能分辨出它们是否有毒，能产生什么疗效。借助这根神鞭，他用草药治好了各种疾病。

炎帝把部落分成几组，带领他们东迁，与黄帝作战，但被黄帝击败了。后来他求助于黄帝并与他结成了联盟，一起打败了蚩尤（传说中的部落首领）。他们常年生活在黄河中下游地区。中国早期历史上的两个重要人物炎帝和黄帝结成的部落联盟，形成了华夏民族的主干，最终演变成汉民族，所以中华民族的后代被统称为"炎黄子孙"。

Yan Emperor Shennong

He was the god who invented farming and was the first to use herbs for medical use. According to the legends, Yan Emperor Shennong had a magical whip. By lashing various kinds of herbs, he could distinguish whether they were poisonous or not, and what effect they might produce. With this whip, he cured diseases with herbs as medicine.

It is said, once Yan Emperor divided his whole tribe into several groups and led them to migrate eastward and fight against Yellow Emperor, but he was defeated. Then he turned to Yellow Emperor and formed a union with him. After they defeated Chiyou, the legendary chief of a tribe, they lived and multiplied in the middle and lower reaches of the Yellow River for many years. The united tribe by Yan Emperor and Yellow Emperor, the two august figures of the earliest Chinese history, formed the main part of the Huaxia nationality which changed itself into Han nationality in the later times, so the later generation of Chinese nationality is called the "descendants of Yan Emperor and Yellow Emperor."

黄帝

黄帝姓姬，号轩辕氏，是大约 4 000 年前生活在黄河中下游地区的联盟部落著名首领，一直被尊为中华民族的始祖。他发明了四轮牛车和制陶艺术，通过修路、建桥和造船改善了交通。他在位期间，宝石、金和铜开始作为货币流通。

Yellow Emperor

Yellow Emperor, whose family name was Ji, literary name Xuan Yuan, a famous chief of a united tribe living in the middle and lower reaches of the Yellow River about 4,000 years ago, has been worshipped as the common ancestor of Chinese nationalities. He invented the wheel and carts drawn by oxen and discovered the art of pottery-making. He improved transportation by building roads, bridges and ships. At that time under his administration, precious stones, gold and copper were introduced to serve as money.

大禹

大禹因治理黄河之水而受到人们的缅怀和尊敬。大约4 000年前，人们遭受着黄河洪水之困。舜帝先派禹的父亲鲧来治理黄河。鲧尝试了各种办法来阻塞洪水。

鲧治水九年之后，情况变得更糟，黄河之水到处泛滥。舜帝很生气，便辞了鲧，任命禹来治水。禹跟随他父亲治水多年，采用新方法来疏浚水道，把水引向大海。他潜心投身于治水，期间三过家门而不入。他花了13年时间终于成功治理了黄河。

Yu the Great

Yu the Great is remembered and respected as the ruler who made the Yellow River under control. He lived about 4,000 years ago when people suffered from big floods of the Yellow River. King Shun, the ruler before Yu, assigned Yu's father Gun to handle the problem initially. Gun tried out many methods of blocking up the water wherever the flooding occurred.

Nine years later, the situation had become even worse with the river overflowing everywhere. King Shun was very angry about what Gun had done, and ended up with dismissing Gun and appointing Yu to control the river. Yu learned techniques from his father but adopted a new way of dredging water channels and conducting the river to the sea. He focused on this project of water control with all his heart. It was said that during this period of time, he passed by his house three times but never went inside. It took him 13 years to tame the river.

中国各个朝代

1. 夏朝（前2070—前1600）

对于禹的功绩，舜帝很是感激，之后把王位让给了他。传说大禹是原始社会最后一个通过政绩推选的领导人。大禹的儿子启违反了这一选举体制。他杀了大禹任命的继位人，自己继承了父亲的王位。启创立了夏朝，开始了君主世袭制。夏朝持续了400多年，从公元前21世纪到公元前17世纪，共有十七个君王十四代人。

虽然这个理想中的大同社会被独裁政权所取代，但建立了夏朝，这意味着中国历史的巨大进步。

1. The Xia Dynasty（2070 BC–1600 BC）

King Shun was impressed by Yu's great efforts and passed his throne to Yu later on. Legend has it that Yu the Great was the last leader of the primitive society, in which the election of the leader followed the merit system. It was Qi, the son of Yu, who violated this practice. He killed the person whom Yu the Great had appointed and succeeded his father's power. Qi founded the Xia Dynasty and initiated the hereditary system of monarchy. The Xia Dynasty lasted over 400 years from the 21st century BC to the 17th century BC. There were seventeen kings over fourteen generations in total.

Although the ideal Society of Great Harmony was replaced with an autocratic regime, the establishment of the Xia Dynasty represents a huge advancement in the evolution of China.

2. 商朝（前 1600—前 1046）

商朝是中国第二个世袭王朝，持续了近六百年，共三十一个君王十七代。商曾经是生活在黄河下游地区一个古老的部落，是夏国的附属国。夏末最后一个统治者桀是一个暴君，他使人们整日生活在痛苦之中。商部落首领汤领导一支反叛军，推翻了夏朝，建立了商朝，定都为亳。

商朝最后一个君王帝辛，即纣王掌权。他在位期间，朝廷内部冲突变得更加严重，邻国开始反抗。公元前 11 世纪，一个叫周的边境国声名大振。在周文王的统治下，周国很快强大起来。文王死后，他的儿子姬发被封为武王，接替王位。公元前 1122 年，武王讨伐商纣王，发起战争。商朝军队在纣王统治时期遭受痛苦，商军变节，带领周军占领了商都。纣王自杀，商朝灭亡。

2. The Shang Dynasty（1600 BC – 1046 BC）

The Shang Dynasty was the second hereditary dynasty in China. It lasted almost six hundred years with 31 kings over 17 generations. Shang used to be an old tribe living in the lower reaches of the Yellow River. It was a tributary of the Xia Kingdom. At the end of the Xia, the last ruler Jie was a tyrant who made his people living in misery. The chief of the Shang tribe, Tang, led an insurgent army and overthrew the Xia Dynasty. Tang then established the Shang Dynasty and made Bo the capital city.

The last monarch in the Shang Dynasty Dixin, normally known as King Zhou, was in power. Internal social conflict became more serious and neighboring states began to rebel. In the 11th century BC, a frontier state called Zhou gained its prominence. Under the rule of King Wen, the kingdom of Zhou became powerful soon. When King Wen died, his son Jifa, known as King Wu, succeeded him. In 1122 BC, King Wu launched a punitive attack against King Zhou of the Shang. Having suffered much during the reign of King Zhou, the Shang army turned coat and led the Zhou army to the Shang capital. King Zhou committed suicide and the Shang Dynasty collapsed.

3. 周朝（前 1046—前 256）

周朝在传统上分为两个时期：西周（前 1046—前 771），定都镐京。东周进一步分为春秋时期（前 770—前 476）和战国时期（前 475—前 221），都城东迁到现在的洛阳。

周朝统治了 800 多年，是中国历史上统治时间最长的王朝。它见证了中国社会从奴隶制度到封建制度的演变，并在文化方面取得了辉煌成就。

中国历史把这一时期称为春秋战国时期。这是一个大混乱时期，许多诸侯国彼此为土地、权力、财富和荣誉而战。

3. The Zhou Dynasty (1046 BC – 256 BC)

Traditionally the Zhou Dynasty was divided into two periods: the Western Zhou (1046 BC – 771 BC) with Haojing as its capital, the Eastern Zhou which was further divided into the Spring and Autumn Period (770 BC – 476 BC) and the Warring States Period (475 BC – 221 BC), when the capital was moved east to present Luoyang.

The Zhou Dynasty reigned over 800 years and was the longest-ruling dynasty in China history. It witnessed the evolution of the China society from a slave system to a feudal one. Especially it was noted for its brilliant achievements in culture.

In Chinese history, this period was called Spring-Autumn Warring-State Period. It was a period of great disorder. There were many kingdoms which fought each other over land, power, treasure and honor.

公元前 770 年到公元前 221 年的春秋战国时期是诸子百家时期，出现了许多著名哲学家和各大流派，成为文化和知识扩张时代。尽管这一时期充满了混乱和血腥战争，但由于大量的思想得以研究和自由讨论，被称为中国哲学的黄金时代。

在这一混乱时期，有一位名为孔子的历史名人。孔子越是看到社会混乱，就越渴望社会和谐。他确立了关于行为、道德和礼仪的理论。他希望有国王愿意实施他的理论。孔子为了自己的伟大事业周游列国，结果却令他失望。国君们都热衷于追求权力和奢侈的生活，没有人对他的崇高道德教义感兴趣。最后，孔子只好在家乡开办私人学堂，宣传自己的教义，成为成功的教育家。据称，他有 3 000 个弟子，其中许多弟子后来成为著名的学者和高官。他和他的弟子们一起编写的教科书成了中国文化典籍。

Hundred Schools of Thought were philosophers and schools that flourished from 770 BC to 221 BC during the Spring-Autumn Warring-State Period, an era of great cultural and intellectual expansion in China. Even if this period was fraught with chaos and bloody battles, it is also known as the Golden Age of Chinese philosophy because a broad range of thoughts and ideas were developed and discussed freely.

During the chaos, there lived a great person in Chinese history who was named Confucius. The more Confucius saw the disorder, the more he craved for the social harmony. So he established a theory of behavior, moral, and etiquette. He hoped he could find out a king who was willing to carry on his theory. For his great cause, Confucius traveled many kingdoms and visited many kings. However, it was a frustrating journey. Those kings were so enthusiastic at power and luxurious life. Nobody had interests in his sublime moral doctrines. At last, disappointed, Confucius set up a private school at his hometown, preaching his own teachings. He became a very successful educationist. It is alleged that he has 3,000 disciples. Many of his disciples became famous scholars and high-rank officials. The textbooks his disciples compiled became classic books in China.

4. 秦朝（前221—前206）

公元前221年，秦王嬴政通过十年战争征服了其他六个诸侯国，结束了战国时期（前475—前221）的暴乱，建立了秦朝。这是中国历史上第一个统一的、多民族的中央集权国家，把陕西西安附近的咸阳定为都城。虽然秦朝是一个短命王朝，仅持续了15年，却开创了中国2 000年封建历史，对后来的各个朝代产生了深远的影响。除了西部边界、西南和东北地区，到现在为止秦的领土依然保存得相当完好。为了保护北部边境，秦始皇下令修筑长城。为了防御北方游牧民族的入侵，成千上万的农民被征募去把北方各国以前的城墙连成5 000公里长城。秦始皇还制定了中央集权制和严格的法律法规来镇压百姓。公元前207年秦始皇去世后的一年，一支农民军推翻了秦王朝的统治。

秦始皇和他的继任者的暴政遭到全国百姓的普遍反对。农民起义冲击着秦朝政权。最后，公元前207年，项羽带领的军队使秦军遭受重大损失；第二年，刘邦带军攻破了秦首府咸阳，秦朝统治结束。

4. The Qin Dynasty (221 BC – 206 BC)

Yingzheng, king of the Qin state, conquered the other six dukes through ten years of wars and brought an end to the riotous Warring States Period (475 BC – 221 BC) in 221 BC. He built up the Qin Dynasty—the first unified, multi-national, autocratic and power-centralized state in China history—by making Xianyang, a city near Xi'an in the Shaanxi Province, his capital city. Although Qin is a short dynasty with a span of only fifteen years, it started off a 2,000-year-long imperial history in China and exerted a far-reaching influence on the subsequent dynasties. Except for frontiers in the west, southwest and northeast, Qin's territory has been kept fairly intact up to now. To protect the northern frontier, Qin Shi Huang ordered the construction of the Great Wall. As a defense against the northern nomads, hundreds and thousands of peasants were conscripted to join up and extend the walls of the former northern states into the 5,000-kilometer-long Great Wall of China. Emperor Qin Shi Huang instituted centralism and a strict set of rules by which people lived in oppression. An army of peasants overthrew the harsh Qin regime just one year after the death of the Emperor Qin Shi Huang in 207 BC.

The tyranny of Emperor Qin Shi Huang and his successor resulted in wide opposition throughout the country. Peasant uprisings struck the regime of the Qin continually. Finally, in 207 BC, Xiang Yu's army inflicted heavy losses on the Qin army. In the following year, Liu Bang broke Xianyang, the capital of Qin, thus putting an end to the Qin Dynasty.

秦朝是中国历史上第一个中央集权的、统一的、多民族的封建国家。

在秦朝，文字得以简化和统一。丞相李斯把全国各地文字标准化为统一的大小和形状，深深地影响了中国几千年后的文化。他创立的小篆体，成为现代汉语的基础，至今仍在图片、海报和广告中使用。

后来项羽和刘邦为了争夺全国的统治权，他们发起了为期4年的楚汉战争。最后，刘邦于公元前202年击败项羽，建立汉朝（前206—220），自称汉帝。

The Qin Dynasty is the first centralized, unified, multi-ethnic feudal state in Chinese history.

The written language was simplified and made unified. Prime Minister Li Si standardized the writing system to be of uniform size and shape across the whole country. This would have a unification effect on the Chinese culture for thousands of years. He is also credited with creating the "lesser-seal" style of calligraphy, which serves as a basis for modern Chinese and is still used in cards, posters, and advertising.

Later, in pursuit of the domination of the country, a four-year war known as the Chu-Han War broke out between Xiang Yu and Liu Bang. Finally, Liu Bang defeated Xiang Yu in 202 BC and established the Han Dynasty (206 BC – 220 AD), after which he proclaimed himself the emperor of the Han.

5. 汉朝（前206—220）

经过与对手项羽四年的战争，刘邦终于掌控了全国局势，并于公元前202年建立了自己的政权——汉。

汉王朝分为两个历史时期。第一时期为西汉（前206—25），定都长安（即现在的陕西西安）。第二时期为东汉（25—220），定都洛阳。

汉朝是中国历史上第二个统一王朝。秦始皇统一中国之后，各种不同文化融合在一起，为汉文化奠定了基础，正是在此期间，汉民族成为中国的主要民族。汉民族更先进的文明，赢得了汉族人民在各族人民中的主导地位。无论过去的几个世纪发生过多少变化，汉民族的优势地位至今仍然存在。

汉武帝的对外扩张政策巩固了汉朝，却也耗尽了国家财库，导致税收急剧增加和对经济的严格控制。从长远来看，这样做会给各朝代带来不好的影响。

5. The Han Dynasty (206 BC – 220 AD)

After four years' war with his rival, Xiang Yu, Liu Bang finally got command of the whole country and established his reign—Han Dynasty in 202 BC.

The Han Dynasty has been divided into two historical periods. The first period is called the Western Han (206 BC – 25 AD) as the capital was Chang'an (the present city of Xi'an in Shaanxi Province). The second period is known as the Eastern Han (25 – 220) as Luoyang became the capital city.

The Han Dynasty ruled over the second unified Chinese empire. Based on the unification created by Emperor Qin Shi Huang, a variety of different cultures were integrated. This laid the foundation for what became the common culture of Han/Cathay. It was during this period that the Han ethnic group established itself as the core nation of China. It was as a consequence of their more advanced civilization that the Han people assumed a dominant position. This dominance still exists in China today, regardless of many changes having taken place over the centuries.

Emperor Wu's expansionist policies strengthened the Empire. Nevertheless, they drained the imperial treasury. This resulted in sharp increases in taxes and tight control over the economy. In the long term, it had the effect of undermining the dynastic influence.

昭帝和宣帝掌权时，尽管经济增长了，潜在的社会危机却开始出现。西汉最后几十年，陆续有几个幼皇帝登基，摄政权落在宦官和后妃的家属手里，导致腐败和阶层分化，最终导致频繁的农民起义。哀帝继承王位之后，西汉王朝衰落。公元 8 年皇后的亲戚王莽废黜了幼皇帝，自称新朝皇帝（9—23）。

王莽尽管被谴责为篡位者，却是一位博学的儒家学者。他希望通过采用一系列儒家经书中描述的政策来恢复汉朝的荣耀（王莽改制）。他更名官位、废除奴隶制、限制土地所有权、垄断工商业、减少朝廷开支。然而，由于他大量发行新币，使黄金储备国有化和频繁地对外宣战，王莽并没有得民心，最后导致社会更加动荡。公元 17 年，一场全国性的起义爆发了。六年后，即公元 23 年，王莽被叛军杀害。

When Emperors Zhao and Xuan were in power, potential social crises began to appear despite economic growth. During the last decades of the Western Han Dynasty, a series of child emperors occupied the throne. These necessitated regencies and power fell into the hands of eunuchs and empresses' relatives, which led to corruption and greater class division resulting in frequent peasant uprisings. Ultimately, the Western Han Dynasty fell after the Emperor Ai succeeded to the throne. In 8 AD, Wang Mang, one of the empress' relatives, deposed infant Emperor and proclaimed himself Emperor of the Xin Dynasty (9 – 23 AD).

Although condemned as a usurper, Wang Mang was a learned Confucian scholar. He wished to retrieve the glory of Han by adopting policies described in the Confucian classics. He renamed officials, outlawed slavery, limited land holdings and monopolized both industry and commerce. He also reduced court expenses. However, Wang Mang's unpopularity due to the issue of new coins, nationalization of gold reserves and frequent declarations of war finally led to more serious social turmoil. In 17 AD, a nationwide rebellion broke out. Six years later, in 23 AD Wang Mang was killed by rebels.

之后不久，汉皇室成员刘秀重新确立汉朝霸权地位，即东汉（25—220）。

平息东汉黄巾之乱之后，涌现出了众多地方军阀争夺国家的掌控权。其中，黄河中下游地区袁绍和曹操的军队是最强的。而在长江以南，孙权和刘备分别占领了东部和西部地区，在第一轮权力争夺战中他们相对较弱。

Very soon, Liu Xiu, a member of the Han imperial family, re-established Han supremacy through what has become known as the Eastern Han Dynasty (25—220).

After the quelling of the Yellow Turbans Uprising of the Eastern Han Dynasty, local warlords and tyrants sprung up everywhere to struggle for the control over the country. Among them, the military groups under Yuan Shao and Cao Cao in the middle and lower reaches of the Yellow River stood out as the strongest. While to the south of the Yangtze River, Sun Quan and Liu Bei occupied the eastern and western areas respectively. They stayed comparatively weaker in the first round of power struggle.

6. 三国（220—280）、两晋（265—420）、南北朝（420—589）

公元263年，魏国征服蜀。蜀国历经42年，两个君主。魏国持续了46年，五个君主。公元265年，魏国一名高官司马炎篡夺了皇权，建立了自己的政权晋（265—420）。后来，晋于公元280年推翻了最后一个幸存王国吴国，三国时期结束。

曹操被称为三国时期著名的政治家、军事家和伟大的文学家。曹操在二十岁的时候就开始了军事生涯。在东汉末年镇压黄巾起义军的过程中，他组建了军队。叛乱平息后，东汉政权有名无实，国家解体成曹操、刘备和孙权三股对抗势力。当时，曹操的势力超过刘备和孙权。

公元196年，曹操把东汉首府从洛阳迁到许昌（都在现在的河南省内）。他自称为丞相，把傀儡皇帝当撒手锏。经过几场与北部地方军阀的决定性战争，他统一了黄河以北地区。

同时，曹操在诗歌方面也取得了巨大成就，他和他的两个儿子一起开启了中国文学新纪元。

6. Three Kingdoms（220 – 280）, Jin（265 – 420）, Southern and Northern Dynasties（420 – 589）

In 263, the Wei Kingdom conquered Shu, which only lasted for forty-two years with two kings in the reign. Wei Kingdom lasted for 46 years with five kings. In 265, Sima Yan, a top official of the Wei, usurped the power and established his reign as Jin（265 – 420）. Later, Jin overturned Wu, the last surviving kingdom in 280 and brought an end to the Three Kingdoms Period.

Cao Cao was known as a famous politician, strategist and a great litterateur during the Three Kingdoms Period. Cao Cao started his military career at the age of twenty. In the process of cracking down the Yellow Turbans Uprising at the end of the Eastern Han Dynasty, he built up his force. After the rebellion, the Eastern Han only reigned in name and the country fell apart into three confronting forces of Cao Cao, Liu Bei and Sun Quan. Cao Cao outstripped the other two.

In 196 AD, Cao Cao had the Eastern Han capital relocated from Luoyang to Xuchang, (both in present Henan Province). He proclaimed himself the prime minister and made the puppet emperor his trump card. After several decisive battles with local forces in the north, he unified the region north of the Yellow River.

Meanwhile, Cao Cao made great achievements in poetry. Together with his two sons, they opened a new era in the history of Chinese literature.

三国（220—280）末期，司马家族在魏国变得更显赫。公元265年，司马炎篡权，建立一个新的王朝晋朝。晋朝在历史上分为两个阶段：以洛阳为首府的西晋和以建康（现在的江苏省南京市）为首府的东晋。

晋朝是魏、晋、南北朝时期（420—589）唯一统一的朝代，尽管统一持续不久。

晋朝虽然短暂且充满冲突，但由于长期的接触和相互影响民族之间的融合不断加速。

东晋末年国内出现许多对抗势力。中国分裂成南北对抗的两大阵营。这一时期，不同朝代的兴衰最为频繁。

At the end of the Three Kingdoms Period (220 – 280), Sima family became prominent in the Wei Kingdom. In 265 AD, Sima Yan usurped the power and founded a new dynasty Jin. Jin was divided into two periods historically: the Western Jin with Luoyang as its capital city and Eastern Jin as Jiankang (present Nanjing in Jiangsu Province) became the capital city.

Jin Dynasty was the only period, which unified the country during the period between the Wei, the Jin and the Southern and Northern Dynasties (420 – 589), though this kind of achievement was not lasting.

Although Jin Dynasty was short and full of conflicts, the mix between nationalities was accelerated through the long-term contacts and mutual influences.

After the Eastern Jin Dynasty, there came many rivaling regimes over the country. China was torn apart into the confrontation between north and south. It was the time that saw the highest frequency of the ups and downs of the different dynasties.

南方相继出现了宋、齐、梁、陈四个朝代，持续了 160 年。因为所有这些南方政权都建都南京，所以把它们统称为南朝。在这段时间里，世袭的大家族经历了自西晋王朝以来的大繁荣到衰落的蜕变。虽然他们仍然地位显赫，却没有了实权而不再干涉政务。帝王们重新获得真正的治国权力。

十六国混乱局面结束时，一个文明程度较低的游牧部落鲜卑族逐渐变得强大起来。386 年，鲜卑族首领建立了北魏政权。439 年，北魏统一了黄河以北地区，定都山西大同。这是北朝时期的开始。

471 年，北魏孝文帝迁都洛阳，大力推行学习汉文化。他命令鲜卑人穿汉服，讲汉语，取汉姓。他还鼓励鲜卑人与汉人通婚，朝廷立汉人为官。此外，在经济上，孝文帝颁布法令来实施土地均衡制。所有这些都促进了社会的发展和中华民族融合的趋势。

In the south, there were four consecutive dynasties, the Song, the Qi, the Liang and the Chen, with 160 years. Since all the southern regimes established their capital in present Nanjing City, they got a general term the Southern Dynasty. During this time, hereditary big families underwent their downfall after long-time social prominence ever since the Western Jin Dynasty. Although they still held the noble status, they could no longer meddle in the state affairs. The emperors retrieved the real power over the country.

At the end of the chaotic period of the Sixteen States, a nomadic tribe, Xianbei, which was little civilized, gradually became powerful. In 386, the chief of the Xianbei set up their regime of the Beiwei (the Northern Wei). In 439, the Beiwei Empire unified the region north of the Yellow River and settled the capital in present Datong, Shanxi Province, marking the beginning of the Northern Dynasty.

In 471, the Emperor Xiaowen of the Wei relocated his capital in Luoyang and vigorously promoted the learning of the Han culture. He ordered the Xianbei people to dress up like the Han people, speak their language and adopt the surname of Han's. He also encouraged the intermarriage between the Xianbei people and the Han and employed many Han officials in the court. Moreover, in economy, Emperor Xiaowen promulgated a decree to implement the land equalization system. All this contributed to the development of the society and the amalgamation of the Chinese nationalities.

然而，孝文帝改革遭到了鲜卑贵族保守势力的强烈反对。孝文帝去世后，他的改革被取消，这加剧了鲜卑贵族和汉贵族统治阶级内部的矛盾。不久后，魏国被一分为二。

南北朝末年，中国经历了约 270 年分裂和混乱局面。

577 年，北周征服北齐，统一了北方。北周由鲜卑族的宇文家族掌权，持续了 24 年，共五个皇帝三代人。

However, the reform encountered strong objection from the conservative force among the Xianbei aristocrats. After the Emperor Xiaowen died, his reform was revoked, which intensified the conflicts inside the ruling class between the Xianbei and the Han aristocrats. Before long, the Wei Empire was broken up into two.

By the end of the Southern and Northern Dynasties, China had witnessed disunity and chaos for about 270 years.

In 577, the Northern Zhou conquered the Northern Qi and reunified the North China. The Northern Zhou, known as the reign of Yuwen family of the Xianbei ethnic group, continued for 24 years with five emperors over three generations.

7. 隋朝（581—618）

经过四百年的分裂，隋朝重新统一中国北部和南部，隋文帝杨坚建立了隋朝，定都长安。

隋朝政府重新确立了由汉朝建立的中央集权的行政体制。他们建立了三省六部制，以通过不同部门之间的监督和协作来加强中央集权。此后，所有朝代都效法这一行政体制。

隋文帝确立了科举制度，根据政绩而不是家庭出生背景来选拔官员以遏制腐败。从隋朝开始的科举考试制度在接下来的 1 300 年里一直沿用，并对后来的人才选拔产生了深远的影响。

7. The Sui Dynasty（581—618）

After four hundred years of disunion the Sui Dynasty reunited northern and southern China. The Sui Dynasty was founded by emperor Sui Wendi, Yang Jian, with the capital at Chang'an.

The Sui government re-established the centralized administrative system created by the Han Dynasty. They set up the system of the "Three Departments and Six Ministries" which strengthened the centralized power by focusing on cooperation and supervision between the different departments and ministries. The dynasties thereafter all followed up this administrative system.

Emperor Wen set up the Imperial Examination System to curtail corruption by ensuring that officials were selected based on merits rather than by birth. The system of civil service examinations that began during the Sui Dynasty would be used by successive Chinese dynasties for the next 1,300 years. The system has a profound impact on the talent pageant later on.

由于隋朝恢复了汉代儒家礼仪，儒家思想重新受到欢迎。隋朝也支持佛教，因此，佛教成为中国文化一股新的凝聚力。

隋朝最突出的成就在社会经济建设方面，主要有：大运河的修建（从北京到杭州）和由工匠李春修建的赵州桥（世界上最古老的石拱桥）。

此外，著名的敦煌莫高窟（位于甘肃省）60%的佛像和一些精致的壁画都出自隋朝。

隋王朝历经38年，两代。历史表明它是一个较短暂的朝代。

Confucianism began to regain popularity, as the Sui Dynasty restored Confucian rituals from the Han Dynasty. The dynasty also supported Buddhism, which has become the unifying force of all groups and cultures in China.

The most outstanding achievements on the social economy: the construction of the Grand Canal (from Beijing to Hangzhou) and Zhaozhou Bridge (the world's oldest stone arc bridge) by Artisan Li Chun.

Additionally, 60 percent of the statues of Buddha and delicate murals in the renowned Dunhuang Mogao Caves (located in the Gansu Province) were created during the Sui Dynasty.

Sui Dynasty lasted for only 38 years with two generations. History shows it was one of the short-lived Chinese dynasties.

8. 唐朝（618—907）

唐朝统治了近300年，是中国历史上最著名的朝代。唐朝经历了三个鼎盛时期，即"贞观之治"，武则天统治时期和"开元盛世"时期。当时，唐帝国是世界上最大、最富有、最强盛的国家。唐朝大大地影响了亚洲、欧洲和非洲。邻国纷纷寻求与唐帝国建立关系往来，当时的长安成为东西方文化交流的中心。

唐朝是中国空前繁荣的朝代，其政治、经济、军事实力和外交超过了前面所有朝代。在文化上，唐朝的文学也超出过往。唐朝的诗歌向世人展示了当时诗人们无与伦比的、辉煌的创造力。

8. The Tang Dynasty（618－907）

The Tang Dynasty, which maintained its rule for nearly 300 years, is probably the most well-known dynasty in Chinese history. Successively witnessing three florescences, namely "the Prosperity of Zhenguan", the reign of Empress Wu Zetian and "the Heyday of Kaiyuan" in its period, the Tang Empire justifiably became the largest, richest and most sophisticated state in the world at that time. Greatly and widely admired abroad, the Tang influence spread into Asia, Europe and Africa. Neighboring countries sought and established ties with the empire and Chang'an became the center of cultural exchange between the East and the West.

This was an epoch that was unprecedented in China. Dominance in the fields of politics, economics, military power and foreign relations exceeded all that had gone before. In terms of culture, the one thing that places the Tang Dynasty above all others is the literature of the age.

The brilliance of poetry during the period attests to an unparalleled and glorious flowering of creativity.

唐太宗李世民是唐朝第二个皇帝，是唐高祖李渊与窦皇后的第二个儿子。唐太宗是他死后的谥号，意思是"至高无上的祖先"。他在位 23 年（627—649），被认为是中国最伟大的皇帝之一。他统治的时期称为"贞观之治"，这是一个非常和平与繁荣的时代，也是唐朝最鼎盛的时期之一。唐太宗的政治生涯有三个重要标志：太原养兵、玄武门宫廷政变、贞观盛世。他的政治改革使国家一步步走向繁荣昌盛。确保他实现政治上的稳定有两个主要因素，一是挑选合适的人选；二是在做决定之前广泛征求他人的意见。他死于 649 年，享年 53 岁，被葬于西安的唐昭陵。

Taizong was the second of the Tang emperors. He was born as Li Shimin to the Empress Dou, the second son of Emperor Gaozu. Taizong is his posthumous temple name and means "Supreme Ancestor". His rule lasted for twenty-three years (627 – 649) and he is considered to be one of the greatest of the Chinese emperors. His reign, which is known as the Prosperity of Zhenguan, was outstanding as an era of peace and prosperity, one of the most flourishing during the Tang period. There are three important landmarks in his political career: Raising an Army in Taiyuan; the Palace Coup of Xuanwumen; Prosperity of Zhenguan. The political reforms he introduced were designed to ensure the ship of state sailed on calm waters. There were two main factors that ensured the political stability he sought to achieve. These can be summarized as to pick the right person for the task and to seek the opinion of others before making a decision. Following his death in 649 at the age of fifty-three, he was buried in the Zhaolin Tomb that is located near the present day city of Xi'an.

武则天是中国历史上唯一一位女皇帝，也是最显著的、最有影响力的、最神秘的女性。这个女人统治了中国半个多世纪，与孔子的教义相违背，因此，她成为十几个世纪以来的争议人物。意见分为两派，一派佩服她所取得的许多成就，而另一派则视她为残酷、无情的阴谋家和独裁者。还有人认为她只是做了自己该做的事，其行为与男性皇帝没有什么不同。孔子认为女性当帝王无异于牝鸡司晨。但不可否认，在这个女人的精心治理下，唐朝达到了空前的繁荣。

唐朝从公元 618 年统治下的昌盛帝国到公元 907 年灭亡。最后一个皇帝（哀帝李柷）的暴政和朝廷阴谋以及经济剥削导致了唐朝的衰落。最终朱全忠夺取政权，建立了新王朝，即后梁。

Empress Wu Zetian was the only female monarch of China, and remains the most remarkable, influential and mysterious woman in Chinese history. Contrary to the teachings of Confucius, this was a woman who ruled the empire for over half a century; while her actions have been a subject for debate for more than ten centuries. Opinion is sharply divided between those who admire her for her many achievements and those who regard her as a ruthless, merciless schemer and autocrat. Others will say merely that she did what she had to do and that her actions were no different from those of male emperors of the period. According to Confucius, having a female monarch is unnatural as "a hen crowing like a rooster at daybreak". However, for what proved to be one of the most glorious periods during the Tang Dynasty, a woman did rule the empire.

The magnificent empire that had existed from 618 AD under the rule of the Tang Emperors finally collapsed in 907 AD. With the inevitable decline brought about through misrule, court intrigues and economic exploitation the scene was set for the overthrow of Ai, the last of the Tang Emperors. Zhu Quanzhong seized power and established a new dynasty that has come to be known as the Later Liang.

接下来五十年国家变得支离破碎。华北地区由五个短命的军事政权控制，而南方则分成十个独立的国家，十国因此而得名。这半个世纪也是中国最荒芜的时期，官员腐败和战争普遍存在。

运河和大坝的失修，对北方影响很大，导致了大范围的洪水泛滥和随之发生的饥荒。然而当时有一个杰出成就，即印刷术。

For the next fifty years, the empire was to become fragmented. Northern China was ruled during this period by five short-lived military regimes, while the South became split into ten independent states. Hence the name was given to this era of history. During this half century, which was to prove one of China's bleakest, warfare and official corruption were endemic.

The North was particularly affected as its canal and dam system fell into disrepair. This led to widespread flooding and consequent famine. However, there was one outstanding accomplishment and this was the widespread development of printing.

9. 宋代（960—1279）

宋朝在历史上的重要性是与唐朝和汉朝（前206—220）齐名的。在这不到325年的历史中，中国经济飞速增长，并在艺术文化上取得了辉煌的成就。因此，这个时期可与当时遍布欧洲的文艺复兴相匹敌，被称为中国的文艺复兴时期。

960年，赵匡胤发动陈桥兵变掌握政权后，他能够有条理地控制和巩固全国局势。由他创立的宋朝分为两个阶段。一是960年到1127年的北宋，定都东京（今河南开封）。二是从1127年到1279年的南宋，定都今天的杭州。

9. The Song Dynasty（960 – 1279）

The Song Dynasty ranks alongside the Tang and also the Han（206 BC – 220 AD）in importance. For a little under three and a quarter centuries under its rule, China enjoyed a period of economic growth coupled with great artistic and intellectual achievement. It is for this reason that the period is referred to as the Chinese Renaissance, comparing it with the Renaissance that spread through Europe.

When Zhao Kuangyin seized power by a coup in Chenqiao in 960 he was able to consolidate and extend his control in a restrained and methodical manner. The Song Dynasty that he founded has been divided into two periods. Firstly, the Northern Song when the capital was in Dongjing（present day Kaifeng City in Henan Province）from 960 to 1127. Secondly, the Southern Song when their capital was in present day Hangzhou from 1127 to 1279.

13 世纪，蒙古大草原上的游牧部落出了个伟大首领铁木真。游牧部落占领了大兴安岭北部山区和额尔古纳河东岸。他们擅长骑术，在铁木真的领导下，他们组建为一股强大的战斗势力。1206 年铁木真正式当选为蒙古可汉，占据了蒙古高原和戈壁沙漠。新当选的可汗开始扩大地盘，将目光投向中原。1227 年，他打败了西夏。1234 年，他打败了金，为少数民族政权首次统一全中国。

During the 13th Century a great leader, Temujin, was to emerge from among the nomadic tribes of the Mongolian steppes. These tribesmen occupied the area between the northern Daxing'an Mountains and the eastern bank of the Argun River. As skilled horsemen, they were to become a formidable fighting force once the tribes had united under Temujin's leadership. In 1206 Temujin was formally elected as ruler over Greater Mongolia, encompassing the Mongolian Plateau and the Gobi Desert. The newly elected Khan set about extending his empire and set his sights on Central Plains. In 1227 he defeated the Western Xia and in 1234 he defeated the Jin. This was to open the way to unify the whole of China for the first time under a minority nationality regime.

10. 元朝（1206—1368）

成吉思汗死后，他的孙子忽必烈继位，于 1271 年建立元朝，定都大都（今北京）。元世祖忽必烈接着进攻南宋，1279 年元军占领南宋都城杭州。

随着元朝稳定确立，元统治者成了这个地域最大的、聚居着多民族的国度的统治者，北面向朝鲜和俄罗斯延伸，南面向缅甸和伊拉克延伸。但是这些统治者没有治国经验，因此，他们沿用了中原的政治和文化模式。

蒙古族由于蒙古诸侯的内战和定居中原所带来的生活方式的转变，军事力量大大降低，在中国的统治最终结束。由于这些外来统治者平息不了大规模农民起义，再加上一场接一场的自然灾害的来袭，天命运程转向了农民起义期间杰出的农民领袖朱元璋。

10. The Yuan Dynasty (1206 – 1368)

Following Genghis' death, his grandson succeeded him and as Kublai Khan, the new leader established the Yuan Dynasty in 1271, with his capital city at Dadu (present day Beijing). Kublai, who was known as Emperor Shizu continued to attack the Southern Song and in 1279 the Yuan forces captured Hangzhou, the capital city of the Southern Song.

With their dynasty now firmly established in the Chinese empire, the Yuan found themselves rulers of a complex group of peoples who inhabited the largest land based empire ever to exist, stretching from what is now Korea and western Russia in the north and from Burma to Iraq in the south. But they were rulers with no experience of administration. Consequently, they adopted Chinese political and cultural models.

Mongol rule in China was brought to an end after civil war among Mongol princes and an increasing conversion to the sedentary Chinese way of life that robbed the Mongol military machine of much of its effectiveness. Repeated natural disasters were followed by a massive peasant rebellion that the alien rulers could not quell. The Mandate of Heaven now shifted to Zhu

Yuanzhang, a peasant leader who became eminent during the rebellions.

11. 明朝（1368—1644）

1368 年，明太祖朱元璋占据元朝大都，在建康（今南京）称帝，确立明朝，重新恢复汉族在中国的统治。明朝是汉族人建立的最后一个王朝。

大型建筑项目如修复长城、修建北京紫禁城开始动工。

在航海方面，郑和远渡东南亚和印度洋，使明朝在世界上有了更大的影响力。

文化在明代也得以迅速发展。中国四大名著中的三部都是在明朝创作的，即施耐庵写的《水浒传》，罗贯中写的《三国演义》和吴承恩写的《西游记》。《永乐大典》是由明朝永乐皇帝组织，按帝王顺序编写的大型百科全书，编写始于 1403 年，于 1408 年完成，是当时世界上最大的百科全书，收录了从古代到明代初期八千种引书，有 22 877 或 22 937 手稿卷或章节，共分装为 11 095 册。编写组一共 2 169 人，由解缙和姚广孝监督编写。

科技方面，明朝出了很多科技书籍，其中最著名的是李时珍的《本草纲目》，宋应星的《天工开物》和徐光启的《农政全书》。

11. The Ming Dynasty（1368 – 1644）

In 1368, Zhu Yuanzhang captured Dadu of the Yuan Dynasty and proclaimed himself emperor in Jiankang（currently Nanjing）establishing the Ming Dynasty and restoring Han nationality rule in China. The Ming Dynasty was also the last of the dynasties established by Han nationality.

Enormous projects of construction such as the restoration of the Great Wall and the establishment of the Forbidden City in Beijing were started.

In navigation, Zheng He's long voyages to Southeast Asia and the Indian Ocean made the Ming much more influential in the world.

Culture was developed quickly in the Ming Dynasty. Three of the Four Great Classical Novels of Chinese literature were produced at that time. They are *Water Margin* by Shi Nai'an, *The Romance of the Three Kingdoms* by Luo Guanzhong and *Journey to the West* by Wu Cheng'en. The *Yongle Encyclopedia*（*Yongle Dadian*）is a large encyclopedia compiled on imperial order of the Yongle Emperor of the Ming Dynasty. The compilation started in 1403 and was completed by 1408. It was the world's largest known general encyclopedia at its time, incorporating eight thousand texts from ancient times up to the early Ming Dynasty. It comprised 22,877 or 22,937 manuscript rolls, or chapters, in 11,095 volumes. The compilation team of 2,169 persons was supervised by Xie Jin and Yao Guangxiao.

In science, many treasurable reference books were produced in the Ming Dynasty, among which the most well-known ones are Li Shizhen's *Compendium of Materia Medica*, Song Yingxing's *Exploitation of the Works of Nature* and Xu Guangqi's *Complete Treatise on Agriculture*.

12. 清朝（1616—1911）

由女真族（满族）人建立的清朝，是第二个由少数民族统治整个中国的王朝。它也是中国历史上最后一个封建王朝。清朝期间，中国实力和影响力盛极一时。

女真人被认为是满族人的祖先，是生活在与现在黑龙江地区相邻的一个游牧部落。明朝末年，努尔哈赤从女真部落脱颖而出。在他的领导之下，女真人迅速联合起来。1616 年建立了后金国，独立于明代。1636 年，首领努尔哈赤的儿子皇太极在沈阳把明朝改名为清王朝，并正式对明宣战。

1644 年，李自成领导的农民军攻下北京，崇祯皇帝自杀。驻扎在山海关的明朝指挥官吴三桂带领清军通过山海关。同年，皇太极的儿子福临在摄政王多尔衮的协助下占领北京。四个月后将都城迁到了北京。这标志着清政府开始统治中国。在接下来的十年左右，满族继续压制本地人的抵抗，1659 年消灭了南明的永历政权，逐渐统一了全国。

12. The Qing Dynasty（1616 – 1911）

The Qing Dynasty, which was founded by the Jurchen (Manchu) people, was run by the second ethnic group to rule the whole of China. It is also the last feudal dynasty in Chinese history. It was during this period that imperial China reached its zenith of power and influence.

The Jurchen people, believed to be the ancestors of the Manchus, had been a nomadic tribe that lived adjacent to the present Heilongjiang region. In the closing years of the Ming Dynasty, Nurhachi, emerged from the Jurchen tribe. Under his leadership, the Jurchen people rapidly united and in 1616, established the Later Jin State which was independent from the Ming. In 1636, Nurhachi's son Abahai, renamed the dynasty as Qing in Shenyang while formally declaring war on the Ming.

In 1644, when the peasant army led by Li Zicheng conquered Beijing, Emperor Chongzhen committed suicide. Wu Sangui, a Ming commander stationed in Shanhaiguan Pass, led the Qing army through the pass. With the assistance of prince regent Dorgun, Fulin, son of Abahai, captured Beijing in the same year and four months later, moved his capital there. This marked the beginning of the Qing reign over China. For the next decade or so the Manchu continued to suppress native resistance, finally destroying the Yongli Regime of Southern Ming in 1659 and gradually unified the whole country.

清朝早期是一个前所未有的繁荣时期。为了缓和阶级矛盾，清朝奉行奖励土地耕种和减免税收的政策。这些政策促进了内陆和沿海地区经济的增长。康熙（1662—1723）、雍正（1723—1736）和乾隆（1736—1796）皇帝统治时期是清朝鼎盛时期。18 世纪中期经济发展达到了一个新的高度。这种新的繁荣使权力更加集中，使国力增强，社会秩序得到良好维护，到世纪末人口达到约 3 亿。康熙皇帝统治时期，台湾成为中国的部分领土，康熙和俄罗斯就边境问题签订了《中俄尼布楚条约》。

清朝是少数民族在中国统治非常成功的朝代，它持续了将近 300 年。清政权因 1840 年的鸦片战争而划分为两个阶段。

In its early years, the Qing Dynasty witnessed a flourishing that was unprecedented by any other age. In order to mitigate class conflicts, the Qing pursued a policy of rewarding land cultivation coupled with a reduction or exemption from taxation. These policies promoted economic growth in the hinterland and on the frontiers of the country. The reigns of Emperors Kangxi (1662 – 1723), Yongzheng (1723 – 1736) and Qianlong (1736 – 1796) saw the Qing at its heyday. By the mid-18th century economic development reached a new height. With this new prosperity power became more centralized, national strength increased, a well-maintained social order and a population that amounted to some 300 million by the end of the century. During the reign of Emperor Kangxi, Taiwan became part of the country and the *Sino-Russian Treaty of Nerchinsk* was signed determining the border between the two countries.

The Qing Dynasty was very successful as an ethnic group reign in China. It lasted for almost 300 years and the duration of the regime was divided into two periods by the Opium War occurred in 1840.

第二节　中国新时期历史文化

Section 2　Chinese Modern Historic Culture

很多历史专家认为，中国现代历史（1840—1949）是中国人民的一段革命史。确切地说，是一部中国人民反侵略、反帝国主义和反封建以获得重新独立和民族复兴的历史。中国现代历史分为两个阶段：从 1840 年鸦片战争爆发到 1919 年五四运动濒临爆发的中国旧民主主义革命阶段和从 1919 年五四运动爆发后，到 1949 年新中国成立前的中国新民主主义革命阶段。在这一时期，中国属于半殖民地半封建社会国家。

Chinese modern history (1840 – 1949) in accordance with many historical professionals' standpoints is a revolutionary history of Chinese people, exactly, a history of anti-invasion, anti-imperialism and anti-feudalism of Chinese people for re-independence and national revival. Chinese modern history is separated into two phases: Chinese Old Democratic Revolution Phase from 1840 when the Opium War broke out to 1919 when May-4th Movement was on the verge of breaking out, Chinese New Democratic Revolution Phase from 1919 after May-4th Movement broke out to 1949 before the foundation of New China. Amid this period, China belonged to the country of semi-colony and semi-feudalism.

从 19 世纪中期起，中国开始受到以英国和法国为代表的西方列强的挑衅和入侵的威胁，并逐渐失去了独立性。中国遭受外国入侵和羞辱，主权和领土的完整性在很大程度上受到外国势力的破坏。19 世纪 70 年代之后，外国加紧侵略中国，中华民族危机变得越来越严重，中国和西方之间的冲突不断加剧。中国在战争中的失败给中国带来无尽的耻辱。无能的、荒唐的清政府为了一时的和平被迫签订了一系列可耻的条约，如 1842 年的《南京条约》、1858 年的《天津条约》、1860 年的《北京条约》、1895 年的《马关条约》和 1901 年的《辛丑条约》等，所有这些都丢尽了中国人的脸。为摆脱侵略，拯救中国，清政府进行了几次大规模的、有影响力的改革，如洋务运动和戊戌变法（或称百日维新）。各地的起义有 1851 年到 1864 年的太平天国起义、1899 年的义和团运动、1911 年的辛亥革命等。1912 年清政府统治结束，社会和民族矛盾与冲突得以缓和，但没有完全把入侵势力赶走。1919 年，巴黎和平会议的主题是第一次世界大战后的利益分配问题，中国作为一

个战胜国参加了会议，但会议上，中国提出的合理要求遭到西方列强和日本的拒绝。这些爆炸性新闻直接导致了五四运动的爆发。中国从此进入了追求独立和民主的新时期。

Since the middle phase of the 19th century, China begun to be intimidated by the provocation and invasion of western powers represented by Britain and France and gradually China lost independence. China suffered foreign invasion and humiliation and the integrality of sovereignty and territory were largely undermined by exotic powers. The conflict between China and western powers was worsened after 1870s when foreign aggression was rather intensified and China's national crisis became increasingly urgent. China's failures in warfare always brought China endless disgrace and ignominy. A series of shameful treaties was forced to sign under the trashy and ridiculous leadership of Qing Government for temporary peace like *Treaty of Nanking* in 1842, *Treaty of Tianjin* in 1858, *Treaty of Peking* in 1860, *Treaty of Shimonoseki* in 1895 and *Treaty of Xinchou Year* in 1901 etc. , all of which humiliated Chinese people too much! For getting rid of aggression and saving China, Qing Government held several large-scale and influential reforms such as Yangwu Movement and Wuxu Reform or the Hundred Days' Reform. The grassroots' insurgence like Taiping Rebellion (Heavenly Kingdom of Great Peace) from 1851 to 1864 and Yihetuan Righteous Harmony Society happened in 1899 and finally, Xinhai Revolution in 1911. In 1912 the reign of Qing government ended, which relieved a little bit of social and national conflicts, but it could not root the foreign aggression out. In 1919, Paris Peace Conference themed with the profit distribution after World War One, China as a winning country attended at the conference, but on the conference, China's justified requirements were not agreed by western powers and Japan. This breaking news directly led the outbreak of the May-4th Movement. China entered the new phase in pursuit of independence and democracy.

1921 年，中国共产党在上海成立，中国出现了实现复兴的新生力量。1931 年九一八事变，中国遭受了严重的民族危机，局部抗日战争开始。1935 年华北事变，为了联合击退日本鬼子的侵略，爱国将领张学良（1901—2001）和杨虎城（1893—1949）发动事变，把国民党领袖蒋介石（1887—1975）软禁了起来。周恩来（1898—1976）和许多其他的爱国者全力以赴，最终这一事变得以和平解决。为保护国家领土和抗击日本侵略者，国民党和中国共产党首次形成了爱国统一战线。1937 年七七卢沟桥事变标志着中华民族的全面抗日战争正式开始。1945 年，中国打败了日本，获得胜利。随后，三年内战爆发，并于 1949 年结束；国民党因腐败和决策错误而失败，后来退守台湾。此后，中国大陆由中国共产党领导。

In 1921, Chinese Communist Party was founded in Shanghai. A new way and power for realizing the revival of China appeared. In 1931, September-18th Incident (Mukden Incident or Manchurian Incident) happened. China suffered the severe national crisis and Anti-Japanese War partly begun. In 1935, North-China Incident happened. For jointly rolling back Japanese Ghost-like Invaders, Patriotic Generals Zhang Xueliang (1901 – 2001) and Yang Hucheng (1893 – 1949) launched an incident that they placed Jiang Kai-shek (1887 – 1975), President of Kuomintang, under the house arrest with the all-out efforts of Zhou Enlai (1898 – 1976) and many other patriots. This interior incident was peacefully resolved and Kuomintang-China Communist Party patriotic united front for protecting homeland and fighting against Japanese invaders firstly appeared. In 1937, July-7th Lugouqiao Incident officially symbolized the complete beginning of Chinese National Anti-Japanese War. In 1945, China defeated Japan and won the victory. Subsequently, three-year civil war broke out, up to 1949; Kuomintang failed and retreated to Taiwan because of its corruption and wrong policymaking, and Mainland China since then has been under the leadership of Chinese Communist Party.

1949 年开始的新中国史，作为中国现代史的开端充满泪水和喜悦，令人难忘。中华人民共和国的成立实现了中国几代人长期为之奋斗的民族再独立。民族复兴之路充满了改革、挫折、失败和成功。许多令人伤心的历史往事如"文化大革命"、"大跃进"、"大饥荒"和"反右派"运动，使中国人积累很多经验并吸取了教训。今天，她仍然进行着民族复兴，在过去的 30 年取得了巨大的经济成就。

As the beginning of Chinese modern history, New China's history beginning at 1949 is also impressive and full of tears and surprises. The foundation of the People's Republic of China realized the re-independence of China which many generations have strived for a long time. But the way to revival abounds with lots of reforms, frustrations, failures and success. After many heartbroken historical events represented by "Cultural Revolution", "Grand Leap Forward", "Great Chinese Famine" and "Anti-Rightist" Movement happened, China has learnt much from the lessons. Today, it is still in progress for national revival but has gotten a great economic achievement over the past 30 years.

新中国成立后的最初十年，中国政府成功地对全国 90% 以上的农业人口实行了土地改革政策，3 亿农业人口因此获得了约 4 700 万公顷的土地。从 1953 年到 1957 年第一个五年计划时期，改革取得了惊人的成就。国民收入的平均年增长率达到 8.9% 以上。

中国为实现全面工业化，创建了如生产飞机、汽车、重型机械、精密机械、电力设备、冶金和采矿设备、高级合金钢和有色金属等基础产业。

During the initial ten years after the foundation of New China, the Chinese government successfully carried out land reform policy in areas accounting for over 90 percent of the total national agricultural population, and 300 million farmers were granted approximately 47 million ha. of land. Amazing achievements were made during the First Five-Year Plan period, from 1953 to 1957. The average annual increase rate of the national income reached over 8.9 percent.

China established basic industries necessary for full industrialization hitherto, producing airplanes, automobiles, heavy machinery, precision machinery, power-generating equipment, metallurgical and mining equipment, high-grade alloy steels and non-ferrous metals.

从 1957 年到 1966 年十年间，中国开始了大规模的社会主义建设。虽然期间出现了决策失误，却取得了很多成绩。国家的工业固定资产总额在 1956 年和 1966 年之间翻了两番，国民收入增加了 58%。工业产品的产量增加了几倍甚至十几倍。大规模的农业基本建设得以启动，技术得以改造。

不幸的是，持续了十年的"文化大革命"（1966 年 5 月—1976 年 10 月）自新中国成立以来使人民遭受了最严重的挫折和损失。

1976 年 10 月粉碎江青反革命集团，标志着"文化大革命"的结束和中国历史新时代的开始。

The ten years from 1957 to 1966 was the period in which China started large-scale socialist construction. Although China suffered from the mistakes in its policies during the period, it also accomplished a great deal. The nation's total industrial fixed assets quadrupled between 1956 and 1966 and the national income increased by 58 percent in constant prices. The output of essential industrial products increased by several or even a dozen times. Large-scale agricultural capital construction and technical transformation got underway.

Unfortunately, the "Cultural Revolution," which lasted for ten years (May 1966 – October 1976), made the state and its people suffer the most serious setbacks and losses since its founding.

The Jiang Qing counter-revolutionary clique was smashed in October 1976, marking the end of the "Cultural Revolution," and the beginning of a new era in Chinese history.

中国共产党恢复邓小平在"文化大革命"期间免去的领导职位。1978 年中国在邓小平的领导下制定了"改革开放"政策，把重点转移到现代化建设上来。

中国为经济和政治体制的改革做出了巨大努力，逐步走上具有中国特色的道路，一条通往社会主义现代化的道路。自改革开放以来，中国已经发生了巨大的变化，出现了前所未有的好局面，其特点是快速、大力推进经济发展，人们生活水平明显改善。

The CCP reinstated Deng Xiaoping, in the leadership posts he had been dismissed from during the "Cultural Revolution." In 1978, China instituted a guiding policy of "reform and opening to the outside world" under Deng's leadership and the focus was shifted to modernization.

Major efforts were made to reform the economic and political systems. China was step by step on a road with Chinese characteristics, a road that would lead to socialist modernization. Profound changes have come about in China since the country embarked on the policy of reform and opening-up. The situation in the country is the best ever, characterized by a swiftly and vigorously advancing economy and markedly improved living standard.

口述题

1. 中国古代历史可分为多少个时期？分别是哪些？
2. 秦朝结束了战乱，统一六国，你对其有什么了解？

Questions

1. How many periods can ancient Chinese history be divided into? What are they?
2. Qin Dynasty ended the war and unified the six countries. What do you know about it?

学习网站

1. 传统文化网（http://www.zhwh365.com/）
2. ANCIENT HISTORY（https://www.ancient.eu/china/）

第四章　儒家与中国传统文化

Chapter 4　Confucianism and Traditional Chinese Culture

第一节　儒家思想的形成

Section 1　The Formation of Confucius' Thoughts

背景

孔子，名丘，字仲尼，尼：神圣的山。公元前551年出生于鲁国的一个贫困家庭。他的父亲是鲁国的一个地方长官，在孔子出生三年后逝世。孔子经历了贫困和屈辱的少年后长大成人，曾做过管理仓库和照看牧场等琐碎工作（吾少也贱，故多能鄙事）。不过孔子接受过良好的教育。他19岁时结婚，并生了一个儿子和两个女儿。

50岁时，孔子被任命为鲁国的大司寇，后来被迫离职流放。他离开鲁国，周游列国，想寻找一个重用他的统治者，却遭冷遇。公元前484年，他回到鲁国边整理古代经典著作，边从事教学度过余生。孔子有弟子3 000名，其中72个弟子成为著名的儒学家。

Background

Confucius, given name: Qiu, academic name: Zhongni, Ni: a sacred hill, was born in a poor family in the state of Lu in the year 551 BC. His father, commander of a district in Lu, died three years after Confucius was born. He had endured a poverty-stricken and humiliating youth upon reaching manhood, been forced to undertake such petty jobs as warehouse management and caring for livestock (I was of humble station when young. That is why I am skilled in many menial things). But Confucius received a fine education. He was married at the age of 19 and had one son and two daughters.

At the age of 50, he was appointed Minister of Crime of the Lu State, then forced to leave office and go into exile. He left Lu and traveled in the states looking for a ruler who might employ him but meeting instead with indifference. In 484 BC, he returned to Lu and spent the rest of his life teaching, putting in order ancient classics. Then he became a professional teacher with 3, 000 students, and among them 72 disciples were famous Confucians.

教育

孔子创办了第一所私塾学校，接受来自全国各地的学生。主要学习礼、乐、射、御、书、数。

哲学

孔子创立的儒家思想不仅深刻地影响了人们的日常生活，而且影响了后人的思想体系。直到今天我们仍然受他的思想的深远影响。孔子的基本道义体现在以下五个汉字之中。

仁：即仁慈，是人性、怜悯、善良之意。

义：公正、正义、义务、友好之意。

礼：仪式、庆典、礼仪、礼貌之意。

智：智慧、足智多谋、智力、有教养之意。

信：忠诚、可靠、负责任、诚信之意。

政治

作为政治家，孔子在鲁国并不曾有过显赫的政治地位。他曾做过代理丞相。然而，他在整个政治生涯中，一直都奔走于他国之间。

当时的有识之士都很关心未来的社会模式，因而中国历史舞台上出现了充满思想活力的百家争鸣的局面，比如法家、道家等。因为没有单一的教条主宰他们的生活，这一时期也是最令有识之士兴奋的时期。

孔子提出克己复礼的主张。他还提出了一系列准则，其中包含的思想后来逐步发展为儒家思想。

Education

Confucius established the first private school in China and accepted the students from everywhere. Subjects: Manners, Music, Archery, Riding, Literature, and Mathematics.

Philosophy

Confucius founded the Confucianism, which deeply influenced not only in the daily lives, but also the ideology of later generations in China. It is far-reaching that we are still living under the shadow of its surroundings. The basic Confucius doctrines are embodied in the following characters:

Ren—benevolence, humanity, mercy, kindness.

Yi—justness, righteousness, obligation, friendliness.

Li—rituals, ceremony, manners, courteousness.

Zhi—wisdom, resourcefulness, intelligence, well-educatedness.

Xin—royalty, reliability, responsibility, faithfulness.

Politics

As a statesman, Confucius didn't play an important role in his homeland. Once had he been the acting prime minister, however, during his whole-life political career, he had to go to other countries back and forth.

The intellectuals of the day were concerned about the future mode of society, hence the most brilliant contention of a hundred schools of thought, such as Legist, Taoist, thrived in a vibrant period in Chinese history. This is often regarded as the most exciting times for Chinese intellectuals as no single doctrine dominated their lives.

Confucius' proposal was to discipline oneself and to revive the ethics of Zhou Dynasty. Therefore, he brought forward a series of norms, which step by step developed into Confucianism.

儒家节日和传统儒家礼仪文化

清明节，也称为踏青节，是指每年阳历 4 月 4 日至 6 日春光明媚、草木吐绿的时节，在这期间，人们开展踏青等一系列体育活动。清明节在古代又称为三月节，已有 2 000 多年的历史。这一传统的中国节日也是最重要的宗教节日。人们在这一天从事扫墓、祭拜已故祖先等活动。

Confucianism Festival and the Traditional Confucian Ritual Culture

The Qingming Festival, also known as Ta-Qing Festival, according to the solar calendar, is on April 4 to 6 each year when vegetation spits green in bright spring days. People carried out a series of sports custom such as Qingming Ta-Qing. Qingming Festival in the ancient times also called the Festival of March, has over 2,000 years of history. This traditional Chinese festival is also the most important religious holiday, and it is time for ancestor worship, commonly known as tomb-sweeping, a deceased worship activity.

孟子（约前 372 年—前 289 年），姬姓，孟氏，名轲，字子舆，战国时期邹国（今山东济宁邹城）人。战国时期著名哲学家、思想家、政治家、教育家，儒家学派的代表人物之一，地位仅次于孔子，与孔子并称"孔孟"。宣扬"仁政"，最早提出"民贵君轻"的思想。

Mencius (about 372 B. C. – 289 B. C.) was a man of Ji surname, Meng shi, whose given name was Ke and his surname was Ziyu. In the warring states period, he was a famous philosopher, ideologist, politician and educator. He was one of the representatives of the Confucian school, ranking second only to Confucius. He advocated "benevolent government", the first to put forward the idea of "people and nobles light".

代表作有《鱼我所欲也》、《得道多助，失道寡助》。《生于忧患，死于安乐》、《富贵不能淫》和《寡人之于国也》被编入中学语文教科书中。

His representative works include *FIsh as I Desire*, and *Just Cause Helps Many a Unjust Cause a Few.* "*Born in sorrow, died in happiness*", "*Riches and Honour Can not be Corrupted*" and "*I am in the Country*" were included in the middle school language textbooks.

儒家语录
Quotes of Confucianism
求知篇（About study）
1. 温故而知新，可以为师矣。

If a man keeps cherishing his old knowledge, so as continually to be acquiring new, he may be a teacher of others.

2. 尽信书，则不如无书。

We would rather be short of book than believe all that they say.

3. 三人行必有我师焉。择其善者而从之，其不善者而改之。

When traveling in company of two other people, I could find my teachers; I would learn from their good points and guard against their bad ones.

4. 学而时习之，不亦说乎。

Isn't it a pleasure that to learn and then review (practice) what you have learned from time to time?

5. 学而不思则罔，思而不学则殆。

Learning without thinking is labor lost; thinking without learning is perilous.

品德篇 (About morality)

6. 老吾老，以及人之老；幼吾幼，以及人之幼。

Expend the respect of the aged in one's family to that of other families; expend the love of the young one in one's family to that of other families.

7. 唯仁者，能好人，能恶人。

Only the humane person is able to really like others or to really dislike them.

8. 克己复礼为仁。

To completely overcome selfishness and keep to Li (propriety) is Ren.

9. 言必信，行必果。

Keep what you say and carry out what you do.

10. 其言之不怍，也为之也难。

He who speaks without modesty will find it difficult to find his words good.

交友篇 (About friendship)

11. 有朋自远方来，不亦乐乎？

It is a great pleasure to meet friends from far away.

12. 君子周而不比，小人比而不周。

The superior man is broad-minded and not a partisan. The small man is a partisan and not broad-minded.

13. 里仁为美。择不处仁，焉得知？

As for a neibourhood, it is its humaneness that makes it beautiful. If you choose to live in a place that lacks humaneness, how can you grow in wisdom?

14. 益者三友，损者三友。友直，友谅，友多闻，益矣。友便辟，友善柔，友便佞，损矣。

There are three kinds of friendship which are beneficial and three kinds which are injurious. Friendship with upright men, with faithful men, and with men of much information; such friendship is beneficial. Friendship with plausible men, with men of insinuating manners, and with glib tongued men: such friendships are injurious.

15. 道不同，不相为谋。

Those whose courses are different cannot lay plans for one another.

育人篇（About education）

16. 有教无类。

In teaching people, there is no discrimination (of class, type, etc).

17. 人莫知其子之恶，莫知其苗之硕。

A man does not know the wickedness of his son; he does not know the richness of his growing corn.

18. 当仁不让于师。

In the face of benevolence, do not give precedence even to your teacher.

19. 过而不改，是谓过矣。

To have faults and not to correct them, this, indeed, is to have faults.

20. 子以四教：文、行、忠、信。

There are four things which the Master taught—letters, ethics, devotion of soul, and truthfulness.

第二节　儒家思想的发展和影响

Section 2　The Development and Influence of Confucianism

儒家思想是中国古代最具影响力的学术和思想流派。儒家文化作为华夏固有价值系统的一大代表，并不是通常意义上的学术或流派，一般来说，儒学并不优越于其他学派，尤其是在先秦时期，儒学只是数百个学术流派之一。汉代以来，儒家思想被大力发扬，成为用于教育和社会管理的主要学术思想和卓越的意识形态。直到今天，中国仍受着儒家思想的广泛影响。

儒家始终坚持"亲亲"、"尊尊"的立法原则，维护"礼治"，提倡"德治"，重视"人治"。因此，自汉朝以后儒家思想被所有封建王朝作为用于治国的主要思想体系。

Confucianism is China's most influential academic and ideological school in ancient time. As the representative of Chinese inherent value system, Confucianism is absolutely superior to the customary meaning and role of academic schools. Generally, especially before Qin Dynasty, Confucianism was just one of hundreds of academic schools and did not have a superiority or privilege over other schools. Since Han Dynasty, Confucianism has been largely promoted to be the dominant academic thought and prominent ideology used for educating and administrating the society. Even up to today, China is still under the extensive influence of Confucianism.

Confucians fundamentally insist the legislative principle of "getting close to man who deserves to be closed up" and "respecting the man who are respectable to uphold their basic idea". Then maintain "rule by rites", advocating "rule by morality", and valuing "rule by man". Hence Confucianism was taken as the dominant ideology to administrate the state by all feudalistic dynasties since Han Dynasty.

礼治：礼治的教义体现在"等级区别"。不同的等级有不同的礼治标准与要求。从整个国家到每个家庭包括皇帝在内的每一个人都必须遵循礼治。国家的稳定与否是由社会地位的稳定与否决定的。儒家的礼治也是一种无形的法律，它是维护封建社会的核心和基础。谁违反了规定便处罚谁。

德治：儒家赞成通过道德的力量改造个人或社会，认为任何性格的人都可以接受教育并得到改造。这种教育通过心理改造来完善和净化人的心灵。

人治：儒家重视人的个性、道德发展潜能和同情心。孔子把"仁"作为最高的道德原则、道德规范和道德水平。"仁"是儒家思想的核心，这一核心在很大程度上直接决定了中国文化的特点和形式。

Rule by rites：The doctrine of rule by rites is embodied in "class". Different classes have different standards and requirements of rule by rites. From the whole country to the single family, each individual including the emperor had to follow the rule by rites. The stability of a country depends on that of social status. In other words Confucian's rule by rites is also an invisible law and the core and base for upholding the feudalistic society. Whoever disobeyed its regulation would be surely penalized.

Rule by morality：Confucians approve of remodeling the individual or society via morality. They agree that all men no matter what kind of character they have can be educated and remodeled. Such an education is to refine and purify man's heart through changing his mind.

Rule by man：Confucians emphasize the specialty of man and his possible morality development as well as his sympathy. Confucius took Benevolence as the top moral principle, moral criterion and moral level. Benevolence is the core of Confucianism and directly models the characteristic and form of Chinese culture largely.

儒家的经典著作最终由孔子修订，但不同朝代的人们对这些经典的看法和理解不同。在汉代，儒家经典过于社会化，滥读滥解释，直接导致后代对它的误读、混淆和看法分歧。到宋代，以朱熹（1130—1200）为代表的儒家学者吸收了道教和佛教思想重新解释这些经典著作，使儒家思想的发展进入一个新阶段，这在学界被称为新儒学。1911年推翻清王朝前，儒家思想一直是政府的意识形态。自共和国成立后，儒家思想被边缘化的同时，还受到了外来新文化的冲击。然而，经历新政府和在西方社会成长起来的知识分子的破坏和反对之后，儒家思想依然是中国人的核心价值思想。同时，儒教也是东亚各国共同的基本文化信仰。儒学也是刺激像西方社会卢梭之类的文化精英所倡导的启蒙运动和西方现代科学的良好发展的重要因素。

现在，全世界都面临着许多问题，如全球变暖、能源危机、环境污染、文明冲突和加剧人类生存危机的紧迫性问题。儒家思想基于其复杂的意识形态系统重新发挥着缓解这些危机甚至提供解决办法的作用。儒家思想为全人类维护和平与和谐，为自然和地球上的其他物种共存指明了方向。

Confucian's classics were finally revised by Confucius, but in different dynasties, the standpoints and understanding to these classics are different. In Han Dynasty, Confucian classics were over-socialized or misunderstood, which directly caused misreading, confusion and difference in view of following generations. In Song Dynasty, a large group of Confucians represented by Zhu Xi（1130 – 1200）re-explained these classics via taking in some thoughts from Taoism and Buddhism and made Confucianism develop into a new stage. It is called Neo-Confucianism in academic circle. Confucianism was the governmental ideology all the time till the overthrow of Qing Dynasty in 1911. Since the foundation of The Republic of China, Confucianism was marginalized and also suffered from the impact of the exotic new culture. However, after the destruction and opposition of the new government and academicians growing up in western society, Confucianism is still the core value of Chinese people. Meanwhile Confucianism is also the basic cultural belief shared in Eastern Asian countries. It is also an important element stimulating the development of the Enlightenment advocated by social and cultural elites like Rousseau in western society and the development of western modern science.

Today, the whole world is facing many problems like global warming, energy crisis, environmental pollution, clash of civilization and the urgency that may worsen the crisis of human survival. Basing itself on its sophisticated ideological systems, Confucianism replays its key role of alleviating these crises and even supplying the solutions. Confucianism has pointed out the direction for human staying in peace and harmony as well as coexisting with nature and other species on the earth.

中国现代史上重要的军事和政治人物继续受儒家思想的影响，如穆斯林军阀马福祥。新生活运动很大程度上依赖于儒学。国民党清除中国教育体制的西方思想，引入儒家思想到课程大纲。教育处于国家控制之下，实际上是国民党通过教育部予以控制，增加了国民党三民主义军事和政治课程。教材、考试、学位和教师以及所有大学都由国家掌控。

孟子（前372—前289）和荀子继续发展了儒家思想。汉武帝在位时儒学被提升为国家意识形态。此后，儒家思想成为中国社会的正统教义。孔子成为圣人而不再是普通人。

魏晋时期，儒教与佛教和道教并存。到隋唐时期，三大教派为争取主导地位竞争激烈。宋代是见证儒学发展的至关重要的时期。接下来的700年间儒教恢复了正统地位。

Important military and political figures in modern Chinese history continued to be influenced by Confucianism, like the Muslim warlord Ma Fuxiang. The New Life Movement relied heavily on Confucianism. The Kuomintang party purged the western ideas in China's education system, introducing Confucianism into the curriculum. Education was under the total control of state. In effect, it was under the control of the Kuomintang party via the Ministry of Education. Military and political classes on the Kuomintang's Three Principles of the People were added. Textbooks, exams, degrees, instructors and all the colleges and universities were all controlled by the state.

Confucianism was further developed by Mencius (372 BC – 289 BC) and Xun Zi. It was in the reign of Emperor Wu during the Han Dynasty that Confucianism was promoted to be the state ideology. Since then, Confucianism has become the orthodox doctrine of Chinese society. And Confucius was glorified as a Saint instead of an ordinary man.

In Wei and Jin dynasties, Confucianism coexisted with Buddhism and Taoism. Up to the Sui and Tang dynasties, the struggle for dominance among the three became heated. The Song Dynasty witnessed a vital period of the development of Confucianism. Confucianism restored its orthodox role for the following 700 years.

1915 年开始的新文化运动，挥舞着科学和民主的旗帜，攻击着封建制度，包括以儒家思想为核心的思想体系。"文化大革命"期间，儒家思想再次受到猛烈攻击。

近年来人们可以用更理性的心理看待儒家思想。有些人甚至建议回到儒家智慧。而反对者认为儒学应该为中国发展的滞后负责，因此不应该恢复它的主导地位。

令大家高兴的是，有许多学者致力于研究儒家思想及其对现代社会的应用。这些研究非常重要，因为在过去的几个世纪里中国语言经历了相当大的变化，古代经典名著没有标点符号，从而使我们难以完全理解孔子的思想。

With the banner of science and democracy, the New Cultural Movement from 1915 attacked the feudal system, including its core ideological system of Confucianism. During the "Cultural Revolution", Confucianism was once again under violent attack.

In recent years people treat Confucianism with a more rational state of mind. Some even suggest returning to Confucianism for wisdom while opponents hold that Confucianism should be responsible for the backwardness of China's development and for that reason its dominance should not be revived.

To our delight, many scholars devote themselves to the study of Confucianism and its application to modern society. Such study is important as the Chinese language has experienced considerable changes over the centuries and the lack of any punctuation in the ancient classics has made it difficult for us to fully comprehend Confucius' ideology.

儒教对中国的影响

儒家思想对中华文明影响之大，让你无法想象中国文化和历史会是什么样子。在整个2 000年间，儒家思想影响了中国人的生活态度、生活模式和社会价值观，确立了培训政府官员的标准，为中国政治理论和制度提供了背景材料。儒家思想旨在获得和保持"文化身份地位"，成为调整世界、教育、自我完善、礼貌和忠孝的杠杆。

儒教对世界的影响

儒家思想不仅影响了东亚，对整个世界也影响极大。儒学，特别是孔子的思想，有助于世界和平与稳定。世界各地建立了很多孔子学院以传播儒家文化。

The Impact of Confucianism on China

Confucianism has so great an impact on the Chinese civilization that you can't imagine how Chinese culture and history will be. In the period of 2,000 years, Confucianism has influenced the Chinese attitude toward life, patterns of living and standards of social value. It has helped to establish standards for training government officials, and to provide the background for Chinese political theories and institutions. The Confucianism aimed at attaining and preserving "cultural status position" and was used as means to adjust to the world, education, self-perfection, politeness and familial piety.

The Impact of Confucianism on the World

Confucianism had an enormous impact on not only East Asia, but also the entire world. The Confucianism, specially the idea of Confucius, contributes a lot to the peace of the world. There are many Confucius Institutes around the world, spreading the Confucianism culture.

口述题

1. 请你讲出一句所知道的儒家语录，并说出你对它的理解。
2. 根据本章节所述并结合自身理解，阐述一下儒家文化对于现在的意义。

Questions

1. Tell me a Confucian quotation you know and your understanding of it.

2. According to this chapter and your own understanding, elaborate the significance of Confucian culture for the present.

学习网站：

1. 中国儒学网（http://www.confuchina.com/）
2. Travel China Guide（https://www.travelchinaguide.com/intro/religion/confucianism/）

第五章　道教、佛教与中国传统文化

Chapter 5　Taoism, Buddhism and Traditional Chinese Culture

第一节　道教与中国传统文化

Section 1　Taoism and Traditional Chinese Culture

道教不是宗教而是一种哲学。道基本是难以定义的，它是指事物自然发展的顺序，是一种生活"方式"，是流经每个人、生物和非生物以及整个宇宙的力量。

道教由与孔子同时代的人物老子（约前571—约前471）创立，并由庄子（前369—前286）加以发展。道教开始是建立在心理学和哲学基础之上，但在公元前440年演变成了宗教信仰而被当作国教。当时老子成为被普遍崇拜的神。道教与佛教和儒家思想一起成为中国的三大宗教之一。

Taoism is not a religion but a philosophy. Tao is basically indefinable. It is the natural order of things. It refers to a "Way" of life, the power that flows through every sentient being living and non-living, and through the entire universe as well.

Taoism was founded by Lao Zi (571 BC – 471 BC), a contemporary of Confucius, and was developed by Zhuang Zi (369 BC – 286 BC). Taoism started as a combination of psychology and philosophy but evolved into a religious faith in 440 BC when it was adopted as a state religion. At that time Lao Zi became popularly venerated as a deity. Taoism, along with Buddhism and Confucianism, became one of the three great religions of China.

老子，也叫老聃，是春秋时期（前770年—前476）最早的伟大思想家和哲学家。他出生于楚国，比孔子早几十年。他是周朝皇室管理藏书的史官。业余主要研究哲学，一生试图寻找可以避免无休止的封建战争和其他扰乱社会冲突的方法。

Lao Zi, also called Lao Dan, the earliest great thinker and philosopher of the Spring and Autumn Period (770 BC – 476 BC) in Chinese history, was born in the State of Chu before Confucius by scores of years. He had been a low-ranking official in the palace of the Zhou Dynasty. Working in the library, he was engaged in philosophical studies, searching for a way that would avoid the constant feudal warfare and other conflicts that disrupted society during his lifetime.

在他的《道德经》一书中，他最终得出这样的结论：宇宙由天空、地球、人类和他所谓的"原则"或"道"组成。他认为道是宇宙的第一成因，宇宙中其他所有东西都是由道派生出来的。而且，宇宙中存在相互对立的平衡，这可以从最常见的道教神学图加以说明，即阴阳图。阴（阴暗面、负面）形成地球之气。阳（阳面、正面）形成天之气。他认为所有事物都受相互矛盾、相互依存的客观自然规律支配。有时坏事可以变成好事，反之亦然。

简单地说，世界充满了相互对立的东西——阴阳、美丑、大小、善恶、年轻和年老、男性和女性、生与死等。没有丑便没有美，没有邪恶便没有善良。阴阳理论可以帮助人们思考自己的生活状态，关注周围的世界以理解宇宙的内在和谐。此外，他建议人应该知足。

道规定着宇宙间的自然过程，协调宇宙的平衡发展，体现了对立面的和谐。

Finally in his book called *Dao De Jing*, he reached the conclusion that the universe consisted of sky, earth, humanity and what he called "principles" or "ways", for which he coined the term Tao. He stated that Tao was the first cause of the universe, from which everything else in the universe was derived. What's more, there was the balance of opposites in the universe, which can be illustrated by the most common graphic representation of Taoist theology—the circular Yin Yang figure. Yin (dark side, negative form) is the breath that formed the earth. Yang (light side, positive form) is the breath that formed the heaven. He believed that all things are equally governed by objective natural laws that are contradictions, and yet depend on each other. Sometimes bad things could turn into good things and vice versa.

Simply speaking, the world is full of opposites—Yin and Yang, anything beautiful and ugly, small and big, good and evil, young and old, male and female, live and die, etc. Without ugliness, there is no beauty. Without evil, there is no good. The Yin Yang theory helps people contemplate their own state of their lives, focus on the world around them in order to understand the inner harmonies of the universe. Moreover, he proposed that man should be easily contented.

In short, Tao regulates natural processes and nourishes balance in the Universe. It embodies the harmony of opposites.

《道德经》

"道"这个概念首先由老子在他的书中用简洁的古汉语提出，没有明确其内涵，使得他的跟随者对"道"衍生出各种解释，也给后人留下关于"道"的翻译问题。

四个独特的概念

（1）未分化的原始状态（混乱）："有物混成，先天地生。"（第25章）"道之为物，惟恍惟惚。"（第21章）"道生一，一生二，二生三，三生万物。"（第42章）

（2）道是原初物："道常无名、朴，虽小，天下莫能臣。"（第32章）

（3）人的肉眼看不见"道"，人的感官感觉不到"道"："视之不见，名曰夷；听之不闻，名曰希；搏之不得，名曰微。"（第14章）

（4）道是指事物的规律："天之道……人之道……"。（第 77 章）

Dao De Jing

The concept— "Tao"（the Way）, first put forward by Lao Zi in succinct ancient Chinese in his book *Dao De Jing*, without clarifying its connotations, has left his successors to develop various interpretations of Tao. This also leaves a translation and interpretation problem for the later generations.

Four Distinctive Notions

（1）The undifferentiated primitive state（chaos）："There was something undifferentiated and yet complete."（Chapter 25）"The thing that is called Tao has no definite form."（Chapter 21）"Tao gives birth to the unified thing（One）, the One splits itself into two opposite aspects（Two）, the Two gives birth to another（Three）, the newborn Third produces a myriad of things."（Chapter 42）

（2）Tao is the proto-material："Tao has no name forever. Though the simplicity seems small, it may be subordinated to nothing under Heaven."（Chapter 32）

（3）Tao is invisible to man's eyes, and imperceptible to man's sense organ："You look at it and it is not seen, it is called the Formless. You listen to it and it is not heard, it is called the Soundless. You grasp it and it is not to be held, it is called the Intangible."（Chapter 14）

（4）Tao means the law of things："The Way（Tao）of Heaven... the Way（Tao）of man."（Chapter 77）

部分名篇

道

道可道，非常道。名可名，非常名。无名天地之始。有名万物之母。故常无欲以观其妙。常有欲以观其徼。此两者同出而异名，同谓之玄。玄之又玄，众妙之门。

Some Famous Chapters

Tao

The Tao that can be spoken of is not the eternal Tao;

The name that can be named is not the eternal name;

The nameless is the origin of Heaven and Earth;

The named is the root of all things.

Therefore, the subtleties of Tao are always apprehended through their formlessness.

The limits of things are always seen through their form.

These two（the form and the formless）have the same source but different names.

Both of them can be called deep and profound;

The deepest and the most profound, the door of all mysteries.

阴阳

天下皆知美之为美，斯恶矣；皆知善之为善，斯不善已。故有无相生，难易相成，长短相形，高下相倾，音声相和，前后相随。是以圣人处无为之事，行不言之教。万物作焉而不辞。生而不有，为而不恃，功成而弗居。夫唯弗居，是以不去。

Yin and Yang

When all people in the world know the beautiful as beauty,

There appears ugliness;

When they know goodness as good,

There appears evil.

Therefore, by opposing each other,

Existence and nonexistence come into being,

Difficult and easy form themselves,

Long and short are distinct,

High and low contrast,

Sound and voice harmonize,

Front and back emerge.

Thus the sage manages affairs by "non-action",

And teaches by "saying nothing".

He leaves all things to grow and change without initiation;

Raises all things without attributing them to his contribution;

And takes no credit for himself when the work is done.

It is because no claim is made that his credit cannot be forfeited.

主要道义

（1）道教遵循无为的思想来传承美德。无为并不意味着没有行动，而是顺其自然。最灵巧的东西，好似最笨拙的；最充盈的东西，好似是空虚的一样；最崇高的人，似乎总是很卑微的；最有活力的看起来呆滞；最简单淳朴的看起来多变，就像人应该保持孩子般的简单淳朴，但并非真正的天真无知。

（2）同情、节制和谦卑是道家的主要追求，通过修养得以实现。

（3）道家重视养生术。道教认为，身体的五个主要器官相当于宇宙的五部分：金（肺）、木（肝）、水（脾）、火（心）和土（胃）。认为气（空气、呼吸）是养身的元气，不仅在体内循环，而且与宇宙相连。

Major Practices

（1）Taoists focus on the development of virtue by following the art of non-action (Wu wei). Non-action doesn't mean no action, but to let nature take its course. One who seems to be clumsy is not really clumsy; the fullness which seems to be empty is not really empty; the lofty which seems to be humble is not humble; the vigorous looks like inert; the simple purity looks changeable, as people are advised to remain pure and simple like a child but not a real naive nor ignorant one.

（2）Compassion, moderation and humility are mainly under pursuit and to be achieved by Taoists for self-cultivation.

(3) Taoists generally have an interest in promoting health and vitality. According to Taoism, five main organs of the body correspond to the five parts of the universe: metal (lung), wood (liver), water (spleen), fire (heart), and earth (stomach). So the Qi (air, breath) is believed to nurture and benefit each person's health, who is practicing its circulation not only in the body but also in connection with the universe.

道教的代表性哲学家有老子、庄子、王弼、郭象、嵇康等。中国人常说"内圣外王"(人的内部世界应像圣人一样；外部世界应像国王一样)。它实际上可分为两个部分：儒家思想的社会标准——外表做一个有很高的道德和才能以及道家精神修养的国王；内在做一个有非凡理解力，可以看清社会世界和自然真理的圣人。总之，道教倾向于个人的内在和精神，外表表现为个性和人品；儒家倾向于整个社会的管理和发展，体现民族实力和社会和谐。

道家首先摆脱儒家的套路，用自己的独立和客观的方式来探索人与自然的统一和物质与精神的和谐。它的这种方式世界上大多数主宰者都不可能接受。它只注重天和人的本性。但另一方面，它深刻地影响了中国绘画、中国书法、中国哲学和中国人的生活方式。坦率地说，这对于整个世界的良性发展比儒家更有用，因为它真正满足了构建整个世界的个人的内心需要和愿望。此外，道教也是人与自然和谐共处的完美倡导者，道家是环保主义者。在他们的经典著作中，自然被视为人类之母！

The representative philosophers of Taoism are Lao Zi, Zhuang Zi, Wang Bi, Guo Xiang, Ji Kang and so on. Chinese people often say "Nei Sheng Wai Wang" (Person's Interior World like a Saint's and Exterior World like a King's). It is actually divided into two segments: Confucianism's social criteria: To be an exterior King or Emperor with high morality and talents as well as Taoism's self-cultivation in spirit. To be an interior Saint with extraordinary understanding to see the social world and natural truth. In a word, Taoism is apt to the individual's internality and spirituality which is characterized of personality and humanity revealed outside; Confucianism is inclined to the whole society's administration and development which is featured with the national power and social harmony.

Taoism firstly gets rid of the road that Confucianism goes along and has its own independent and objective way to explore the oneness of human and nature and the harmony of spirituality and materiality. In this way, it is impossibly accepted by majority of dominators in the world. It just pays attention to the heaven's nature and human's nature. But on the other hand, it has the predominant influence on Chinese painting, Chinese calligraphy, Chinese philosophy and Chinese people's lifestyle. It is frankly more useful than Confucianism to the whole world's virtuous development, because it really satisfy the inner need and desire of individuals, who constitute the whole world. Besides, Taoism is also a perfect advocator of harmonious co-existence of human and nature. Taoists are environmentalists anyway. In their classics, nature is regarded as the mother of human being.

顺便说一下，道教与儒教这个在中国从来没有被认为是一种宗教的思想不同，它大约在汉代后期成为一种宗教信仰。道教作为一种宗教，其真正的创始人是张道陵（34—156），发起人是葛洪。道教作为一种宗教不同于道教作为一个哲学流派，虽然他们都宣称老子和庄子是其先驱。作为一种宗教，道教追求永生，变得神秘莫测，许多历史人物成为超自然人形象，如汉武帝、老子、庄子。他们于道教理论基础之上，再造出一个梦幻般的人类精神永恒世界。

By the way, different from Confucianism, which is never considered to be a religion in China, Taoism later became a religious belief roughly in late Han Dynasty. The real founder of Taoism as a religion was Zhang Daoling (34 – 156) and the greatest promoter was Ge Hong. Taoism as a religion is different from Taoism as a philosophical school, though they both claim Lao Zi and Zhuang Zi as their forerunners. Taoism as a religion was turned into mystery and pursuit of immortality. In this Taoist religion, many historical figures became the supernatural beings like Emperor Wu, Lao Zi and Zhuang Zi. They, based on the theory of Taoism, re-create a dream-like permanent world in spiritual world of humankind.

第二节　佛教在中国的传播、发展与影响

Section 2　Buddhism and Its Spread, Development and Influence in China

佛教最初是印度教的一个分支。在学术界，佛教被认为是一种"有神论宗教"。其神为释迦牟尼；其学说基于轮回之上。跟随其哲学、宗教和修行的人超过 3 亿，是基于佛的教义。

佛教在汉朝传入中国。一般来说，佛教在中国的发展可以分为四个时期：

西汉晚期（前 202），佛教从古印度传入中国。经过长时间的传播和发展，佛教在中国逐渐成为一个强大的国有化的宗教。因为传入时间、路线、地区、民族文化以及社会和历史背景的差异，中国佛教形成三个鲜明的分支：汉传佛教、藏传佛教和在云南地区巴利语中传播的小乘佛教。

Buddhism was originally a branch of Hinduism. Among the academics, Buddhism is considered a "theistic religion". Its Deity is Sakyamuni; its doctrine is based on transmigration. Its philosophy, religion, and spiritual practice were followed by more than 300 million people, based on the teachings of the Buddha.

Buddhism was spread to China during the Han Dynasty. In general, the development of Buddhism in China can be divided into four periods.

In late Western Han Dynasty (202 BC), Buddhism came into China from ancient India. After a long time spread and development, Buddhism gradually became a strongly nationalized religion in China. Because of the difference of the entrance time, routes, areas, ethnic cultures as well as social and historical background, Chinese Buddhism formed three vivid branches: Han

Buddhism, Tibetan Buddhism and Theravada Buddhism in Pali spread in Yunnan Area.

汉传佛教：传播到汉民族地区的佛教称为汉传佛教。通过长期的佛经翻译、解释和整理，佛教自然而复杂地与中国传统文化联系在一起，逐渐形成了各种各样具有汉民族文化特色的教派和支派。这种被民族化的汉传佛教自然传到了韩国、日本和越南。

佛教被传到汉民族地区的时间至今仍然不确定。据历史记录，在秦朝时期，汉民族区域接近佛教区域，一些僧侣到过汉民族区域。在西汉时期，特别是从公元前139年到公元前126年，丝绸之路的开创者张骞（前164—前114）被派往西部地区执行外交任务。途中张骞从蜀地人们所穿的服装看出中国和印度之间存在着民间交流，佛教可能随之传入中国。武帝开辟了海上航道，与印度东海岸一些地方建立了联系。近年来的考古发现了雕刻出来的佛像。历史记录佛教进入中国汉民族区域在西汉晚期，主要集中在西安、洛阳和徐州等地方。佛教最初被认为是一种长寿的秘诀，所以人们当时把佛等同为老子和黄帝。

Han Buddhism: Buddhism spread to area of Han Nationality was called Han Buddhism. Through a long-term sutra translation, explanation and coordination, Buddhism naturally and complicatedly associated with Chinese Traditional Culture, and gradually formed a variety of schools and sub-branches vividly featured with Chinese Culture of Han Nationality. Spontaneously, the nationalized Han Buddhism spread to Korea, Japan and Vietnam.

The time that Buddhism was transported into Han Nationality Area has not been fixed yet. In accordance with some historical records, in Qin Dynasty, the Han Nationality Area had been close to Buddhism and some monks had come into Han Nationality Area of China. In Western Han Dynasty, especially during the period from 139 BC to 126 BC, Zhang Qian (164 BC – 114 BC), the opener of the Silk Road, was sent to western area on a diplomatic mission. During his itinerary, Zhang Qian saw the clothing of Shu Area, which meant the existence of folk communication between China and India and possibly the Buddhism also entered China amid the connection. Emperor Wu also opened the seaway and connected with some points of east coast of India. Via the recent years' discovery of archeology, the Buddha statues had been carved out. Buddhism recorded in history entered Han Nationality Area of China around late Western Han Dynasty. It centered on Xi'an, Luoyang and some other places like Xuzhou. Initially, Buddhism was considered as a secret technique for longevity, so people at the time equated Buddha with Lao Zi and Yellow Emperor.

第二个时期是三国魏晋南北朝时期。这是佛教在汉民族地区盛行的黄金时间，佛教超越当地其他信仰，成为主要的宗教信仰。佛教受到甚至包括皇帝在内的广泛欢迎和信任，有些国家因此耗费了国家所有财力而沦陷。因此，寺庙经文和佛教经典翻译受到重视。佛经翻译尤其对中国音乐、诗歌、哲学和社会制度作出了贡献。此外，信佛成为当时一种时尚，几乎大多数高官和文化名流都认为佛教是境外传入但已国有化的宗教。盛行于东西两晋时期的中国玄学也从佛教中吸收了不少营养。中国哲学的发展在很大程度上基于佛教的发展。

第三个时期是在唐宋时期，佛教在汉族人中影响力很大。中国文学和政治体制从佛教吸收了大量营养。新儒学大都来自佛教，我们称之为程朱理学。同时，佛教的内部理论体系也趋于成熟，出现了许多分支，除了大乘佛教（梵语"更大的车辆"）和小乘佛教以外，还有禅宗、天台教派、净土教派或极乐教派、密宗作教派、华燕教派等。总之，佛教在中国实现了培养世俗世界的凡夫俗子的目的。

The second period is in the period of Three Kingdoms and Wei-Jin and Southern and Northern Dynasties. It was the golden time of Buddhism to popularize in area of Han Nationality, it became the superior religious belief over other local beliefs. Buddhism was widely welcomed and believed by many people, even including the emperors, and some states were collapsed by expending the whole national finance. Hence the temple complexes and Buddhist sutra translations were both highlighted. Especially the sutra translation devoted much to Chinese music, Chinese poetry, Chinese philosophy and Chinese social system. In addition, believing Buddhism was a fashion at the time, nearly majority of the high-ranked officials and cultural elites believed in this inbound but nationalized religion. Chinese Xuan Xue Ideology flourished in Western Jin and Eastern Jin dynasties assimilated a lot from Buddhism. To a great degree, the development of Chinese philosophy is based on the development of Buddhism.

The third period is in Tang and Song dynasties. Buddhism influentially spread among Han People. Chinese literature and political system absorbed much from Buddhism. The neo-Confucianism largely learnt from Buddhism, and we call it Cheng-Zhu Li Xue. At the same time, the internal theoretical system of Buddhism also trended to maturity. Many branches appeared such as Zen, Tiantai Sect, Pure-land or Sukhāvatī Sect, Mi Sect, Huayan Sect and so on, apart from Mahayana Buddhism (Sanskrit for "Greater Vehicle") and Theravada Buddhism. Anyway, Buddhism in China realizes its aim at cultivating the mass on the earthly world.

然而，封建社会后期，由于社会动荡，中国佛教发展缓慢。新中国成立后，实施宗教信仰自由的政策，中国佛教迎来其新的成长期。现在，中国佛教正处于快速发展期，国际学术交流正在扩大。

藏传佛教，也称为金刚乘佛教，传统上认为是 10 世纪后期形成的佛教教义和机构的本体。13 世纪中期，藏传佛教在蒙古地区蔓延。

小乘佛教，是在中国另一个有重要影响力的佛教，在中国西南地区广泛传播，尤其是在云南省。

中国佛教带给我们一个可敬的本土佛像，即菩萨或称观音菩萨，是使中国人免受灾难和绝望的菩萨。它是唯一活在人们心中的佛教菩萨。此外，中国石刻艺术直接受佛教的影响，敦煌莫高窟、大同云冈石窟、洛阳龙门石窟都是中国佛教文化的宝藏。

However, in the late feudal society, because of the social unrest, Chinese Buddhism was slow in development. After the founding of People's Republic of China and the implementing of the policy of freedom in religion belief, Chinese Buddhism embraced its new growing age. Now it is developing greatly and the international academic exchanges are expanded.

Tibetan Buddhism, also called Vajrayana Buddhism, traditionally considered as the original body of Buddhist religious doctrine and institutions finally formed in the late period of the 10th century, and in the middle period of the 13th century, Tibetan Buddhism spread in Mongolian Area.

Theravada Buddhism, is another important locally influential branch of Buddhism in China, it is widely spreading and believed in Southwestern China, especially in Yunan province.

Chinese Buddhism additionally also gives us a honorable locally-born Buddha, Kwan-yin or Avalokitesvara, who is Chinese people's own Buddha for saving the people from disasters and despair. It is the only Buddhist Bodhisattva living in people's hearts. Besides, Chinese art is directly influenced by Chinese Buddhism. Dunhuang Mogao Grottos, Datong Yungang Grottos and Luoyang Longmen Grottos are all the treasures of Buddhist culture in China.

对中国文化的影响

通过古代中国和印度之间的文化交流，佛教已给中国各地区带来了巨大的影响。它也给中国哲学带来了巨大的影响。

新儒学提出的哲学概念深受佛教观念的影响。例如，像"清心"，"包括人在内世界上的一切都有'太极'"和"现象可能各不相同，原因却只有一个"，跟佛教术语"清心能见道"和"心就是佛性"有关。

佛教给中国文学带来了深刻影响。晋、唐时期的小说受佛经和《百喻经》的影响。佛教也影响着中国古代诗人如陶渊明、王维、白居易、苏轼的作品。它无疑丰富了中国的语言和文化。

佛教影响了中国古典艺术的不同方面。中国佛教寺庙和宝塔的建筑风格表明了佛教文化给中国建筑带来了巨大的影响。河南省嵩山嵩月寺砖制宝塔，山西省应县木佛塔和福建省开元庙石塔，所有这些都被看成中国古代建筑史有价值的研究对象。

佛教还给中国天文学和医学带来影响和贡献。根据隋唐时期的史书记载，有十多种医学和药学书籍由印度语译成汉语。

Influence on Chinese Culture

Through the cultural exchange between China and India in ancient times, Buddhism has given a tremendous influence to the various areas of Chinese. It had given a deep and tremendous influence to the Chinese philosophy.

The philosophic concepts put forward by Neo-Confucianism were deeply influenced by Buddhist ones. For instance, concepts like "pure heart", "everything in this world including man has a 'Taiji'" and "phenomena might differ from one and the other yet reason just one", which have something to do with those Buddhist terms like "with a clear heart (mind) one sees true" and "mind is nothing but Buddha".

Buddhism had given a deep influence to the Chinese literature as well. The novels in the Jin and Tang dynasties were inspired very much by those Buddhist sutras and the Sutra of *The 100 Parables*. It had also given an influence over the works of those ancient Chinese poets such as Tao Yuanming, Wang Wei, Bai Juyi and Su Shi. It has no doubt enriched the Chinese language and culture.

Buddhism had also given an influence to the classic Chinese art in various aspects. The architectural style of the Buddhist temples and pagodas in China shows a great influence of Buddhist culture over the Chinese Architecture. The Brick Pagoda of Songshan Songyue Temple of China's Henan Province, the Wood Pagoda of Yingxian of Shanxi Province and the Stone Pagoda of Kaiyuan Temple of Fujian Province, all of these have served as the valuable objects for the study of history of the ancient Chinese architecture.

Buddhism has contributed a great deal and given an influence to China's astronomy and medicine. According to those historical books of both the Sui and Tang dynasties, there are over 10 kinds of medicine and pharmacy books that were translated from Indian languages into Chinese.

第五章

口述题

1. 举例说出你所知道的道教代表性人物。
2. 说一说佛教对中国文化的影响。

Questions

1. Give an example of the representative Taoist figures you know.
2. Talk about the influence of Buddhism on Chinese culture.

学习网站

1. ASIAN ART (https://www. burmese-art. com/blog/chinese-buddhism)
2. ANCIENT HISTORY (https://www. ancient. eu/Taoism/)

第六章　中国文学文化

Chapter 6　Chinese Literature

第一节　中国文学文化概览

Section 1　Overview of Chinese Literature

中国文学就像中国历史和中国文化一样，是一个多元化的大主题。中国文学基本是基于中国文化、汉字、中国哲学和中国历史之上的。它是展示中华文明和魅力的一个重要窗口。与中国文化相类似，中国文学在几乎所有领域都有别于西方文学。中国文学由四个部分组成：文学大师、最受欢迎的文学经典、文学教材以及文学论文和期刊。这是以不同的主题来分类的。

根据文学演化的不同时期，中国文学可以分为四个部分：远古时代、古时中世纪时代、距离现代最近的古代和现代。具体来说，这四个阶段还可以进一步分为八个部分：黄帝、炎帝、蚩尤时期、秦代和汉代（公元前 3 世纪），这属于远古时代。中世纪指从魏晋到明代中期，确切地说包括从魏晋到唐代中期，从唐朝中期至南宋后期，从元代早期到明代中期。距离现代最近的古代指从明朝中期到五四运动时期，确切地说包括明朝晚期到鸦片战争（1840），从鸦片战争到五四运动（1919）。现代指从 1919 年到今天，包括从 1919 年至 1949 年，国内视为在新中国成立前期文学和从 1949 年到现在，这一阶段被认为是新文学时期，文学颓废期。

Chinese literature is a topic as large and diversified as Chinese history and Chinese culture. Chinese literature is approximately based on Chinese culture, Chinese characters, Chinese philosophy and Chinese history. It is an important show window exhibiting Chinese civilization and charm. Similar to Chinese culture, Chinese literature is also distinguished from western literature in nearly all fields it connected. Chinese literature is comprised of four sections in the sub-homepage: Masters of Literature, Popular Literary Classics, Textbook of Literature and Papers and Journals of Literature. This is classified from different themes.

In accordance with the phase of evolution, Chinese literature can be categorized into four parts: the remote phase of ancient time, the medieval phase of ancient time, the ancient time nearest to the present and the modern times. And specifically, four phases also can be further divided into eight sections: the phase of Three Ancestral Periods, Qin Dynasty and Han Dynasty

(3 BC), which belongs to the phase of the remote times. The medieval period ranges from Wei and Jin dynasties to middle phase of Ming Dynasty, which exactly consists of the time from Wei and Jin dynasties to middle time of Tang Dynasty, the phase from the middle time of Tang Dynasty to late Southern Song Dynasty, and the phase from the early period of Yuan Dynasty to middle period of Ming Dynasty. The ancient times nearest to the present extends from the middle times of Ming Dynasty to the accident of May-4th Student Movement, exactly covers the period from late Ming Dynasty to the Opium War (1840), and the period from the Opium War to May-4th Movement (1919). The modern times includes the period from 1919 to today, which exactly includes: the phase from 1919 to 1949, domestically considered as the pre-liberation literature in mainland China, and the phase from 1949 to the present, which is considered to be the period of new literature, a ruin period of literature.

所有类型的文学都起源于先秦时期。散文起源于甲骨文时期。散文和诗可以追溯到《诗经》、《楚辞》和汉朝的乐府诗。小说起源于神话传说。论说文起源于《左传》（左丘明）和《史记》（司马迁）等历史作品以及思想家和作家的各种寓言故事。中国戏曲起源于《九歌》。此外，中国文学的思想基础也是在此期间形成的，特别是受到了儒教和道教思想的影响。儒教强调文学社会价值，而道教重视文学的美学功能。士大夫变成了文学的主要创作者。宋朝之前，文学从来没有偏离中国的精英文化。这一阶段的纯文学类型以汉代的赋为代表，代表人物有司马相如、枚乘、王褒等。

All types of literatures were originated from the pre-Qin period, and the prose could be traced back to the inscriptions of the oracle bones, and the prose and poem date from *The Book of Songs* (*Shi Jing*), *Chu Ci* (*Verses of Chu*) and Yuefu Poem of Han Dynasty (*Verses and Poems of Music Bureau of Han Dynasty*), the novel from the mythic legend, the essay from the historical works like *Zuo Zhuan* (created by Zuo Qiuming) and *Records of the Grand Historian* (first great official history created by Sima Qian), as well as the diverse fable stories from various thinkers and writers, even the origin of Chinese opera is partially inspired by the works of *Jiu Ge* (*Nine Songs*). Furthermore, the ideological base of Chinese literature also formed in this period, especially influenced by Confucianism and Taoism. Confucianism emphasizes the social importance of literature, while Taoism attaches importance to the aesthetics of literature. Besides, scholar-bureaucrats turned to be the main creators of literature, and then the literature was never away from the elite culture of China until the coming of Song Dynasty. The pure type of literature in this phase is highly represented by Fu masterpieces of Han Dynasty, and the representatives were Sima Xiangru, Mei Cheng and Wang Bao, etc.

一般来说，中世纪是中国文学的觉醒时期，它是中国文学独立的正式标志。诗、词、曲、赋、散文和小说代表了所有文学类型。杰出的文学家代表包括三曹（曹操、曹丕、曹植）、魏时七大作家和晋朝陶渊明、谢灵运、庾信；初唐时期四个优秀作家郑子昂、王维、孟浩然、高适；还有唐朝中后期的李白、杜甫、白居易、韩愈、李商隐。出现了两个有生气的文学现象——建安风骨和盛唐气象。宋代是中国文学的顶峰时期，代表有苏东坡、欧阳修、柳永、周邦彦、李清照、辛弃疾、姜夔、秦观、黄庭坚和陆游，他们大都既是学者又是诗人。散文和杂文方面则以唐宋八大家为典型代表。

自元代开始，戏曲蓬勃发展。明清时期的小说家成为文学的主人，代表性小说包括《水浒传》、《三国演义》、《西游记》和《红楼梦》，被视为中国古代四大小说名著。戏剧也达到顶峰，以《牡丹亭》、《长生殿》和《桃花扇》为代表。

Generally speaking, the medieval period is the self-consciousness time of Chinese literature, and it was the official symbol of the independent literature of China. All types of literature represented by poems, ci, qu, fu, prose and novels. The outstanding representatives of litterateurs include Three Writers of Cao Family (Cao Cao, Cao Pi and Cao Zhi), Seven Great Writers of Wei and Tao Yuanming, Xie Lingyun of Jin Dynasty and Yu Xin; Four Excellent Writers of Early Tang Dynasty, Cheng Zi'ang, Wang Wei, Meng Haoran and Gao Shi; Li Bai, Du Fu, Bai Juyi, Han Yu and Li Shangyin of Middle and Late Tang Dynasty. Two vivid phenomena of literature appeared—Jian An Feng Gu (the Power and Strength of Literature of Jian'an Period) and Sheng Tang Qi Xiang (the Great Atmosphere of Peak-time Tang Dynasty). In Song Dynasty, which was the summit period of Chinese literature, the representatives were Su Dongpo, Ouyang Xiu, Liu Yong, Zhou Bangyan, Li Qingzhao, Xin Qiji, Jiang Kui, Qin Guan, Huang Tingjian and Lu You. The scholars and poets were generally the same people. In the aspect of prose and essay, Eight Great Writers of Tang and Song dynasties were the typical representatives.

Since Yuan Dynasty, the operas flourished, and in Ming and Qing dynasties, novelists became the heroes of literature, and the represented novels included *Outlaws of the Marsh*, *The Romance of the Three Kingdoms*, *Journey to the West* and *A Dream of Red Mansions*, all of which are together considered as Four Great Classical Novels of Ancient China, also the operas were in the peak time represented by *Peony Pavilion*, *Longevity Palace* and *Peach Blossom Fan*.

当代文学改变了文学创作的传统方式。文学的西化风格主导着中国文学的发展。诗转变为自由体。由于胡适发起的白话文运动，古汉语的古典文学被现代汉语的现代文学所取代，代表有徐志摩、鲁迅、闻一多、戴望舒、林语堂、周作人、张恨水、王国维等。1949年后，文学明显被政治化而不再独立。

The modern literature changes the traditional way of literary creation, and the westernized style of literature dominated the development of literature in China. The poem was modernized to be the free style of poem, and the classical literature of traditional Chinese language is replaced by the modern literature weaved by the modern Chinese language, due to Hu Shi's Colloquial Writing Movement. The representatives were Xu Zhimo, Lu Xun, Wen Yiduo, Dai Wangshu, Lin Yutang, Zhou Zuoren, Zhang Henshui, Wang Guowei and so on. After 1949, the literature is obviously politicized, and it is not independent any more.

第二节　中国文学文化的辉煌成就

Section 2　Brilliant Achievement of Chinese Literature

唐诗

唐诗指的是中国唐朝（618—907）期间或前后写的诗，遵循某种风格，常常被视为中国诗歌的黄金时代。据编撰，全唐诗包括 2 200 多位作者所写的约 50 000 首唐诗。在唐代，诗歌仍然是社会各阶层社会生活的重要组成部分。文人要求掌握这些诗歌以参加文职选拔考试，但理论上人人都能接触这门艺术。因此出现了大量的诗作和诗人，其中部分诗作保留至今。这一时期两个最著名的诗人是杜甫和李白。

古体诗和近体诗

唐代诗歌可分为古体诗和近体诗。近体诗是在前唐时期形成，形式更严格，诗体结构有规律。古体诗和近体诗的著名代表分别为李白和杜甫。

Tang Poetry

Tang poetry refers to poetry written in or about China's Tang Dynasty (618 – 907) and follows a certain style, often considered as the Golden Age of Chinese poetry. According to a compilation, the Quantangshi included almost 50,000 Tang poems written by over 2,200 authors. During the Tang Dynasty, poetry continued to be an important part of social life at all levels of society. Scholars were required to master poetry for the civil service examinations, but the art was theoretically available to everyone. This led to a large record of poetry and poets, a partial record of which survives today. Two of the most famous poets of the period were Du Fu and Li Bai.

Gutishi and *Jintishi*

Tang poetry can be divided into the original *gutishi* (old stylistic poetry) and *jintishi* (new stylistic poetry). The latter is a stricter form developed in the early Tang Dynasty with rules governing the structure of a poem. The greatest writers of *gutishi* and *jintishi* are often held to be Li Bai and Du Fu respectively.

古体诗
Old Style of Poems

（五言古诗）李白：春思

Li Bai：IN SPRING

燕草如碧丝，

秦桑低绿枝。

当君怀归日，

是妾断肠时。

春风不相识，

何事入罗帏？

Yan's grasses are as blue as jade,

Our mulberries here curve green-threaded branches.

And at last you think of returning home,

Now when my heart is almost broken.

O breeze of the spring, since I dare not know you,

Why part the silk curtains by my bed?

（五言古诗）王维：渭川田家
Wang Wei：A FARM-HOUSE ON THE WEI RIVER

斜光照墟落，

穷巷牛羊归。

野老念牧童，

倚杖候荆扉。

雉雊麦苗秀，

蚕眠桑叶稀。

田夫荷锄至，

相见语依依。

即此羡闲逸，

怅然吟式微。

In the slant of the sun on the country-side,

Cattle and sheep trail home along the lane；

And a rugged old man in a thatch door

Leans on a staff and thinks of his son, the herd boy.

There are whirring pheasants, full wheat-ears,

Silk-worms asleep, pared mulberry-leaves.

And the farmers, returning with hoes on their shoulders,

Hail one another familiarly.

No wonder I long for the simple life

And am sighing the old song, Oh, to go back again！

（七言古诗）陈子昂：登幽州台歌
Chen Zi'ang：ON A GATE-TOWER AT YOUZHOU

前不见古人，

后不见来者。

念天地之悠悠，

独怆然而涕下。

Where, before me, are the ages that have gone?

And where, behind me, are the coming generations?

I think of heaven and earth, without limit, without end,

And I am all alone and my tears fall down.

（七言古诗）李白：宣州谢朓楼饯别校书叔云

Li Bai：A FAREWELL TO SECRETARY SHUYUN AT THE XIETIAO VILLA IN XUANZHOU

弃我去者，昨日之日不可留；

乱我心者，今日之日多烦忧。

长风万里送秋雁，

对此可以酣高楼。

Since yesterday had to throw me and bolt，

Today has hurt my heart even more.

The autumn wild geese have a long wind for escort

As I face them from this villa，drinking my wine.

蓬莱文章建安骨，

中间小谢又清发。

俱怀逸兴壮思飞，

欲上青天揽明月。

抽刀断水水更流，

举杯消愁愁更愁。

人生在世不称意，

明朝散发弄扁舟。

The bones of great writers are your brushes，in the School of Heaven，

And I am a Lesser Xie growing up by your side.

We both are exalted to distant thought，

Aspiring to the sky and the bright moon.

But since water still flows，though we cut it with our swords，

And sorrows return，though we drown them with wine，

Since the world can in no way answer our craving，

I will loosen my hair tomorrow and take to a fishing boat.

（乐府）孟郊：游子吟

Meng Jiao：A TRAVELLER'S SONG

慈母手中线，

游子身上衣。

临行密密缝，

意恐迟迟归。

谁言寸草心，

报得三春晖？

The thread in the hands of a fond-hearted mother

Makes clothes for the body of her wayward boy.

Carefully she sews and thoroughly she mends,

Dreading the delays that will keep him late from home.

But how much love has the inch-long grass

For three spring months of the light of the sun?

（乐府）李白：将进酒

Li Bai：BRINGING IN THE WINE

君不见，黄河之水天上来，

奔流到海不复回！

君不见，高堂明镜悲白发，

朝如青丝暮成雪！

人生得意须尽欢，

莫使金樽空对月。

天生我材必有用，

千金散尽还复来。

烹羊宰牛且为乐，

会须一饮三百杯。

See how the Yellow River's waters move out of heaven.

Entering the ocean, never return.

See how lovely locks in bright mirrors in high chambers.

Though silken-black at morning, have changed by night to snow-white.

Oh, let a man of spirit venture where he pleases.

And never tip his golden cup empty toward the moon!

Since heaven gave the talent, let it be employed!

Spin a thousand pieces of silver, all of them come back!

Cook a sheep, kill a cow, whet the appetite.

And make me, of three hundred bowls, one long drink！

岑夫子，丹丘生，

将进酒，杯莫停。

与君歌一曲，请君为我倾耳听。

钟鼓馔玉不足贵，

但愿长醉不复醒。

古来圣贤皆寂寞，

惟有饮者留其名。

陈王昔时宴平乐，

斗酒十千恣欢谑。

主人何为言少钱？

径须沽取对君酌。

五花马，千金裘，

呼儿将出换美酒，

与尔同销万古愁。

To the old master, Cen, and the young scholar, Danqiu,

Bring in the wine! Let your cups never rest!

Let me sing you a song! Let your ears attend!

What are bell and drum, rare dishes and treasure?

Let me be forever drunk and never come to reason!

Sober men of olden days and sages are forgotten,

And only the great drinkers are famous for all time.

Prince Chen paid at a banquet in the Palace of Perfection

Ten thousand coins for a cask of wine, with many a laugh and quip.

Why say, my host, that your money is gone?

Go and buy wine and we'll drink it together!

My flower-dappled horse, my furs worth a thousand,

Hand them to the boy to exchange for good wine,

And we'll drown away the woes of ten thousand generations!

近体诗

近体诗或称律诗，形成于 5 世纪之前。到唐朝时，发展为固定的平仄形式，以确保每一联句中的中古汉语四个声调之间的平衡，即平声、上声、去声、入声。唐朝近体诗达到最高峰，王维和崔颢是近体诗最著名的代表，而杜甫是最精通近体诗的典范。

近体诗的基本形式是律诗，有八行。除了声调的限制外，第二联和第三联的诗行要形式对仗。诗行要内容对称，其中每个词的词性要相同。

近体诗的另一种形式是绝句或四行诗，有律诗前四行的声调，形式无须对应。

Jintishi

Jintishi (new stylistic poetry), or regulated verse developed from the 5th century onwards. By the Tang Dynasty, a series of set tone patterns had been developed, which were intended to ensure a balance between the four tones of Middle Chinese in each couplet: the level tone, and the three oblique tones (rising, departing and entering). The Tang Dynasty was the high point of the *jintishi*. Wang Wei and Cui Hao were notable pioneers of the form, while Du Fu was its most accomplished exponent.

The basic form of *jintishi* is *lvshi*, with eight lines. In addition to the tonal constraints, this form required parallelism between the lines in the second and third couplets. The lines in these couplets had to contain contrasting content, with the characters in each line usually in the same part of speech.

Another form is the *jueju*, or quatrain which followed the tonal pattern of the first four lines of the *lüshi*. This form does not require parallelism.

（五言律诗）王勃：送杜少府之任蜀州

Wang Bo：FAREWELL TO VICE-PREFECT DU SETTING OUT FOR HIS OFFICIAL POST IN SHU

城阙辅三秦，

风烟望五津。

与君离别意，

同是宦游人。

海内存知己，

天涯若比邻。

无为在歧路，

儿女共沾巾。

By this wall that surrounds the three Qin districts，

Through a mist that makes five rivers one，

We bid each other a sad farewell，

We two officials going opposite ways，

And yet，while China holds our friendship，

And heaven remains our neighbourhood，

Why should you linger at the fork of the road，

Wiping your eyes like a heart-broken child？

（五言律诗）杜甫：春望

Du Fu：A SPRING VIEW

国破山河在，

城春草木深。

感时花溅泪，

恨别鸟惊心。

烽火连三月，

家书抵万金。

白头搔更短，

浑欲不胜簪。

Though a country be sundered，hills and rivers endure；

And spring comes green again to trees and grasses

Where petals have been shed like tears

And lonely birds have sung their grief.

After the war-fires of three months，

One message from home is worth a ton of gold.

I stroke my white hair. It has grown too thin

To hold the hairpins any more.

（七言律诗）崔颢：黄鹤楼

Cui Hao：THE YELLOW CRANE TERRACE

昔人已乘黄鹤去，

此地空余黄鹤楼。

黄鹤一去不复返，

白云千载空悠悠。

晴川历历汉阳树，

芳草萋萋鹦鹉洲。

日暮乡关何处是？

烟波江上使人愁。

Where long ago a yellow crane bore a sage to heaven,

Nothing is left now but the Yellow Crane Terrace.

The yellow crane never revisited earth,

And white clouds are flying without him for ever.

Every tree in Hanyang becomes clear in the water,

And Parrot Island is a nest of sweet grasses；

But I look toward home, and twilight grows dark

With a mist of grief on the river waves.

（七言律诗）杜甫：登高

Du Fu：A LONELY CLIMBING

风急天高猿啸哀，

渚清沙白鸟飞回。

无边落木萧萧下，

不尽长江滚滚来。

万里悲秋常作客，

百年多病独登台。

艰难苦恨繁霜鬓，

潦倒新停浊酒杯。

In a sharp gale from the wide sky apes are whimpering,

Birds are flying homeward over the clear lake and white sand,

Leaves are dropping down like the spray of a waterfall,

While I watch the Yangtze River always rolling on.

I have come three thousand miles away.

Sad now with autumn and with my hundred years of woe,

I climb this height alone. Ill fortune has laid a bitter frost on my temples,

Heart-ache and weariness are a thick dust in my wine.

（七言律诗）李商隐：无题

Li Shangyin：TO ONE UNNAMED

相见时难别亦难，

东风无力百花残。

春蚕到死丝方尽，

蜡炬成灰泪始干。

晓镜但愁云鬓改，

夜吟应觉月光寒。

蓬山此去无多路，

青鸟殷勤为探看。

Time was long before I met her, but is longer since we parted,

And the east wind has arisen and a hundred flowers are gone,

And the silk-worms of spring will weave until they die

And every night the candles will weep their wicks away.

Mornings in her mirror she sees her hair-cloud changing,

Yet she dares the chill of moonlight with her evening song.

It is not so very far to her Enchanted Mountain.

O blue-birds, be listening！Bring me what she says！

（五言绝句）王之涣：登鹳雀楼

Wang Zhihuan：AT HERON LODGE

白日依山尽，

黄河入海流。

欲穷千里目，

更上一层楼。

Mountains cover the white sun,

And oceans drain the Yellow River；

But you widen your view one thousand miles

By going up one flight of stairs.

（五言绝句）孟浩然：春晓

Meng Haoran：A SPRING MORNING

春眠不觉晓，

处处闻啼鸟。

夜来风雨声，

花落知多少。

I awake light-hearted this morning of spring,

Everywhere round me the singing of birds.

But now I remember the night, the storm,

And I wonder how many blossoms were broken.

（七言绝句）刘禹锡：乌衣巷
Liu Yuxi：BLACKTAIL ROW

朱雀桥边野草花，

乌衣巷口夕阳斜。

旧时王谢堂前燕，

飞入寻常百姓家。

Grass has run wild now by the Bridge of Red-Birds；

And swallows' wings, at sunset, in Blacktail Row

Where once they visited great homes,

Dip among doorways of the poor.

（七言绝句）杜牧：泊秦淮
Du Mu：A MOORING ON THE QIN HUAI RIVER

烟笼寒水月笼沙，

夜泊秦淮近酒家。

商女不知亡国恨，

隔江犹唱后庭花。

Mist veils the cold stream, and moonlight the sand,

As I moor in the shadow of a river-tavern,

Where girls, with no thought of a perished kingdom,

Gaily echo *A Song of Courtyard Flowers*.

词

词（或辞）是一种抒情诗，也称为长短句和诗余。

每行的字数和声调取决于 800 套固定模式，都与特定的曲调名相关，称为词牌。起先填词是用来唱曲的，有固定的节奏、韵律和速度。因此，词牌名可能与内容毫无关系。有些词用次词牌名（或注释，有时长达一段）来表明内容。

Ci（poetry）

Ci is a kind of lyric Chinese poetry. It is also known as *Changduanju*（"lines of irregular lengths"）and *Shiyu*（"that is beside poetry"）.

Typically the number of characters in each line and the arrangement of tones were determined by one of around 800 set patterns, each associated with a particular title, called *cipai*. Originally they were written to be sung to a tune of that title, with set rhythm, rhyme, and tempo. Therefore, the title may have nothing to do with its contents. Some *ci* would have a "subtitle"（or a commentary, sometimes as long as a paragraph）indicating the contents.

苏轼【江城子】

Su Shi：JIANG CHENG ZI

十年生死两茫茫。

不思量，自难忘，

千里孤坟，无处话凄凉。

纵使相逢应不识，

尘满面，鬓如霜。

Ten years living and dead have drawn apart.

I do nothing to remember,

But I cannot forget

Your lonely grave a thousand miles away.

Nowhere can I talk of my sorrow—

Even if we met, how would you know me,

My face full of dust,

My hair like snow?

夜来幽梦忽还乡。

小轩窗，正梳妆，

相顾无言，唯有泪千行。

料得年年断肠日，

明月夜，短松冈。

In the dark of night, a dream: suddenly, I am home

You are by the window

Doing your hair

I look at you and cannot speak

Your face is streaked by endless tears

Year after year must they break my heart

These moonlit nights?

That low pine grave?

苏轼【水调歌头】

Su Shi：SHUI DIAO GE TOU

明月几时有？

把酒问青天。

不知天上宫阙，

今夕是何年？

我欲乘风归去，

又恐琼楼玉宇，

高处不胜寒。

起舞弄轻影，

何似在人间？

The moon—how old is it?

I hold the cup and ask the clear blue sky,

But I don't know, in palaces up there

When is tonight?

If only I could ride the wind and see—

But no, jade towers

So high up, might be too cold

For dancing with my shadow—

How could there, be like here?

转朱阁，

低绮户，

照无眠。

不应有恨，

何事长向别时圆？

人有悲欢离合，

月有阴晴圆缺，

此事古难全。

但愿人长久，

千里共婵娟。

Turning in the red chamber

Beneath the carved window,

The brightness baffles sleep,

But why complain?

The moon is always full at parting

A man knows grief and joy, separation and reunion,

The moon, clouds and fair skies, waxing and waning—

And old story, this struggles for perfection!

Here's to long life,

This loveliness we share even a thousand miles apart!

辛弃疾【青玉案】

Xin Qiji: THE LANTERN FESTIVAL

东风夜放花千树，

更吹落、星如雨。

宝马雕车香满路。

凤箫声动，

玉壶光转，

一夜鱼龙舞。

Lanterns look like thousands of flowers aglow；

Later like stars, from the skies, fallen below.

On main streets, horses and carriages ply.

There, ladies shed perfume, as they pass by.

Orchestral music and song greet our ears,

As the moon, slow and steady, eastward veers.

Of the Spring Festival, this night marks the end.

The whole night, capering, carps and dragons spend.

蛾儿雪柳黄金缕，

笑语盈盈暗香去。

众里寻他千百度。

蓦然回首，

那人却在，

灯火阑珊处。

Adorned with ribbons or paper flowers on their head,

Clad in their best raiment, something bright or red,

Women squeeze their way among the festive crowd,

As they talk and laugh；even giggle aloud.

Rouged and powdered；perfumed to their heart's content,

They cannot but leave behind a subtle scent.

Up and down the main streets, I must have run—

A thousand times or more in quest of one,

Who I have concluded, cannot be found；

For, everywhere, no trace of her can be seen,

When, all of a sudden, I turned about,

That's her, where lanterns are few and far between.

李清照【如梦令】
Li Qingzhao：TO THE TUNE OF "LIKE A DREAM"

昨夜雨疏风骤，

浓睡不消残酒。

试问卷帘人，

却道海棠依旧。

知否？知否？

应是绿肥红瘦。

Last night a sprinkling of rain, a violent wind.

After a deep sleep, still not recovered from the lingering effect of wine,

I inquired of the one rolling up the screen;

But the answer came:

"The cherry-apple blossoms are still the same."

"Oh, don't you know, don't you know?

The red must be getting thin, while the green is becoming plump."

李清照【一剪梅】

Li Qingzhao: A TWIG OF MUME BLOSSOMS

红藕香残玉簟秋。

轻解罗裳，

独上兰舟。

云中谁寄锦书来？

雁字回时，

月满西楼。

The jade-like mat feels autumn's cold,

I change a coat. And 'mid the fading fragrance'

Of lotus pink alone I boat.

Will wild returning geese bring letters through the cloud?

When they come, with moonbeams

My west chamber's o'erflowed.

花自飘零水自流。

一种相思，

两处闲愁。

此情无计可消除，

才下眉头，

却上心头。

As water flows and flowers fall without leaving traces,

One and the same longing

O'erflows two lonely places.

I cannot get rid of this sorrow: kept apart

From my eyebrows,

It gnaws my heart.

曲

中国文学中，曲或元曲是由散曲和杂剧构成。散曲包括诗歌，而杂剧是中国戏剧的一种形式。曲在南宋后期开始流行，元朝达到鼎盛时期。因此常称为元曲。散曲和词都是抒情诗，有特定的调子，但散曲又不同于词，它更口头化，可添加衬字。散曲还可以分为小令和散套，散套由多个调子组成。

Qu（poetry）

In Chinese literature, *qu* or *yuanqu* consists of *sanqu* and *zaju*. Along with *shi* and *ci*, the former comprises Chinese poetry. The latter is a form of Chinese opera. *Qu* became popular during the late Southern Song Dynasty, and reached its highest popularity in Yuan Dynasty, therefore it is often called *yuanqu*. Both *sanqu* and *ci* are lyrics written to fit a particular melody, but *sanqu* differs from *ci* in that it is more colloquial, and is allowed to contain *chenzi* ("filler words" which are additional words to make a more complete meaning). *Sanqu* can be further divided into *xiaoling* and *santao*, with the latter comprising of more than one melody.

马致远【天净沙】秋思

Ma Zhiyuan: AUTUMN THOUGHTS TO SAND AND SKY

枯藤老树昏鸦，

小桥流水人家。

古道西风瘦马，

夕阳西下，

断肠人在天涯。

Sear bine coiled the tree while the crow was singing in the eventide,

River flew through the bridge while nearby a house stood,

The thin horse walked in the old road while the wind was blowing from the west,

Sunset in the far west,

There were still heartbroken people tramping far away from home.

古文运动

晚唐和宋代的古文运动主张清晰和准确而不主张华丽的骈体文或自汉代以来流行的平行散文风格。平行散文结构呆板，过于华丽而忽视内容，因此受到批评。

古文风格倡导者的目的是要继承前汉散文的精神，而不是直接模仿。他们使用口语元素，使文字变得更直接。

古文运动的第一大发起人是韩愈和柳宗元，他们不仅是大作家也是大理论家，为古文运动奠定了基础。两人都热衷于促进古文运动，热衷于教年轻人，使运动得以发展。

Classical Prose Movement

The Classical Prose Movement of the late Tang Dynasty and the Song Dynasty in China advocated clarity and precision rather than the florid *piantiwen* or parallel prose style that had been popular since the Han Dynasty. Parallel prose had a rigid structure and came to be criticized for being overly ornate at the expense of content.

The aim of the *guwen* stylists was to follow the spirit of pre-Han prose rather than to imitate it directly. They used elements of colloquial language to make their writings more direct.

The first great promoters of the movement were Han Yu and Liu Zongyuan who were not only great writers but also great theorists, providing the foundation of the movement. Both were enthusiastic to promote the movement and were keen to teach young people, so the movement could develop.

明清小说
四大古典名著

中国文学四大古典名著是中国最伟大、最有影响力的四部中国古典小说。按时间顺序，他们是 14 世纪的《三国演义》和《水浒传》，16 世纪的《西游记》和 18 世纪后期的《红楼梦》，也称《石头记》。

学者们通常将四部古典小说看成中国后现代小说的顶峰。在明清文学创作蓬勃发展时期写的这四部小说至今仍然很受欢迎。即使是现在，它们还继续影响中国各地和其他东亚地区如日本、韩国和越南等地的文学作品、电影、游戏和其他娱乐形式。它们还被翻译成不同的语言，或被删节或简化出版，在全世界享有大批观众。

Novels in Ming and Qing Dynasties
Four Great Classical Novels

The Four Great Classical Novels of Chinese literature are the four novels commonly counted by scholars to be the greatest and most influential in classical Chinese fiction. In chronological order, they are *Romance of the Three Kingdoms* (*San Guo Yan Yi*) written in the 14th century, *Water Margin* (*Shui Hu Zhuan*, also known as *Outlaws of the Marsh*) in the 14th century, *Journey to the West* (*Xi You Ji*) in the 16th century, and *A Dream of Red Mansions* (*Hong Lou Meng*, also known as *The Story of the Stone*) in the late 18th century.

The Four Great Classical Novels are generally regarded by scholars to be the pinnacle of China's post-modern fiction. Written during the Ming and Qing dynasties when literary creativity flourished, these four novels—*Romance of the Three Kingdoms*, *Outlaws of the Marsh*, *Journey to the West* and *A Dream of Red Mansions*—remained very popular to this day. Even now, they have continued to influence many Chinese literary works, movies, games and other forms of entertainment throughout China and other parts of East Asia such as Japan, Korea and Vietnam. They have also been translated into different languages, as well as published in abridged or simplified versions, to be enjoyed by a wider audience throughout the world.

《三国演义》

14 世纪罗贯中写的《三国演义》是一部中国历史小说，是基于汉朝（前 206—220）末期和三国时期（220—280）动荡岁月基础上写的。

三国时期是指中国汉代衰落后的那段时期。以三个敌对国——魏国（220—265）、蜀国（221—263）和吴国（222—280）的斗争为标志而得名。魏国最强大，于 263 年征服了蜀国。当司马家族从曹操家族夺取了魏以后，司马炎于 265 年正式登上王位，并建立了晋朝（265—420）。吴国后来于 280 年被征服，中国统一。

Romance of the Three Kingdoms

Romance of the Three Kingdoms, written by Luo Guanzhong in the 14th century, is a Chinese historical novel based on events in the turbulent years toward the end of the Han Dynasty (206 BC – 220 AD) to the Three Kingdoms period (220 – 280).

Three Kingdoms refers to a period of time after the fall of the Han Dynasty in China. It was so named because it was marked by the struggle of three rival kingdoms—the Kingdom of Wei (220 – 265), the Kingdom of Shu (221 – 263) and the Kingdom of Wu (222 – 280) —for control of China. Wei was always the most powerful kingdom and conquered the Shu Kingdom in 263. As the Sima clan had effectively wrested control of Wei away from the Cao family, Sima Yan formally seized the throne in 265 and established the Jin Dynasty (265 – 420). The Kingdom of Wu was later conquered in 280 resulting in the unification of China.

小说的结构以蜀国、吴国之间的冲突为中心，故事情节围绕魏、蜀和吴三国之间的权力斗争而展开。蜀国由以匡扶天下自居的汉室后裔刘备领导。他的敌人是魏国首领曹操，一个残忍但有才气、会写诗的将军。刘备由有骑士精神的关羽和愚忠、鲁莽的张飞帮助。最出色的是诸葛亮，他是道教学者，是一位有超自然力的谋略家。

The structure of the novel centers on the conflict between the two kingdoms, Shu and Wu, with the plot evolving around the struggles between the three powers, Wei, Shu, and Wu. The kingdom of Shu was lead by Liu Bei, a descendant for the Han nobility with the strongest claim for legitimacy in the pursuit for power. His archenemy is Cao Cao, a ruthless but brilliant, poem-writing general who led the kingdom of Wei. Liu Bei is aided by Guan Yu, the epitome of chivalry, and Zhang Fei, a fiercely loyal but rash warrior. Rounding out the top players is Zhuge Liang, a taoist scholar and master strategist with almost supernatural abilities.

小说是罗贯中根据分别由曹操、刘备和孙权建立的魏、蜀和吴三国之间的冲突的民间传说和历史记录写成的。魏、蜀、吴三国位于华北、四川西部和长江中下游以南。这本小说记载了诸侯和将领的生活以及他们统领全国的战略和战争情况，还生动地描述了人物性格和壮观的战争场面。它用简明扼要的语言塑造了 1 798 个人物形象，每个人物都有独特的个性。小说充斥着勇猛战士间的遭遇战、杰出的军事战略和悬疑的阴谋，但基本是关于人的动机、忠义和对权力的贪婪的叙述。

这本小说融入了历史记录、唐代诗歌作品和元代戏曲等。它还强调罗贯中时期儒家的道德价值观，如对家人、朋友和君主要忠诚。小说在情节的发展上注意保持一致性，充满了复杂性和变化性。它的结构既宏伟又紧凑，在中国古典小说中很少见。这本小说通过生动描述一系列错综复杂的故事讲述了不同政治派系之间的战争和冲突。作者罗贯中写小说时结合了现实主义和浪漫主义风格。基本表现手法是现实主义，但一些情节的安排及历史人物塑造有时充满了浪漫色彩。

Luo Guanzhong based his novel on both folk tales and historical records of the conflicts between the kingdoms of Wei, Shu and Wu, established by Cao Cao, Liu Bei and Sun Quan, respectively. The kingdoms of Wei, Shu and Wu were based in Northern China, Western Sichuan and south of the lower Yangtze River. The novel chronicled the lives of these leaders and their generals, the strategies and wars that competed for the domination of China. It also vividly described character profiles and spectacular war scenes. Using simple and succinct language, Luo created 1,798 figures with each having a unique personality. In the novel, there are many encounters between fierce warriors, brilliant military strategies, and suspenseful intrigues, though it is ultimately about human motivation, loyalty and the greed for power.

The novel incorporated available historical records, poetic works from the Tang Dynasty and operas from the Yuan Dynasty. It also highlighted Confucian moral values, which were prominent during Luo's time, such as loyalty to one's family, friends and superiors. The novel, while maintaining consistency in the development of plot, is full of complexities and variations. Its structure achieves a combined grandness and compactness rarely seen in Chinese classic novels. The novel describes all types of struggles and warfare among different political cliques through the vivid recounting of a series of intricate stories. The author Luo Guanzhong combines realist and romantic styles in writing the novel. The basic expressive technique is realist, but the arrangement of some plots and the portraying of the historical figures are at times full of romantic color.

《水浒传》

《水浒传》是明朝（1368—1644）初年施耐庵所著。《水浒传》暗指历史强盗宋江和他的三十六个同伴的故事。将南宋（1127—1279）时期关于宋江的民间故事和梁山土匪故事作为元朝（1206—1368）戏剧的主题，很受大众欢迎。在此期间，《水浒传》的素材演变成今天的样子。宋江的土匪们扩容到 108 位，虽然他们来自不同的背景，但最终都是为了占据梁山。小说详细描述了 12 世纪初期 108 个好汉所经历的考验和磨难。

Water Margin

Water Margin (*Shui Hu Zhuan*, also known as *Outlaws of the Marsh*) was written in the early Ming Dynasty（1368 – 1644）by Shi Nai'an. *Water Margin* is vaguely based upon the historical bandit Song Jiang and his thirty-six companions. Folk stories about Song Jiang circulated during the Southern Song（1127 – 1279）and stories about the bandits of Liangshan became popular as subject for Yuan Dynasty（1206 – 1368）drama. During this time the material on which *Water Margin* was based evolved into what it is today. Song Jiang's bandits were expanded to number 108, and though they came from different backgrounds, all eventually come to occupy Liangshan. The novel details the trials and tribulations of 108 outlaws during the early 12th century.

这部小说是对官员腐败和封建压迫的强烈讽刺。它生动地阐述了"不法之徒"怎样聚集梁山，支持穷人反对腐败的统治阶级，充满感人的爱情、友谊和善良的故事。在击败压制他们的帝国军队以后，最终徽宗皇帝授予大赦，招募他们组成一个军事特遣队，并展开宣传抵抗外国侵略的运动。

《水浒传》写的是一系列连接松散的故事，因此不会因缩写而蒙受损失。108 条好汉并非同时出场。其实，这本书写的就是好汉们如何凑到一起，加入一个或多个群体，以躲避贪官污吏们做出的一些非正义的事。它是中国历史上第一部章回体白话小说，是一种每一章由一组联句说明主旨内容的传统式中国小说，共描述了787个人物，每个人物都有自己的性格特点和详细描述。人们说《水浒传》中描写了绿林好汉主要人物的故事，是中国最伟大的富有骑士精神的小说。最重要的是这本小说描述了他们志同道合和充满正义的精神，符合农民的传统理想。因此《水浒传》获得了包括城市居民在内的广泛接受。

The novel is a powerful satire on official corruption and feudal oppression. The novel provided vivid accounts of how these "outlaws", who had gathered at Liangshan Marsh, stood up for the poor against the corrupt ruling class, as well as moving stories of love, friendship and kindness. After defeating the imperial armies sent to suppress them, they were eventually granted amnesty by Emperor Hui Zong, who recruited them to form a military contingent and embark on campaigns to resist foreign aggression.

Water Margin is written as a series of loosely connected stories and therefore may not lose as much from abridgement. 108 superheroes do not appear all at once. In fact the book is about how the bandits get together and join the group one at a time or in small groups to escape some injustice perpetrated by corrupt officials. It is the first vernacular novel in Chinese history written in Chapter Style, which is a type of traditional Chinese novel with each chapter headed by a couplet giving the gist of its content. In total, the novel describes 787 characters, with each having its own characteristics and detailed descriptions. People say that the story of heroes of the greenwoods who are leading characters of Water Margin is China's greatest novel of chivalry. Most importantly the novel depicts comrades among these men and the spirit of justice and accordance to the traditional ideals of the peasants. Therefore, Water Margin has gained wide acceptances among the city dwellers as well.

《西游记》

《西游记》由明代吴承恩（1504—1582）所写。作为中国文学中的四部著名小说之一，它被评为最优秀的中国神话小说。

《西游记》写的是唐朝时期和尚玄奘如何忍受各种怪兽和魔鬼施加的重重困难的故事，他的三个弟子孙悟空、猪八戒和修道士沙僧为保护他，与成群的想要抓住他，吃他的肉成仙的恶魔作战。他在三个弟子的协助下西行，最终到达印度。

Journey to the West

Journey to the West was written in the Ming Dynasty by Wu Cheng'en (1504 – 1582). As one of the four famous novels in Chinese literature, it is referred to as the most brilliant Chinese mythological novel.

Journey to the West tells the story of how Xuan Zang, a Buddhist monk of the Tang Dynasty, endures countless difficulties imposed by various monsters and demons. His three disciples Monkey King, Pigsy, and Friar Sha have to guard their master and battle hordes of demons who all want to capture him and eat his flesh for immortality and finally Xuan Zang travelled west to India assisted by his three disciples.

孙悟空是小说中最精彩的人物。他热爱自由，有战斗精神。他自傲，对神和佛不屈不挠，但他非常忠诚于他的主人。玄奘既是虔诚的佛教僧侣，又是顽固的封建文人。作者通过孙悟空的勇敢和机智的性格批评玄奘的怯懦和无能。猪八戒是小说中的重要衬托人物。他粗鲁、贪恋美色，他的傲慢和自怜自哀的行为给小说带来了喜剧性调剂效果。

The Monkey King is the most brilliant figure in the novel. He loves freedom and has a fighting spirit. He is arrogant and unyielding in the face of gods and Buddha, but at the same time is very obedient and loyal to his master. Xuan Zang's character embodies both the piety of a Buddhist monk and the stubbornness of a feudal scholar. The author criticizes Xuan Zang's timidity and incompetence by contrasting his character to Monkey King's bravery and resourcefulness. Pigsy is an important foil in the novel. He is rude and avaricious, and lusts after women. His arrogance and self-pitying behavior brings much comic relief to the novel.

这部小说深受中国神话和传统价值观念的熏陶，虽然许多人尤其是儿童普遍认为这是一个冒险故事，它也可以被视为个人朝圣得以教化的故事。有学者还认为小说是对明代当时的现实描写和对政治和社会状况的批判。

Deeply steeped in Chinese mythology and traditional values, the novel, while commonly viewed by many, particularly children, as an adventure story, can also be seen as an individual pilgrimage towards enlightenment. The novel is also regarded by scholars as a realistic portrayal and critique of the political and social circumstances of the Ming Dynasty at the time.

《红楼梦》

《红楼梦》是 18 世纪晚期的曹雪芹（1715—1763）所著。人们认为这部小说是半自传体，反映了曹家的命运。在第一章中，作者详细说明了自己是想纪念他年少时认识的一些女性：朋友、亲戚和佣人。曹雪芹出生于富贵权势家庭，一生却经历了从极其兴盛到贫穷的过程。童年的奢侈生活使他了解到贵族家庭和统治阶层的生活方式，而后来的贫困生活使他能够更清楚更深入地观察生活。由于他对生活的理解以及他的进步思想、认真的态度和高超的才艺，能够创作《红楼梦》这部被认为是中国古典小说顶峰的小说。

小说按情节详细地记录了都城比邻的两家大院的大家庭生活。他们的祖先是诸侯。在小说的开头，两院都是都城最负盛名的家族。最初极其富裕，有很大的社会影响力。家有女子成为皇妃，最终两家失宠于皇帝，其豪宅被突击搜查和没收。这部小说围绕 30 多个主要人物和 400 多个次要人物，描绘了这一大家庭从显赫到败落的过程。

A Dream of Red Mansions

A Dream of Red Mansions was written in late 18th century by Cao Xueqin (1715 – 1763). The novel is believed to be semi-autobiographical, mirroring the fortunes of Cao's own family. As the author details in the first chapter, it is intended to be a memorial to the women he knew in his youth: friends, relatives and servants. Cao was born into a noble and powerful family, which was reduced from extreme prosperity to poverty in his lifetime. The life of luxury in his boyhood acquainted him with the ways of noble families and the ruling class, while poverty in his later life enabled him to observe life more clearly and penetratingly. Basing on his own understanding of life and with his progressive ideas, serious attitude, and high craftsmanship, he was able to create *A*

Dream of Red Mansions, a book regarded as the pinnacle of the Chinese classical novel.

The novel itself is a detailed, episodic record of the lives of the extended family, which occupies two large adjacent family compounds in the capital. Their ancestors were made Dukes and, at the beginning of the novel, the two houses still comprised one of the most illustrious families in the capital. Originally extremely wealthy and influential, with a female member made an imperial concubine, the family eventually fell into disfavor with the emperor, and had their mansions raided and confiscated. The novel is a charting of the family's fall from the height of their prestige, centering around some 30 main characters and more than 400 minor players.

这部小说分为 120 回，其中前 80 回由曹雪芹所写，后 40 回由高鹗和程伟元所写。以贾宝玉与林黛玉的悲惨爱情故事为主题，描述了四个封建贵族家庭的命运。这本小说反映的是曹雪芹家庭和清王朝的兴衰。

故事描写了出身于富贵而有权势的家族、无忧无虑的青少年贾宝玉，他生活在表姊妹和女佣包围的悠闲之家，爱上了他的表妹林黛玉，但他后来被骗，娶了表姐薛宝钗。三个主要人物之间的关系暗示了贾家的衰败，构成了小说故事的主线。这部小说非同一般，不仅因为其庞大的人物阵容（大部分为女性）和心理审视，还因为其对 18 世纪中国贵族的生活和社会结构特征精确和详细的观察。

The novel consists of 120 chapters, of which the first 80 were written by Cao Xueqin and the remaining 40 by Gao E and Cheng Weiyuan. Recounting the tragic love story of Jia Baoyu and Lin Daiyu as the main theme, it also describes the fate of four feudal noble families. The novel is believed to reflect the rise and fall of Cao Xueqin's own family and the Qing Dynasty.

The story is about Jia Baoyu, a carefree adolescent from a rich and powerful family who lived in an idyllic household surrounded by his female cousins and maids. Jia was also in love with his cousin Lin Daiyu but he was subsequently tricked into marrying another cousin. The relationship among the three main characters against the backdrop of the Jia family's decline forms the main story in the novel. The novel is remarkable not only for its huge cast of characters (most of them are females) and psychological scope, but also for its precise and detailed observation of the life and social structures typical of 18th-century Chinese aristocracy.

口述题

1. 在你的认知中，哪一首诗词是最令你印象深刻的，并给出你的理解。
2. 根据对本章节的了解，说出你对四大名著的认识。

Questions

1. Which poem is the most impressive in your understanding?
2. According to the understanding of this chapter, state your understanding of the four famous works.

学习网站

1. CHINASAGE（https://www.chinasage.info/poetry.htm）
2. 古诗文网（https://www.gushiwen.org/）

第七章　中国饮食文化

Chapter 7　Chinese Food Culture

第一节　饮食原料和饮食特征

Section 1　Raw Material and Characteristics of Food

中国菜是中华民族文明和智慧的结晶，是民族文化宝库的珍宝。中国广阔的地貌和悠久的历史创造出了丰富的中国菜肴。因此，中国的烹饪文化在世界上享有最高的声誉，中国、法国和土耳其被称为"世界三大主要烹饪王国"。

中国菜的做法大致分为北部和南部做法。一般来说，北方以面食为主，面条、馄饨、包子、煎饺和馒头都是北方人青睐的面食。北方菜肴则油而不腻，里边的醋和大蒜的味道往往比较浓郁，北京菜、天津菜和山东菜是最著名的北部地区风格菜。

Chinese cuisine, a crystallization of the civilization and wisdom of all Chinese nationalities, is a gem in the nation's cultural treasury. The vastness of Chinese geography and history created the varieties of Chinese cuisine. Thus, China gains the highest reputation in the world for its culinary culture, and is known as the "three major culinary kingdoms" together with France and Turkey.

Chinese food can be roughly divided into the Northern and Southern styles of cooking. Pasta plays an important role in Northern Chinese cooking; noodles, ravioli-like dumplings, steamed stuffed buns, fried meat dumplings, and steamed bread are favored flour-based treats. In general, Northern Chinese cooking dishes are oily without being cloying, and the flavors of vinegar and garlic tend to be more pronounced. The cooking of Beijing, Tianjin, and Shandong are perhaps the best known area styles of Northern Chinese cuisine.

菜的芳香能激起食欲。令人垂涎的香料包括葱、生姜、大蒜、辣椒、酒、八角茴香、肉桂、胡椒、香油、干香菇等。烹饪极为重要的一点是保鲜和保持食材的自然风味，去除不好的腥味或气味。在西式菜肴中，经常用柠檬去除腥味；而中国菜常用葱和姜。酱油、糖、醋和其他调味料可增加菜的风味而不会掩盖其风味。精心准备的多油脂的菜肴适合那些喜欢味道浓的人；不太辣的菜适合那些喜欢味道清淡的人；鲜甜的菜适合那些喜欢甜味道的人；辣菜适合那些喜欢辛辣味的人。

A dish with a fragrant aroma will whet the appetite. Ingredients that contribute to a mouthwatering aroma are scallions, fresh ginger root, garlic, chili peppers, wine, star anise, stick cinnamon, pepper, sesame oil, dried Chinese black mushrooms, and so forth. Of foremost importance in cooking any dish is preserving the fresh, natural flavor of the ingredients, and removing any undesirable fishy or gamey odors. In Western cooking, lemon is often used to remove fishy flavors; in Chinese cooking, scallions and ginger serve a similar function. Soy sauce, sugar, vinegar, and other seasonings add richness to a dish without covering up the natural flavor of the ingredients. A well-prepared dish will be rich to those who like strong flavors, not over spiced to those who like a blander taste, sweet to those who like a sweet flavor, and hot to those who like a piquant flavor.

色、香、味并不是中国菜唯一遵循的原则，中国菜最关注的是营养。食材的搭配原理可以追溯到殷商王朝（公元前 16 到 11 世纪）学者伊尹。他认为甜、酸、苦、辣、咸五味能满足人体五个主要器官系统（心、肝、脾/胰腺、肺和肾脏）营养的需要，强调五味能保持身体健康。事实上，很多中国菜中使用的葱、生姜、大蒜、干百合花、树菌等有预防和缓解各种疾病的属性。中国文化传统上相信食物的药用价值，认为食材和药材是同源的。这一观点可以被视为中国营养学的前卫思想。在这一理论中，值得注意的是蔬菜与肉的比例要适当；蔬菜类菜肴应该有三分之一的肉食。做汤的用水量应为容器的十分之七。简而言之，做每个菜或汤必须坚持正确的成分比例，以确保其充分的营养价值。

Color, aroma, and flavor are not the only principles to be followed in Chinese cooking; nutrition is of course the first concern. A theory of the harmonization of foods can be traced back to the Shang Dynasty (16th to 11th century BC) scholar Yi Yin. He related the five flavors of sweet, sour, bitter, piquant, and salty to the nutritional needs of the five major organ systems of the body (the heart, liver, spleen/pancreas, lungs, and kidneys), and stressed their role in maintaining good physical health. In fact, many of the plants used in Chinese cooking, such as scallions, fresh ginger root, garlic, dried lily buds, tree fungus, and so forth have properties of preventing and alleviating various illnesses. The Chinese culture has a traditional belief in the medicinal value of food, and that food and medicine share the same origin. This view could be considered as a forerunner of nutritional science of China. Notable in this theory is the concept that a correct proportion of meat to vegetable ingredients should be maintained; one third of meat-based food should be vegetable ingredients, and one-third of vegetable-based dishes should be meat. In preparing soups, the quantity of water used should total seven-tenths the volume of the serving bowl. In short, the correct ingredient proportions must be adhered to be in the preparation of each dish or soup in order to ensure full nutritional value.

中国文化有一些与吃有关的规定和习俗。例如，必须坐着吃；男子、妇女、老人和青年谁先就座有先后顺序；每张桌子通常坐十到十二人，主菜必须吃完。典型的宴会包含四个开胃菜，如冷盘或饭前点心；六到八个主菜；最后是一道美味鱼和甜点。做菜方法包括煸、炖、蒸、煎、油炸、平底锅煎等。菜可以咸、甜、酸或辣。每道菜的主要颜色包括红色、黄色、绿色、白色和焦糖色。装饰菜如雕西红柿、雕白萝卜、雕黄瓜等，能增加视觉上的美感。所有这些食材能使中国菜真正成为吸引人的眼球、鼻子以及味蕾的盛宴。

The Chinese culture has a number of rules and customs associated with eating. For example, meals must be taken while seated; there is a set order of who may be seated first among men, women, old and young; the main courses must be eaten arranged on a per table basis, with each table usually seating ten to twelve persons. A typical banquet consists of four appetizer dishes, such as cold cut platters or hors d'oeuvres; six to eight main courses; then one savory snack-type fish and a dessert. The methods of preparation include stir-frying, stewing, steaming, deep-frying, flash-frying, pan-frying, and so forth. A dish may be savory, sweet, tart, or piquant. The main colors of a dish may include red, yellow, green, white and caramel color. Food garnishes, such as cut or sculptured tomatoes, Chinese white radishes, cucumbers, and so forth, may be used to add to the visual appeal of a dish. All of these elements contribute to making Chinese food a true feast for the eyes and nostrils as well as the taste buds.

中国烹饪艺术的特征

原料和配料的选择：

中国菜肴强调原料和辅料的选择。不同季节有不同的成分和调料。夏天吃牛肉、羊肉和芥末；冬天吃腌制的食物和辣椒。

调味料的使用：

中国菜调味的特点在于调料品种丰富，使用得当。古代关于调味的理论认为，五味（甜、酸、苦、辣和咸）的恰当比例可以做出最佳风味。

五味的基本调料详情如下：

甜——红糖、蜂蜜、蔗糖、糖精和麦芽糖等。

酸——醋和姜、酸柠檬、西红柿酱等。

苦——干橙皮等。

辣——胡椒粉、芥末、洋葱、红辣椒、野山椒和咖喱粉等。

咸——盐、酱油、腐乳等。

Features of Chinese Culinary Arts

The choice of raw materials and ingredients：

Chinese cuisines stress the choice of raw materials and auxiliary materials. In different seasons, there will be different ingredients and seasonings. Beef, mutton, and mustard are for summer and preserved food and pepper are for winter.

The use of seasonings：

The feature of seasoning in Chinese cooking lies in the variety of condiments and the proper use of them. According to the ancient theories about seasoning, the harmonious proportion of the five tastes (sweet, sour, bitter, pungent and salty) could produce the best flavor.

The basic seasonings with the five flavors are as follows：

Sweet—molasses, honey, sucrose, saccharin and maltose, etc.

Sour—vinegar and ginger, lemon acid, tomato sauce, etc.

Bitter—dried orange peel, etc.

Hot—pepper, mustard, onion, chilli, wild pepper and curry powder, etc.

Salty—salt, soy, fermented soya beans, etc.

菜肴的制作：

烹饪美食主要包括切、火候、烹饪技术和原材料的保护性措施。

切：切成小方块，切成碎片，捣碎，切成薄片或切成丝、片、立方块等，是烹饪中常用的切法。

时间和温度：嫩、半生熟、全熟或刚好。

烹调技巧：炒、干煸、油炸、烘焙、烤、煨、蒸、炖、熬、焖、煮、汆等。

保护性措施：裹上一层淀粉，沾上奶油面糊和浇注淀粉酱以保护原材料。

The making of cuisines：

The cooking of cuisines mostly involves cutting, temperature, the cooking techniques and the protective treatment of raw materials.

Cutting: Dicing, shredding, mashing, slicing, or cutting into strips, pieces, cubes, etc. are the cutting methods often used in cooking.

The time and temperature: tender, medium, overdone or just done to a turn.

Cooking techniques: frying, dry-fry, deep-frying, baking, broiling, simmering, steaming, stewing, decocting, braising, boiling, quick-boiling and so on.

The protective treatments: Rolling in starch, dipping in batter and pouring starchy sauce over the dish are the protective treatments of raw materials in the process of cooking.

根据不同信仰或要求做药膳和素食菜。

药膳：中国人有个老说法，"药疗不如食疗"。许多食物不仅包含人体所需的营养成分，也可用于预防或治疗疾病。

药膳也称食物疗法，把食物和传统医学结合起来，把苦药变成美味菜肴。这种食疗可以缓和饥饿，预防或治愈疾病。在一般情况下，长期食疗还可以帮助改善健康状况。中华饮食中最常见的药膳包括莲子粥、八宝粥、三味汤。

药膳有很多种类，包括各种菜肴、汤、饮料、粥和糕点。食疗按照每个人的体质、病症、季节的变化、偏爱和对不同食物的反应来执行。

基于传统中医的脏腑理论，药膳最基本的作用是增强身体抵抗力，以加强免疫功能。随着生活方式的改进和烹饪技巧的进步以及对新食物药疗性的进一步研究，药膳将对促进中国以及世界其他地区人类的健康发挥更大的作用。

Medicinal food and vegetarian food according to different beliefs or demands：

Medicinal food: As old Chinese sayings such as "It is better to depend on food than on tonics for nutrients than on medicines". Many foodstuffs not only contain nutrients needed by the body, but are also useful for preventing or curing diseases.

Chinese medicinal food, also known as dietotherapy, combines foodstuffs with certain kinds of traditional medicine. Turning bitter medicine into delicious dishes, such dietotherapy can both appease hunger and prevent or cure diseases. Under ordinary circumstances, dietotherapy can also help promote health if taken over a long period. The most common medicinal foods in the Chinese diet include lotus seed porridge, eight-treasure rice budding and three-delicacy soup.

There are many varieties of medicinal food in China. They include various dishes, soups, drinks, porridge and pastries. Dietotherapy is administered in accordance with the constitution of each individual, the nature of his ailment, the change of seasons and his preference for and reaction to different foods.

Based on the principle of syndrome differentiation followed in traditional Chinese medicine, the most fundamental aspect of medicinal food is to improve the body's resistance and strengthen its immunity function. With lifestyle improvements, progress in cooking techniques and the study of new foods that have therapeutic potential, medicinal food will play an even greater role in promoting health in China as well as the rest of the world.

素食菜

长期以来，素食菜一直是中国文化中的重要食物，自宋代以来一直很受欢迎，明、清得以发展。素食有三大派系——寺院素食、宫廷素食和民间素食。素食的主要特征是做法独特、健康。

主要成分是绿叶蔬菜、水果、蘑菇、豆制品。通常用植物油做调料，因为它不仅可口，营养丰富，它还可以帮助消化，防止癌症。虽然有很多素食菜肴的名称里面有"肉"、"鱼"，比如"红烧素咕噜肉"，"素食虾"，但并不真正有鱼肉、猪肉、鸡肉，而只把它们是加工成外观像鱼和肉的样子。

Vegetarian Food

Vegetarian food has been an important food in the Chinese culture for a long time. It has been a popular choice of food since the Song Dynasty and was developed further in the Ming and Qing dynasties. There are three types of schools—monastery vegetarian food, court vegetarian food and folk vegetarian food. The main characteristic of this type of food is to be uniquely cooked and healthy.

The main ingredients are green leafy vegetables, fruits, mushrooms and bean curd products. Vegetable oil is usually a condiment, as it is not only delicious and nutritious, it also helps the digestion process and prevents cancer. Although lots of vegetarian dishes get the names with "meat", "fish" like "Braised Vegetarian Meat", "Vegetarian Shrimps", they do not contain real fish, meat, chicken, just processed and cooked to look and taste like the real things.

第二节　中国八大菜系

Section 2　Chinese Eight Cuisines

中国菜有许多种类，但最有影响力、最为人熟知的是八大菜系：山东菜、四川菜、广东菜、福建菜、江苏菜、浙江菜、湖南菜和安徽菜。形成这些菜系的原因包括历史因素、烹调特点、地理因素、气候、资源和生活方式等。不同地区的菜系差别很大，有时即便是地理位置相邻，菜的风格却迥异。

Chinese cuisine has a number of different genres, but the most influential and typical known by the public are the "Eight Cuisines". These are as follows: Shandong Cuisine, Sichuan Cuisine, Guangdong Cuisine, Fujian Cuisine, Jiangsu Cuisine, Zhejiang Cuisine, Hunan Cuisine, and Anhui Cuisine. The essential factors that establish the form of a genre are complex and include history, cooking features, geography, climate, resources and life styles. Cuisines from different regions are so distinctive that sometimes despite the fact that two areas are geographical neighbors their styles are completely alien.

鲁菜或山东菜

鲁菜是中国影响最大、普及地区最广的菜系之一。鲁是山东省的简称，山东是中国古文化发祥地之一，地处黄河下游，气候温和，境内山川纵横，河湖交错，沃野千里，物产丰富。其粮食产量目前居中国第三位，蔬菜种类多，品质优良，是中国重要的蔬菜产地。山东是孔子故乡的所在地，鲁菜处处体现着孔子"食不厌精，脍不厌细"的饮食理念，讲究调味纯正，口味偏咸鲜，具有鲜、嫩、香、脆的特色。常用的烹调技法有30多种，尤擅"爆、炒、烧、塌、扒"。明、清两代，鲁菜已是宫廷御膳主体。以清代国宴规格设置的"满汉全席"，使用全套银餐具，196道菜，全是山珍海味，可谓奢华至极。作为北方第一菜系，喜庆寿诞的高档宴席和家常菜的许多基本菜式都是由鲁菜发展而来的，不仅如此，鲁菜对京、津、东北等地特色风味菜肴的形成也有着重要的影响。山东人豪爽好客，特别讲究待客之道，唯恐客人吃不饱、吃不好，因此菜量很大，在山东人家做客要有一吃到底的心理准备。

Shandong or Lu Cuisine

Lu cuisine is one of the most influential and popular cuisines in China. "Lu" is short for Shandong Province, which is one of the cradles of Chinese ancient culture. With mountains towering and rivers meandering throughout the province, it boasts vast fertile fields and abundant produce. Its grain output ranks third in China, and it also has many kinds of high-quality vegetables. Shandong is the home province of Confucius, and Shandong Cuisine embodies the dining concept of "Eat no food but what's of the best quality; eat no meat but what's finely minced". It emphasizes purity of the seasonings and is a little salty. It features freshness, tenderness, aroma and crispness. There are over 30 kinds of common cooking techniques, of which, "bao (quick stir-frying), chao (frying), shao (stewing), ta (boiling) and pa (braising)" are outstanding. In the Ming and Qing dynasties, Shandong cuisine was the main style of imperial meals. The "Feast of Complete Manchu-Han Courses", established in accordance with the state banquet of the Qing Dynasty court, adopted a banquet of 196 courses served on silver platters, including delicacies of every kind as luxurious as possible. As the first cuisine of north China, many basic courses of high-class feasts prepared for festivals and birthdays were developed based on Shandong cuisine. It also had an important influence on the formation of the local cuisines of Beijing, Tianjin and northeast China. The people of Shandong Province are good-hearted, keep open doors, and pay special attention to treating guests well to ensure they leave full and well satisfied. Hence, the dishes served are more than sufficient, and family guests never go hungry.

糖醋黄河鲤鱼：此菜选用黄河鲤鱼烹制而成，成菜后外焦里嫩，香酥、酸甜、稍咸。

德州扒鸡：鸡皮光亮，色泽红润，肉质肥嫩，热吃时，手提鸡骨一抖，骨肉随即分离，香气扑鼻，味道鲜美，是德州传统风味。

Yellow River Fish are cooked in a particular way, so that they are crisp outside and tender inside. The dish is savory and crisp, sour and sweet and a little salty.

Dezhou Stewed Chicken: The chicken skin is bright and ruddy, and the meat is fat and tender. When eating it hot, diners simply grip the feet and shake it, and the meat separates from the bones. Sweet-smelling and tasty, it is the traditional flavor of Dezhou.

典型的山东菜：

Typical menu：

扒原壳鲍鱼	Braised Abalone
糖醋鲤鱼	Sweet and Sour Carp
八仙过海闹罗汉	Eight Immortals Crossing Sea Teasing Arhats

广东菜

广东菜源于华南地区的广东省和香港。那些来来回回用餐车推着的中餐小点心，就始于这一地区。点心的意思是打动人们的心。广东菜最为新鲜。在烹活鱼和海鲜之前先养在水箱里。粤菜酱汁味道很淡，所以不会盖过食材的鲜味。最受欢迎的粤菜包括蒸全鱼、脆皮鸡、鱼翅羹和烤乳猪。

粤菜或广东菜采用精细和稀有的食材，做法考究，风格别致。它强调味道清而不淡，鲜而不俗，嫩而不粗。夏秋尚清淡，冬春求浓郁。除了猪肉、牛肉和鸡肉，广东菜包含了几乎所有食用肉类，包括动物内脏、鸡脚、鸭舌、蛇和蜗牛。然而，广东不像北方或西方，人们很少吃羊肉。它使用很多烹调方法，其中蒸和炒最受青睐，因为这样能

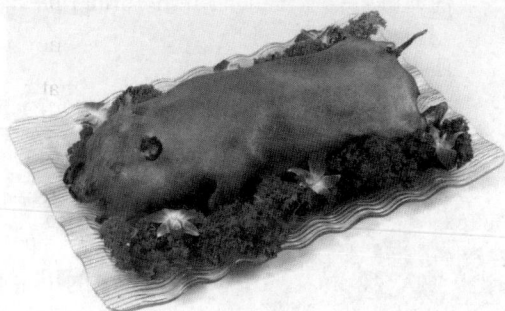

方便、迅速地把食材最新鲜的味道做出来。其他做法包括浅层油炸、煮、焖和深层油炸。

Guangdong Cuisine

Guangdong cuisine originated from the areas of Guangdong Province and Hong Kong in southern China. Dim sum meaning touching the heart, the Chinese meal of small tidbits of food presented on roving carts, began in this region. Freshness is supreme to the Cantonese. Live fish and seafood are held in tanks just before being dispatched immediately for cooking. Cantonese sauces are mild and subtle so as not to overpower the freshness of the ingredients. Popular Cantonese dishes include steamed whole fish, crispy-skinned chicken, shark's fin soup, and roast suckling pig.

Guangdong cuisine takes fine and rare ingredients and is cooked with polished skills and in a dainty style. It emphasizes a flavor which is clear but not light, refreshing but not common, tender but not crude. In summer and autumn it pursues clarity and in winter and spring, a little more substance. Besides pork, beef, and chicken, Cantonese cuisine incorporates almost all edible meats, including organ meats, chicken feet, duck tongue, snakes, and snails. However, lamb and goat is rarely eaten, unlike in cuisines of Northern or Western China. Many cooking methods are used, steaming and stir-frying being the most favored due to their convenience and rapidity, and their ability to bring out the flavor of the freshest ingredients. Other techniques include shallow frying, double boiling, braising, and deep frying.

典型的广东菜：
Typical menu：

菊花鱼	Chrysanthemum Fish
烩蛇羹	Braised Snake Porridge
脆皮乳猪	Roast Suckling Pig（Crispy BBQ Suckling Pig）

其他著名的广东菜：
Other famous Guangdong dishes：

龙虎斗	Dragon Duel Tiger
清蒸鲈鱼	Steamed Bass
脆皮乳鸽	Crisp Spring Pigeon
油泡鲜虾仁	Fresh Shrimp Meat in Oil

四川菜

四川菜用辣椒和胡椒来刺激味蕾、抵御寒冬。四川菜很辣，吃后不会立即感觉到辣，而是过一会儿会慢慢感觉很辣。这一地区的蔬菜和肉类经过浸制和腌制可以保留一个寒冬。醋味和甜味混杂的油炸食品就起源于中西部地区。著名的川菜有四川牛肉、炒青豆、花生汁冷面和麻婆豆腐。

川菜把成都和重庆美食结合在一起。早在清朝，书中就系统地收录了 38 种烹调方法，如煎、炒、炸、烤、腌制、炖煮和卤等。其特点是调料很辣，著名的调料有"三椒"（花椒、胡椒和辣椒）、"三香"（葱、姜和大蒜）和"七滋八味"。

Sichuan Cuisine

Chili peppers and red peppercorns are used in Sichuan cooking to stimulate the taste buds and counter the bitter cold of winter. Sichuan dishes are considered spicy, although the heat is not immediate, it can creep up on you. Through pickling and salt-curing, the vegetables and meats of this region are preserved to last through the harsh winter. The combined flavors of vinegar with sweetly fried food originate in this central western region. Well-known Sichuan dishes are Sichuan beef, stir-fried green beans, cold noodles with peanut sauce, and spicy stir-fried Mapo tofu.

This combines the cuisines from Chengdu and Chongqing. From as early as the Qing Dynasty, books had systematically recorded a total of 38 cooking methods like to saute, stir-fried, fry, bake, pickle, stew, and bittern, etc. It features pungent seasonings which were famed as "Three Peppers" (Chinese prickly ash, pepper and hot pepper), "Three Aroma" (shallot, ginger, and garlic), "Seven Tastes and Eight Flavors".

典型的四川菜：

Typical menu：

麻婆豆腐	Mapo Tofu, Stir-fried Tofu with Minced Beef in Spicy Bean Sauce
灯影牛肉	Lamp-shadow Beef
夫妻肺片	Lung Pieces by Couple
宫保鸡丁	Kung Pao Chicken

一些知名的川菜描述如下：

锅巴肉片：锅巴指的是沾在饭锅底部的脆米饼。锅巴堆放在铁板上，服务生把滚热的汤浇在锅巴上，锅巴发出噼啪声，冒完蒸汽后发出咝咝声。美味极了！加进来的肉和蔬菜汤把锅巴软化为脆脆的米饭。

樟茶鸭子：就是指用茶树叶和樟树叶熏鸭子。把本地鸭泡在糯米汁里，掺盐、花椒和辣椒。然后把浸泡好的鸭从汁里拿出。用茶树叶和樟树叶熏鸭子直到鸭皮变成棕色。最后一步是蒸或深煎，这样的鸭子闻起来香吃起来嫩。

宫保鸡丁：就是指辣子鸡炒花生。它是一道名菜，几乎所有当地餐馆都有。主要成分包括鸡胸肉、干花椒、花生。厨师将鸡胸肉切成小方块，把花椒和其他必要的食材放入热油中炸。准备好后，添加花生。据说一个从贵州省来的名叫丁宫保的人发明了这道菜。清朝期间他曾在四川省当官，他的厨师经常用干红辣椒炒鸡。丁很喜欢这道菜，他同他的厨师一起把这道菜加以改良，后来这道菜在四川广为流传，当地人以他的名字命名了这道菜。

Some well-known Sichuan dishes are described below：

Guoba Roupian：Guoba refers to the crispy bits of rice that get stuck to the bottom of the rice pot. Guoba is put on a hot plate in stack, and then a service person proceeds to baptize the rice with piping hot soup. The dish erupts in fireworks when the steam and sizzle has cleared, leaving the mirage on the table. Delicious! Soupy additions are meat and vegetables, which soften the rice to a crunchy texture.

Zhangcha Yazi：Sichuan Duck Smoked with Camellia and Camphor Leaves. Local ducks are soaked in glutinous rice juice mixed with salt, Chinese prickly ash, and peppers. Then the soaked ducks are removed out of the juice. They are smoked with camellia and camphor leaves until the ducks' skin become brown. The final step is to steam or deeply fry the brown ducks, which smell good and taste tender.

Gongbao Jiding：Spicy Chicken Fried with Peanuts. It is a well-known dish, which is served by almost all the local restaurants. The main ingredients consist of chicken chest meat, dry peppercorns and peanuts. A cook puts the chest meat in diced size, peppercorns and other necessary ingredients into hot oil to fry. As the dish is ready, peanuts are added. It is said that a man whose name was Ding Gongbao from Guizhou province invented this dish. When he served as a governor of Sichuan Province during the Qing Dynasty, his cook often cooked the fried chicken with dry red pepper. Ding enjoyed this dish very much and he worked with his cook to further improve the quality of the dish. Finally the recipe of the dish was widely spread in Sichuan and local people named the dish after Ding Gongbao.

麻婆豆腐：麻婆指的是一位脸上有麻子的女子。麻婆豆腐是四川的一道家常菜，其特色是调料用很多柿子椒和红辣椒。它是由小方块豆腐加大蒜、碎牛肉，再加入辣酱做成的。据说一个世纪前一位脸上有麻子的女子与她的丈夫在成都的桥边开了一家店。那女子做好这种炖辣豆腐卖给过往的小贩和船夫。后来她的这些客人把她做的豆腐叫做麻婆豆腐。

Mapo Tofu：Mapo refers to a lady with a pockmarked face. Toufu means bean-curd. Mapo Tofu is one of the common dishes in Sichuan, characterized by the use of many spices and liberal application of pimiento and hot red peppers. Mapo Tofu is a small square of bean curd, with garlic, minced beef, all prepared in a chilly sauce. It is said that a lady with a pockmarked face set up a shop with her husband near a bridge in Chengdu a century ago. The lady served itinerant peddlers and boatmen with her red-hot stew bean-curd when they passed by. Gradually her customers named her bean-curd as Mapo Bean-Curd.

小吃

川菜中有大量有名的小吃，或称为小点心。小吃非常便宜。下面列出几款最知名的小吃：

Snacks

Sichuan cuisine includes a number of famous snack dishes, specialties originated from *xiao chi* or finger food. The snack dishes cost you next to nothing. A few of the more renowned snack dishes are listed here below：

赖汤圆：这道小吃是一个名叫赖源鑫的小贩于 1894 年发明的。赖源鑫开始只是一个街头摊档小贩，他卖的汤圆好看又很甜。后来，赖源鑫自己开了家店铺卖汤圆，当地人命名为赖汤圆。传统上一碗有四个汤圆，配一小碗芝麻酱。每个汤圆有不同的甜馅料，吃前应蘸糖芝麻酱。

担担面：它是一种五香汤面，里边有虾米酱、腌制蔬菜、花生、芝麻、辣椒油、醋和大蒜。担担是指扁担。以前有个小贩用扁担挑着两筐面和酱走在街上叫卖，以方便行人。他的面很便宜，当地人称它为担担面。

Laitangyuan（*Lai Rice-dumpling*）: This dish was invented in 1894 by a vendor whose name was Lai Yuanxin. Lai started off as a street stall vendor, and his rice dumpling had a delicate visual appeal and tasted sweet. Later, Lai set up his own shop and local people named the rice dumpling after Lai. Traditionally four dumplings are in a soup with a side dish of sesame sauce. Each dumpling has a different sweet stuffing inside and it should be dipped in the sugar sesame sauce before devouring.

Dandan Mian: It is a kind of hot-spiced noodles in soup favored with a sauce containing dried shrimp, shredded preserved vegetables, peanuts, sesame seeds, chili oil, vinegar and garlic. Dandan refers to shoulder poles. In the earliest time a noodle peddler shouldered his pole with two baskets at the either side while walking along streets. The baskets contained his noodles and sauce. He sold his noodles for the convenience of passers-by. His noodles cost almost nothing and gradually local people called it Dandan Noodle.

夫妻肺片：夫妻指丈夫和妻子。据说是名叫郭朝华的人和他的妻子发明了这道菜。人们称它为夫妻肺片。通常四川厨师把煮熟的牛肉切片再加一些牛的内脏，并将它们放在一个盘子上，然后加麻辣酱到牛肉和牛内脏上。

Fuqi feipian（*Slices of Beef and Assorted Entrails of Oxen*）: Fuqi refers to a husband and his wife. It is said that a husband and his wife, whose name was Guo Chaohua invented this dish. People named it Husband and Wife's Slices of Beef and Assorted Entrails of Oxen. Usually Sichuan chefs slice cooked beef and some oxen entrails, and place them on a plate. Then they add numbingly spicy sauce to the beef and entrails on the plate.

四川火锅：据说火锅起源于重庆市。在 20 世纪 20 年代，重庆市长江北面有几个宰牛场。屠房经常以低廉的价格向河渡口附近的商贩卖牛内脏，商贩清洗好内脏，切成小块放入锅里，炖熟加辣椒和酱，然后卖给船夫、民工和小贩。这种牛杂汤便宜又好吃，然而只能趁热吃。

随着天气变化，河边风起，汤很快就凉了，牛杂变得没味道。后来，一些船夫搭起了一口大炒锅，加满热香油，把切片的内脏加入铁锅内趁热吃。这种吃火锅的方式逐渐传播到整个四川省。现在，四川主要餐馆都有火锅。

Sichuan Hotpot: It is said that the hotpot originated in Chongqing city. In 1920s, there were several oxen slaughterhouses located in the northern side of the Yangtze River in Chongqing. The slaughterhouses often sold oxen entrails in cheap price to vendors who owned stalls near the river ferry. The vendors cleaned the entrails and cut them into small pieces before putting them into pots to stew with hot pepper and other sauce. The vendors sold the stewed entrails in soup to boatmen, laborers and peddlers. It was cheap and tasty. However, the sliced oxen entrails in soup could only be eaten while it is hot.

As weather changed and wind blew from the river, the soup soon became cool and the entrails didn't taste good. Later, some boatmen set up a big wok full of hot, spiced oil. They skewed sliced entrails and eat them hot as the entrails were ready in the wok. This way of hotpot eating gradually spread far and wide in Sichuan Province, and at the present time, it has been introduced into main restaurants as an important part of Sichuan cuisine.

成都的人行道边有火锅摊，也有精致的火锅餐厅。店主在桌子的中央矗一口大锅，里边加满热的五香油汤吸引路人坐下来吃火锅。锅附近放着一碟碟切得很薄的肉片和其他食材，顾客可以拿起烤肉叉自助用餐。

与其他四川食品一样，并不是所有的火锅都会使客人辣得额头冒汗或舌头灼热。火锅也有做得清淡的，如酸辣蔬菜、鱼酱、羊肉汤、啤酒鸭、辣椒鸡汤。冬季或夏季火锅料几乎相同，有各种肉类、海鲜及丰富的蔬菜。

In Chengdu there are many sidewalk hotpot operations and exquisite hotpot restaurants. In the center of the table stands a big wok full of hot, spiced oil or hot rich soup alluring passers-by to sit down. Around the wok are placed a dozen plates of paper-thin slices of raw meat and other ingredients, and the customers pick up skewers of raw ingredients and make a do-it-yourself.

Like other Sichuan food, not all of the hot-pot is spicy-hot, with skewered food making your forehead drip or tongue searing. The development of the particular hotpot cuisine has been toned down for tourists with other flavorings such as sour vegetables, fish sauce, mutton soup, beer and duck flavor and hot pepper chicken soup. In winter or summer the skewered items tend to be almost the same with a variety of meat, seafood and rich vegetables.

湖南菜

湖南菜很辣。有时很难区分湖南菜和四川菜，两种菜的口味很吻合是因为这两个省相邻。湖南人做菜重油、大蒜和辣椒酱。炒肉之前往往先炸一下，做出香浓的调味汁和菜肴。最受欢迎的湖南菜是陈皮牛肉、陈皮鸡、鱼香茄子和脆皮鱼。

湖南菜（或湘菜）包括湘江、洞庭湖和湖南西部地区的菜。湖南菜有三地风格：湘江风格，由长沙、湘潭和衡阳菜构成；洞庭湖风格，由岳阳、常德菜构成；湖南西部风格，由张家界、吉首、怀化菜构成。湖南菜重油、重色，脆、软、嫩、开胃、香。1958 年毛主席和其他领导人高度称赞过湖南菜。

Hunan Cuisine

The food from Hunan is hot, hot, hot. It's often difficult to distinguish Hunan from Sichuan cuisine. The cuisines dovetail nicely as the two provinces also are neighbors. The Hunanese use preserved basics such as hearty oils, garlic, and chili-based sauces. The stir-fried meats are often seared prior to stir-frying, creating sauces and dishes that exude comfort. Popular dishes from Hunan are orange beef or chicken, spicy eggplant in garlic sauce, and hot crispy fish.

Hunan cuisine consists of the cuisines of the Xiang River region, Dongting Lake and western Hunan Province, in China. Hunan cuisine consists of three styles: Xiang River style which is represented by dishes of Changsha, Xiangtan, and Hengyang, Dongting Lake style which is represented by dishes of Yueyang and Changde, and western Hunan style which is represented by dishes of Zhangjiajie, Jishou, and Huaihua. Hunan cuisine lays a stress on the use of oil, dense color, and techniques that produce crispness, softness and tenderness as well as the savory flavors and spices. Chairman Mao, together with other leaders highly praised the Hunan cuisine in 1958.

湖南菜很辣是因为湖南气候非常潮湿，人体湿气很重，湖南人爱吃辣椒，以驱寒祛湿。湖南菜主要的烹饪方法是烧、炖、蒸、煮。它也以经常食用腊肉而著称。

Hunan food is hot because the climate of Hunan is very humid, which makes it difficult for human body to eliminate moisture. The local people eat hot peppers to help remove dampness and cold. The main cooking methods for Hunan dishes are braising, double-boiling, steaming and stewing. It is also renowned for its frequent use of preserved meat in cooking.

大米是湖南的主食，但北方风格点心和馅料也很普及，如豆腐馒头卷、饺子和美味面包。

典型的湖南菜包括：东安鸡、辣子鸡、炒牛肚片、牛肚鸭汤、莲子冰糖、潇湘龟、蒸腌肉、辣青蛙。

Rice is the staple in Hunan, but northern-style side dishes and fillers are also popular: bean curd "bread" rolls or dumplings and savory buns.

Typical courses include: Dong'an chick, peppery and hot chick, stir-fried tripe slivers, tripe in duck's web soup, lotus seed with rock candy, Xiaoxiang turtle, steamed pickled meat, and hot and spicy frog leg.

江苏菜

江苏菜，简称苏菜，是中国菜主要菜系之一，由扬州、南京、苏州、镇江菜式组成。它以其独特的风味享誉全世界，在长江下游地区尤其受欢迎。

江苏俗称"鱼米之乡"，食材丰富。江苏菜的特点是选材严格、工艺精湛、造型典雅、文化特征丰富。典型的食材是鲜活的水产品，它强调食材的新鲜度。其他食材包括精选茶叶、竹笋、蘑菇、梨和枣。刀功很精湛，特别是雕瓜艺术众所周知。由于做菜方法为炖、蒸、快炸、炙和酒汁腌制，再加糖作为调味品，江苏菜新鲜、清淡、味醇。

江苏菜可分为苏州—无锡菜式和镇江—扬州菜式。苏州风格菜肴的特点是保持原有的自然风味，咸甜混合。镇江—扬州风格菜的特点是"汤很清淡，可以看到碗底，酱汁浓而呈乳白色"。

Jiangsu Cuisine

Jiangsu cuisine, also known as Su Cai for short, is one of the major components of Chinese cuisine, and consists of the styles of Yangzhou, Nanjing, Suzhou and Zhenjiang dishes. It is very famous in the whole world for its distinctive style and taste. It is especially popular in the lower reach of the Yangtze River.

Known as "a land of fish and rice" in China, Jiangsu Province has a rich variety of ingredients available for cooking. Jiangsu cuisine has the characteristics of strictly selected ingredients, exquisite workmanship, elegant shape, and rich culture trait. The typical raw materials are fresh and live aquatic products. It highlights the freshness of ingredients. Other cooking ingredients are often carefully selected tea leaves, bamboo shoots, mushrooms, pears, and dates. Its carving techniques are delicate, of which the melon carving technique is especially well known. Due to using the methods of stewing, braising, quick-frying, stir-frying, wine sauce pickling and adding some sugar as condiments, Jiangsu dishes taste fresh, light and mellow.

Jiangsu dishes can be classified into that of Suzhou-Wuxi style and Zhenjiang-Yangzhou style. The feature of Suzhou-style dishes is their natural flavor in original stock and a mixture of salty and sweet taste. The characteristics of Zhenjiang-Yangzhou style food are best described by the saying that "the soup is so clear that you can see the bottom of the bowl and the sauce is so thick that it turns creamy white".

典型的江苏菜有金陵盐焗鸭、水晶肉、蟹肉丸、扬州蒸肉干、三套鸭、腊鸭和霸王别姬。

Typical courses of Jiangsu cuisine are Jinling salted dried duck, crystal meat (pork heals in a bright, brown sauce), clear crab shell meatballs (pork meatballs in crab shell powder, fatty, yet fresh), Yangzhou steamed jerky strips (dried tofu, chicken, ham and pea leaves), triple combo duck, dried duck, and Farewell My Concubine (soft-shelled turtle stewed with many other ingredients such as chicken, mushrooms and wine).

南京盐焗鸭：这道菜有一千多年的历史。鸭子外表肥硕，脆、鲜、香，油而不腻，非常诱人。600年前发明了此烹鸭方法。盐焗鸭是先在鸭子上涂一层厚厚的烤盐，再放在浓盐水中浸泡，烤干，然后用盖压一段时间；成品盐焗鸭皮为奶油色和红色，肉嫩。清朝时这道菜是皇宫的贡品。

Nanjing Style Dried Salty Duck: It has a long history of over 1,000 years. Apart from its plumpness in appearance, the duck tempts people with characteristics of tasting crisp, fresh, fragrant, and rich but not greasy. The cooking method of the duck was invented 600 years ago. The salted duck is slathered with roasted salt, steeped in clear brine, baked dry and then kept under cover for some time; the finished product should have a creamy-colored skin and red, tender flesh. It was the tribute to the royal palace during the Qing Dynasty.

松鼠鳜鱼：这道菜的来历是，乾隆六下江南时，在古城苏州微服私访，忽然觉得饥饿难忍，便进了一家名为松鹤楼的饭店，看见店家的水牌上有一道名为松鼠鳜鱼的菜，就随口点了这道菜。厨师知道皇帝来了，于是使出浑身解数做调味品调味。为能免除杀"圣鱼"的罪恶，他把鲤鱼做成松鼠的样子，其头、尾高高翘起。做好的暗红色鱼外脆里嫩，酸酸甜甜，很合乾隆皇帝的口味，皇帝大加赞赏，于是这道菜家喻户晓。此菜原料的特点是肉质柔软、骨头稀少。经过刮鳞和煎炸，鱼嘴张开，鱼头显得很大，尾巴弯曲向上，鱼肉像松鼠直立的毛发。如果上面撒一层虾肉、干笋、番茄酱，吃起来发出的声音就会像松鼠吱吱叫。松鼠鳜鱼色、香、味、声俱全，人见人爱。

Squirrel-shaped Mandarin Fish：Tradition has it that once stopping at the Crane House during his sixth south Yangtze tour, Emperor Qian Long saw a carp frisking on the holy table and ordered it cooked for him. The chef, knowing it was the emperor's order, spared no effort in flavoring and seasoning. In order to be exempted from the sin of killing the "holy fish", the chef made the carp into the shape of a squirrel with its head and tail soaring high. The dark reddish brown fish, crisp outside and tender amid, was sour and sweet enough to the taste of emperor, whose appreciation raised the name of Squirrel-shaped Mandarin Fish to the world. Being the raw material, the mandarin fish is characterized by its tenderness of the flesh and sparseness of the bones as well. After scaling and frying, the head of the fish looks big with its mouth wide open, the tail bends upwards, and the flesh imitates the erecting hair of a squirrel. It will be squeaking like a squirrel if it is sprinkled with shrimp meat, dried bamboo shoots and tomato ketchup. Thus the Squirrel-shaped Mandarin Fish is complete in color, smell, flavor and sound, and it is to arouse the appetite of whoever sees it.

扬州炒饭：米饭是这道菜的主要原料。先把米饭捣碎，然后炒虾、火腿、鸡蛋、豌豆和时令蔬菜。加入各种时令蔬菜，吃起来口感和风味奇妙！

"狮子头"蟹黄肉丸：这道菜是淮扬菜的象征，做工复杂。先把猪肉泥、鸡蛋白、蟹肉、米酒、盐、葱和姜和成稠状。然后将其分成4份，每份滚进一个肉丸。加白菜、鸡汤入砂锅，用小火久熬。这道菜有猪肉和蟹肉的香味，亮如橙色，味道肥而不腻。

无锡排骨：无锡排骨是最受欢迎的地方特色菜。加入米酒和酱油做成酱红色，掺入姜、茴香、丁香和黑胡椒，最后加入番茄酱，以丰富口感。

Yangzhou Style Fried Rice：Rice is the main ingredient in this dish. It is first pounded and then stir-fried with shrimp, ham, egg, peas and seasonal vegetables. Because a variety of seasonal vegetables are used, you can taste a variety of wonderful flavors and textures!

"Lion-Head" Meatball with Crab Roe：This dish is the symbol of Huaiyang cuisine and it requires very complicated procedure. First mix the ground pork, egg white, crabmeat, rice wine, salt, scallions and ginger into a rather stiff mixture. Then divide it into 4 portions and roll each portion into a meatball. Add cabbage, chicken broth together with meatballs into casserole and place on low heat and simmer for long time until it's done. It has the fragrance of the pork and crab and the color of the dish is as bright as orange. It tastes rich but not greasy.

Wuxi Sweet and Salty Spare Ribs: Wuxi Spare Ribs is the most popular local dish. It features the common eastern technique of "red cooking" in a stock of rice wine and soy sauce and spiced with ginger, anise, cloves and black peppercorns and has unique red-sweet sauce on the top in order to give rich taste.

浙江菜

浙江菜（或浙菜）包括浙江省主要城市的佳肴，它结合了杭州菜的精美多样、宁波菜的柔软新奇、绍兴菜的乡村野趣。杭州曾经是南宋的都城，人们习惯把菜配上秀美的地名。烹饪采用油炸、快炒、煸炒、炖和蒸等方法，既开胃又有益于健康。

浙江菜是中国八大著名菜系之一。浙江菜由杭州、宁波、绍兴菜组成，不油腻，因其新鲜、嫩、软、滑和香而久负盛名。杭州菜是三地菜中最著名的。

杭州菜的特点是烹调方法多样化，如煸、蒸、炒和油炸。杭州菜味道新鲜脆嫩，随季节而变化。宁波菜咸而美味，海鲜经过蒸、烤、焖以后，保留原有的新鲜、嫩和软。绍兴菜因有新鲜的水产品和家禽，使其具有特别的农村风味，气味芳香，软、黏，时令肉汤浓。

Zhejiang Cuisine

As Zhejiang cuisine consists of hundreds of small delicacies from its main cities, it takes in Hangzhou's fineness and diversification, Ningbo's softness and originality, and Shaoxing's pastoral interests. Hangzhou, once the capital of the Southern Song Dynasty, it is customary to endow cuisine with dainty place-names. The chief techniques of cooking lie in the methods used such as frying, quick-fry, stir-fry, braising, and steaming thus rendering the dishes both salubrious and savory.

Zhejiang cuisine, is one of the eight famous culinary schools in China. Comprising the specialties of Hangzhou, Ningbo and Shaoxing, Zhejiang cuisine, not greasy, wins its reputation for freshness, tenderness, softness, and smoothness of its dishes with mellow fragrance. Hangzhou cuisine is the most famous one among the three.

Hangzhou cuisine is characterized by its varying techniques of cooking, such as sauting, stewing, and stir- and deep-frying. Hangzhou food tastes fresh and crisp, varying with the change of season. Ningbo food is a bit salty but delicious. Specializing in steamed, roasted and braised seafood, Ningbo cuisine is particular in retaining the original freshness, tenderness and softness.

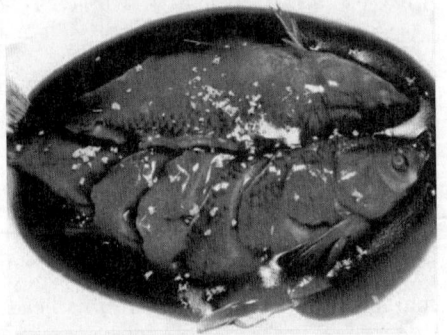

Shaoxing cuisine offers fresh aquatic food and poultry that has a special rural flavor, sweet in smell, soft and glutinous in taste, thick in gravy and strong in season.

传说叫花鸡是由杭州小偷发明的。因为小偷没有炉子，他把偷来的鸡用黏土包住，放入地洞中烤；还有一种说法是饥饿的盗贼发明了一种做鸡的方法，以保持鸡的香味。

Legend has it that Beggar's Chicken was invented by a Hangzhou thief. The story goes that because the thief had no stove, he wrapped the stolen bird in clay and baked it in a hole in the ground; another version explains that he was a hungry thief who found a way to cook his bird and keep it and its aroma!

典型的浙江菜：

Typical menu：

西湖醋鱼	West Lake Fish in Vinegar Gravy
龙井虾仁	Shelled Shrimps Cooked in Longjing Tea
东坡肉	Dongpo Rou
叫花鸡	Jiaohua Ji or Beggar's Chicken

福建菜

福建菜，简称闽菜，在中国烹饪艺术中占有重要地位。福建省的经济和文化在南宋后开始蓬勃发展。18 世纪清朝中期，著名福建官员和文人促进了福建菜的发展，把福建菜推广到了中国其他地区。

福建菜由福州、闽南和闽西三地菜组成。它们之间略有不同。福州菜流行于闽东、闽中、闽北地区，更鲜、更美味，不咸不甜不酸；闽南菜则广传于厦门、泉州、漳州、闽南金三角，又甜又辣，用辣酱、奶黄和橘子汁作调料；闽西菜又咸又辣，具有浓郁客家地区的乡土风味。由于福建人移民海外，福建菜在国外成为最受欢迎的菜。一般来说，福建菜微甜、酸、不咸，常用红酒糟调味。

Fujian cuisine, also called Min Cai for short, holds an important position in China's culinary art. Fujian's economy and culture began flourishing after the Southern Song Dynasty. During the middle Qing Dynasty around 18th century, famous Fujian officials and literati promoted the Fujian cuisine so it gradually spread to other parts of China.

Fujian cuisine comprises three branches—Fuzhou, South Fujian and West Fujian. There are slight differences among them. Fuzhou dishes, quite popular in eastern, central and northern Fujian Province, are more fresh, delicious, and less salty, sweet, and sour; South Fujian dishes, popular in Xiamen, Quanzhou, Zhangzhou and the golden triangle of South Fujian, are sweet and hot and use hot sauces, custard, and orange juice as flavorings; West Fujian dishes are salty and hot, prevailing in Hakka region with strong local flavor. As Fujian people emigrate overseas, their cuisine become popular abroad. Generally speaking, Fujian dishes are slightly sweet and sour, and less salty, and often use the red distiller's grain for flavoring.

福建菜有以下四个特点：

（1）食材以海鲜和山珍为主：由于福建地势倚山傍海，北部多山，南部面海，苍茫的山区盛产菇、笋、银耳等山珍野味；沿海地区盛产167种鱼类，90种龟类和贝类。还有食用燕窝、墨鱼、鲟鱼，给闽菜提供了丰富的原料资源。本地人都擅长烹饪海鲜，特色做法有炖、煮、焖、快煮和蒸等。

Fujian cuisine is characterized by the following four aspects：

（1）Ingredients of seafood and mountain delicacies：Fujian cuisine emphasizes seafood and mountain delicacies. Fujian Province has a favorable geographical location with mountains in its north and sea to its south. Many mountain delicacies such as mushroom, bamboo shoots and tremella are often found here. The coastal area produces 167 varieties of fish and 90 kinds of turtles and shellfish. It also produces edible bird's nest, cuttlefish, and sturgeon. These special products are all used in Fujian cuisine. The local people are good at cooking seafood, featuring in methods of stewing, boiling, braising, quick-boiling, and steaming, etc.

（2）刀工巧妙：闽菜注重刀工，有"片薄如纸，切丝如发"之美称，而且一切刀工均围绕着"味"下功夫，使原料通过刀工的技法，更体现出原料的本味和质地。大多数菜都是海鲜做的，如果海鲜切不好，菜便失去本真的味道。

（2）Fine slicing techniques：Fujian cuisine stresses on fine slicing techniques so much that it is reputed as sliced ingredients are as thin as paper and shredded as slim as hairs. Everything sliced serves its original aroma. Fine slicing techniques may better show the aroma and texture of food. Most dishes are made of seafood, and if the seafood is not cut well, the dishes will fail to have their true flavor.

（3）汤菜考究，变化无穷：闽菜重视汤菜，与多烹制海鲜和传统食俗有关。人们长期积累的经验认为，最能保持原料本质和原味的当属汤菜。有的汤白如奶汁，甜润爽口；有的汤清淡如水，色鲜味美；有的汤金黄澄透，馥郁芳香；有的汤汤稠色酽，味厚香浓。

（3）Various soup and broth：Fujian cuisine stresses on soup, which is associated with the seafood cooking and traditional eating custom. The accumulated experience tells that soup can best maintain the essence and flavor of raw materials. Some soup is as white as milk, sweet and refreshing；some is as clear as water with fresh color and tasty flavor；some is as golden orange with aromatic fragrance；some is thick, strong and aromatic.

（4）精湛的烹饪艺术：福建菜美味是因为制作过程考究，包括选料、调味、控制时间和火候。菜不太咸时，味道更鲜美。甜味使菜味道更好，而酸味则有助于去除海鲜的腥味。

（4）Exquisite culinary art：Fujian dishes are tasty because of their emphasis on a series of delicate procession：selecting ingredients, mixing flavors, timing the cooking and controlling the heat. When a dish is less salty, it tastes more delicious. Sweetness makes a dish tastier, while sourness helps remove the seafood smell.

典型的福建菜：

Typical menu：

最著名的福建菜是佛跳墙，菜名的意思是佛闻到菜香跳过墙来尝一尝。它由海鲜、鸡、鸭、猪肉混合放入米酒缸里，用小火慢慢煨成。

Buddha-jumping-over-the-wall is the most famous; the name implies the dish is so delicious that even the Buddha would jump over a wall to have a taste once he smelled it. A mixture of seafood, chicken, duck, and pork is put into a rice-wine jar and simmered over a low fire.

徽州菜

徽州菜或徽菜主要是由徽州本地和沿长江流域与淮河流域的风味菜组成。在徽菜菜单上你会发现菜肴很少是油炸或快炒的而是炖的或焖的。人们往往添加火腿和糖作为调料以丰富其鲜味。

徽菜的大部分食材，如石蛙、蘑菇、杨梅、茶叶、竹笋、枣等，都是来自山区。黄山食材丰富。黄山肉驴肉嫩味甜，可以清汤煮或红烧，能除热提神。又白又嫩的笋子可以制成非常美味的食物。老树上的头等香菇也非常美味。

Huizhou Cuisine

It is mainly composed of local flavors of Huizhou and other areas along the Yangtze River and the Huai River. Among the dishes on the Anhui cuisine menu, you will find less fried or quick-fried dishes than those that are braised. People here are inclined to add ham as seasoning and sugar to enrich the freshness.

Most ingredients in Anhui cuisine, such as stone frog, mushroom, bayberry, tea leaves, bamboo shoot, dates, etc. are from mountain area. Huangshan Mountain has abundant products for dish cooking. Huangshan Chukka has tender flesh and a sweet taste. It can be boiled in clear soup or braised in soy sauce. The dishes help relieve internal fever and build up vital energy. The white and tender bamboo shoots produced on Huangshan Mountain can be made into very delicious food. Xianggu, a kind of top-grade mushroom grows on old trees, is also very tasty.

典型的徽州菜：

Typical menu：

火腿炖甲鱼：把软壳龟、猪肉、火腿、竹笋、蒜、葱、姜、酱油、盐、丁香、稻米酒、黑胡椒、猪油放一起在木炭火上炖。这道菜不油腻，让食客回味无穷。

Stewed soft shell turtle with ham: One whole soft shell turtle, pork, ham, bamboo shoots, a clove of garlic, shallot, ginger, soy sauce, salt, clove, rice wine, black pepper, lard are all stewed together in a pot on charcoal fire. The dish is not greasy and can lead diners to endless aftertastes.

蒸石蛙：石蛙是栖居在黄山山洞里特有的食材。重量约 250 克，其腹部呈白色，背部

有黑色条纹。石蛙有丰富的蛋白质、钙等。它有清热、改善营养和提高视力等功能。

Steamed stone frog: Inhabited in caves, stone frog is a special product in Huangshan Mountain. It weights 250 grams or so, whose belly is white and back black with stripe. Stone frog is rich in protein, calcium and so on. It has the functions of clearing heat, improving nutrition and vision.

火腿香菇炖鞭笋：它是徽州山区的一道传统风味菜。竹笋加入香肠、香菇烹煮则更香。它味美好看、多汁汤浓。

Bamboo shoots cooked with sausage and dried mushroom: It is one traditional flavor in Huizhou mountainous area. Cooked with sausage and dried mushrooms, the bamboo shoots are more fragrant. It is delicious, and noted for its good color, juicy meat and thick soup.

李鸿章大杂烩：这道以安徽省著名人物李鸿章命名的菜很受欢迎。李鸿章是晚清时期的一位高级官员。他曾访问美国，宴请美国友人。中国菜可口美味而深受欢迎。开宴不久，李鸿章即命厨师加菜，但正菜已上完，厨师只好将所剩海鲜等余料混合下锅，有海参、鱿鱼、豆腐、火腿、香菇、鸡肉和其他难以辨认的食材。美国友人尝后赞不绝口。

Li Hongzhang Hotchpotch: Li Hongzhang hotchpotch is a popular dish named after one of Anhui's famous personages. Li Hongzhang was a top official of the late Qing Dynasty. When he was in office, he paid a visit to the US and hosted a banquet for all his American friends. As the specially prepared dishes continued to flow, the chefs, with limited resources, began to fret. Upon Li Hongzhang's order, the remaining kitchen ingredients were thrown together into an impromptu stew, containing sea cucumber, squid, tofu, ham, mushroom, chicken meat and other less identifiable food materials. His friends praised it a lot after tasting it.

其他典型的徽州菜：

Other typical menu:

| 火腿炖甲鱼 | Braised Turtle with Ham |
| 符离集烧鸡 | Fuliji Grilled Chicken |

淮扬菜：上海菜、江浙菜（扬州、镇江、淮安）

淮扬菜起源于先秦时期，隋唐变得有名，明代和清朝期间成为地方特色菜。此菜系包括淮安菜、扬州菜、苏州菜和上海菜。

Huai-Yang Cuisine: Shanghai Cuisine and Jiangzhe Cuisine (Yangzhou, Zhenjiang and Huai'an)

Huai-Yang Cuisine originated from the Pre-Qin Period, became famous during the Sui and Tang dynasties, and was recognized as a distinct regional style during the Ming and Qing dynasties. This cuisine includes dishes from Huai'an, Yangzhou, Suzhou, and Shanghai.

淮扬菜的原料有鲜活的水产品。刀工精湛，最知名的是西瓜雕刻艺术。淮扬菜风味轻淡、鲜甜。其烹饪特点是炖、焖和长时间小火蒸。用这种方式做的名菜有栗子黄焖鸡、荷叶蒸肉、八宝鸭、扬州狮子头和蝴蝶海参（海参切成蝴蝶形状，用香料烹成）。其他名菜包括清炖蟹粉狮子头、大煮干丝、三套鸭、水晶肴肉、松鼠鳜鱼、干煸鳝丝和梁溪脆鳝。

Raw materials of Huai-Yang dishes include fresh and live aquatic products. The carving techniques are delicate, of which the melon carving technique is especially well-known. The flavor of Huai-Yang cuisine is light, fresh and sweet. Huai-Yang cuisine is characterized by stewing, braising, and steaming over a low fire for a long time. Famous dishes cooked this way are chicken braised with chestnuts, pork steamed in lotus leaf, duck stewed with eight treasures, meatballs with crab meat in Yangzhou style, and butterfly sea cucumber (sea cucumber cut into butterfly shapes and cooked with flavorings). Other famous dishes include stewed crab with clear soup, long boiled dry shredded meat, crystal meat, squirrels with mandarin fish, sauteed eel shreds and Liangxi crisp eel.

淮扬小吃和点心很精致，如水煮豆腐、凉拌豆腐、干豆腐，蒸肉饺。

其特点是选材考究、注重食材清鲜，还注重刀工、搭配、烹饪和摆放。清淡、新鲜、香甜、性温，特别注重保持原料的天然汁液和味道。

Huai-Yang snacks and refreshments are exquisite, such as boiled, shredded, dried bean curd, steamed dumplings with minced meat and gravy.

They are characterized by the strictness in material selection, the emphasis of cleanliness and freshness of its ingredients, as well as the fine workmanship in cutting, matching, cooking, and arranging. Lightness, freshness, sweetness, and mildness of taste are the features of these dishes, and special attention is paid to retaining the ingredient of natural juices and flavors.

口述题

1. 你知道中国八大菜系有哪些吗？
2. 八大菜系中你最喜欢吃哪种？为什么？

Questions

1. Do you know any of the Chinese Eight Cuisines?
2. Which of the eight cuisines do you like best? Why?

学习网站

1. 舌尖上的中国（http://www.cctv.com/）
2. China HIGHLIGHTS（https://www.chinahighlights.com/travelguide/chinese-food/）

第八章　中国医药文化

Chapter 8　Chinese Medicine Culture

第一节　中医药文化的形成与特点

Section 1　The Formation and Characteristics of Chinese Medicine Culture

中医简介

中国传统医学（中医）有 2 000 到 3 000 年的历史，已经形成了一个独特的诊断和治愈疾病的系统。中医疗法基本上不同于西方医药疗法。正如道教所述，中医对人体的理解是基于对宇宙的全面理解之上的，疾病的治疗主要基于诊断和症状变异。

中医疗法把脏腑作为人体主要器官。人体内的组织和器官通过经脉和血管相连。气作为载体通过经络系统向外传达信息。病理上，脏腑器官的功能障碍可能通过经络反映在体表，同时，体表组织疾病也可能影响相关脏腑器官。受影响的脏腑器官也会通过内部连接相互影响。传统中医药治疗基于对整个人体系统的分析，然后通过调整脏腑器官的功能着重处理病变。

对综合征的评估不仅包括原因、机制、位置和疾病的性质，也包括致病因素和身体抵抗力之间的对抗。治疗不仅基于症状，而且基于症状的变异。因此，相同的疾病可以用不同的方法治疗，而不同的疾病可能导致同样的症状，可以用相似的方法治疗。

Introduction to TCM

With a history of 2, 000 to 3, 000 years, Traditional Chinese Medicine (TCM) has formed a unique system to diagnose and cure illness. The TCM approach is fundamentally different from that of Western medicine. In TCM, the understanding of the human body is based on the holistic understanding of the universe as described in Daoism, and the treatment of illness is based primarily on the diagnosis and differentiation of syndromes.

The TCM approach treats zang-fu organs as the core of the human body. Tissue and organs are connected through a network of channels and blood vessels inside human body. Qi (or Chi) acts as some kind of carrier of information that is expressed externally through jingluo system. Pathologically, a dysfunction of the zang-fu organs may be reflected on the body surface through the network, and meanwhile, diseases of body surface tissues may also affect their related zang or fu organs. Affected zang or fu organs may also influence each other through internal connections. Traditional Chinese Medicine treatment starts with the analysis of the entire system, then focuses on the correction of pathological changes through readjusting the functions of the zang-fu organs.

Evaluation of a syndrome not only includes the cause, mechanism, location, and nature of the disease, but also the confrontation between the pathogenic factor and body resistance. Treatment is not only based on the symptoms, but also differentiation of syndromes. Therefore, those with an identical disease may be treated in different ways, and on the other hand, different diseases may result in the same syndrome and are treated in similar ways.

中国传统医学中的临床诊治主要基于阴阳和五行理论。这些理论把自然现象和规律运用于生理活动与身体病变及两者的相互关系的研究。典型的中医疗法包括针灸、中药治疗和气功锻炼。针灸治疗是通过刺激体表的特定穴位完成的。中药治疗是针对体内的脏腑器官治疗，而气功是通过运气来疏通经络气血，调整阴阳。这些疗法虽然大不相同却对人体的性质和它在宇宙中所处的位置有相同的设想和观察。有些科学家把通过草药、针灸、气功治疗疾病的方法描述为"阴阳疗法"。

The clinical diagnosis and treatment in Traditional Chinese Medicine are mainly based on the yin-yang and five-element theories. These theories apply the phenomena and laws of nature to the study of the physiological activities and pathological changes of the human body and its interrelationships. The typical TCM therapies include acupuncture, herbal medicine, and qigong exercises. With acupuncture, treatment is accomplished by stimulating certain areas of the external body. Herbal medicine acts on zang-fu organs internally, while qigong tries to restore the orderly information flow inside the network through the regulation of Qi. These therapies appear very different in approach yet they all share the same underlying sets of assumptions and insights in the nature of the human body and its place in the universe. Some scientists describe the treatment of diseases through herbal medication, acupuncture, and qigong as "yin-yang therapy".

传统中医泛指有相同理念的治疗方法，这些理念在中国得到了发展，已有两千多年的传统，包括各种形式的传统中药、针灸、按摩、气功和食疗。这些疗法在整个东亚地区都很普遍。

中医理论来源于《黄帝内经》和《伤寒杂病论》等书以及阴阳和五象等宇宙学概念。20 世纪 50 年代开始，这些概念逐渐现代化，它被融入了医学中的解剖学和病理学概念。然而，许多假定的概念，包括体型或疾病概念，现代医学都不支持。

中医不注重人体解剖结构，而主要关注功能器官（主管消化、呼吸、老化等）的诊断。人们认为健康是这些器官与外界的和谐互动，而疾病被解释为不和谐的互动。中医诊断包括检查症状和潜在的不和谐模式，主要包括把脉和观察舌头。

Traditional Chinese Medicine refers to a broad range of medicine practices sharing common theoretical concepts which have been developed in China and are based on a tradition of more than 2,000 years, including various forms of herbal medicine, acupuncture, massage, exercise (qigong) and dietary therapy. These practices are a common part of medical care throughout East Asia.

The doctrines of Chinese medicine are rooted in books such as *Huang Di's Inner Canon* and *Treatise on Febrile and Miscellaneous Diseases*, as well as in cosmological notions like Yin-Yang and the Five Phases. Starting in the 1950s, these precepts were modernized in the People's Republic of China so as to integrate many anatomical and pathological notions from scientific medicine. Nonetheless, many of its assumptions, including the model of the body, or concept of disease, are not supported by modern evidence-based medicine.

TCM's view of the body places little emphasis on anatomical structures, but is mainly concerned with the identification of functional entities (which regulate digestion, breathing, aging, etc.). While health is perceived as harmonious interaction of these entities and the outside world, disease is interpreted as a disharmony in interaction. TCM diagnosis consists in tracing symptoms to an underlying disharmony pattern, mainly by palpating the pulse and inspecting the tongue.

中国传统医学（"中医"）是中国文化的组成部分。它为中国的繁荣昌盛作出了巨大贡献。今天，在中国，中医和西医都为医疗和保健提供服务。

Traditional Chinese Medicine is an integral part of Chinese culture. It has made great contributions to the prosperity of China. Today both of TCM and western medicine are being used in providing medical and health services in China.

中医的起源
中医学始于神农氏这位中国古代著名的草药大师，他大约生活在 6 000 年前，这是中医学的萌芽阶段。

中医典籍
秦王朝之前，《神农本草经》中记录了 365 味中药，总结了中药材的种类，并根据它们的基本疗法、功能和毒性将它们分为三类。这是中国有史以来发现的最早药典。但我们谈论药典，绝不能忽视李时珍的著作《本草纲目》。《本草纲目》是现代中医的基础。

Origin of TCM
Traditional Chinese Medicine originated with Shen Nong, the celebrated herbal master of ancient China who lived about 6,000 years ago, a time which is believed to be the embryo stage in the development of traditional Chinese medicine.

Great Books on TCM
Shen Nong's Herbal Classic, prior to the Qin Dynasty records 365 work that sums varieties of medicinal herbs and classifies them into three categories in accordance with their respective primary treatments, functions and toxic character. This is the earliest pharmacopoeia ever found in China. But when we talk about the pharmacopoeia, we cannot neglect Li Shizhen's work *Compendium of Material Medica*. It is so great that we use it as the basis of the modern TCM.

著名医生
在中医学发展的高峰期出现过许多老少皆知的医生，如扁鹊、华佗、张仲景、孙思邈。其传奇故事激励着我们，使我们对传统文化充满自信。

神农：《神农本草经》并不是神农本人所写，它是在战国或秦汉时期完成的。神农尝百草，发现了中药。这本书是现存最早的医学专著。

Famous Doctors

At the peak of Traditional Chinese Medicine, there come forth many brilliant doctors known by the young and the old, such as Bian Que, Hua Tuo, Zhang Zhongjing, Sun Simiao. Their legends inspire us and make us confident of our traditional culture.

Shen Nong：*Shen Nong's Herbal Classic* wasn't written by himself; it was finished in Warring States Period or Qin and Han Dynasty time. Shen Nong tasted hundreds of grass and found herbs. This book was the earliest extant medical monograph.

黄帝：针灸鼻祖，与神农相似，《黄帝内经》也不是他本人写的。据说它可能是在秦汉时期完成的。

华佗：外科手术鼻祖，生活在东汉末年。他以外科手术和麻沸散（草药做的一种麻醉药）而著名。他基于虎、鹿、熊、猿和鹤的动作，开创了健身操五禽戏。

Huang Di：He is the earliest ancestor of acupuncture and moxibustion. It was similar to Shen Nong, *Huang Di's Inner Canon* was also not written by himself. It's said that it might be finished in Qin and Han Dynasty time.

Hua Tuo：He is the earliest ancestor of surgery, lived in late Eastern Han Dynasty. He was famous for surgical operation and *ma fei san* (a kind of narcotic made of herbs). He created a body building exercise called *Five Animals Exercise*, which is based on the movements of tiger, deer, bear, ape and crane.

扁鹊：中医界的脉学介导者，生活在春秋战国时期。四诊合参——望、闻、问、切是由他开创的。

孙思邈：药王，生活在唐朝。他著的《备急千金方》是中国最早的临床医学百科全书。

Bian Que：He is the sphygmology mediator of Traditional Chinese Medical Science and lived in Spring and Autumn and Warring States Period. The four diagnostic methods were created by him.

Sun Simiao：He is the king of medicine, lived in Tang Dynasty. He finished the book *Golden Prescriptions for Emergencies*, which was the earliest clinical medicine encyclopedia in China.

张仲景：医圣，生活在东汉时期。他著有著名的医学专著《伤寒杂病论》。

宋慈：法医之祖，生活在南宋时期。他写的《洗冤全集》中提出滴血认亲的方法，是当时的一个伟大构想。

Zhang Zhongjing：He is the herbalist doctor saint, lived in the Eastern Han. He finished the famous medical monograph *Treatise on Febrile and Miscellaneous Diseases*.

Song Ci：He is the earliest ancestor of medical jurisprudence, lived in the Southern Song

Dynasty. He wrote the book *Record of Redressing Mishandled Cases* in which he put forward the method of identify direct relative through blood, which was a great idea at that time.

钱乙：儿科鼻祖，生活在北宋时期，著有第一部儿科专著《小儿药证直诀》。

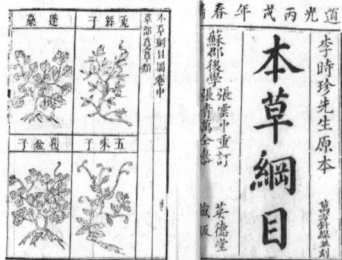

李时珍：《本草纲目》是明代李时珍的不朽杰作，书中包括1 892种药材，11 096个处方和1 162幅插图。

Qian Yi：He is the earliest ancestor of department of pediatrics, lived in Northern Song Dynasty. He is the author of the first monograph of pediatrics *Key to Therapeutic of Children's Disease*.

Li Shizhen：Li Shizhen of the Ming Dynasty, whose monumental masterpiece, *Compendium of Material Medica*, includes 1, 892 medicinal substances, 11, 096 prescriptions, and 1, 162 illustrations.

第二节　中医药理论与治疗

Section 2　Theories and Treatment of Traditional Chinese Medicine

阴阳理论

中医哲学起源于道教的信条。道教很多思想都是基于对自然世界和它运作的方式的观察，所以中医系统广泛采用自然隐喻并不足为怪。中医基于对自然的观察基础上的人体隐喻观点通过"阴阳"理论和五行系统完全明确地表达了出来。

汉语中阴和阳的直接含义是物体的明亮和阴暗两面。中国哲学用阴和阳来表示宇宙中普遍相反的属性：冷与热、慢与快、静与动、男与女、低与高等。总之，任何移动的、上升的、明亮的、进步的、活跃的特性，包括身体的功能性疾病，都属阳。任何静止的、下降的、黑暗的、退化的、不活跃的特性，包括器质性疾病，都属阴。

阴和阳的作用是以对立统一规律为导向的，换句话说，阴和阳是相冲突的，但同时又是互相依赖的。阴和阳的性质是相对的，两者都不能孤立存在。没有"冷"就没有"热"；没有"动"就没有"静"；没有"黑暗"就没有"光亮"。阴阳相互依存的最突出例证是物质与机能之间的相互关系。只有拥有充裕的物质，人体机能才能保持健康；只有机能进程处于良好状态，基本物质才能恰当地得到补充给养。

The Theory of Yin-Yang

The philosophical origins of Chinese medicine have grown out of the tenets of Daoism (also known as Taoism). Daoism bases much of its thinking on observing the natural world and manner in which it operates, so it is no surprise to find that the Chinese medical system draws extensively on natural metaphors. In Chinese medicine, the metaphoric views of the human body based on observations of nature are fully articulated in the theory of "Yin-Yang" and the system of Five Elements.

The direct meanings of yin and yang in Chinese are bright and dark sides of an object. Chinese philosophy uses yin and yang to represent a wider range of opposite properties in the universe: cold and hot, slow and fast, still and moving, masculine and feminine, lower and upper, etc. In general, anything that is moving, ascending, bright, progressing, hyperactive, including functional disease of the body, pertains to yang. The characteristics of stillness, descending, darkness, degeneration, hypo-activity, including organic disease, pertain to yin.

The function of yin and yang is guided by the law of unity of the opposites. In other words, yin and yang are in conflict but at the same time mutually dependent. The nature of yin and yang is relative, with neither being able to exist in isolation. Without "cold" there would be no "hot"; without "moving" there would be no "still"; without "dark", there would be no "light". The most illustrative example of yin-yang interdependence is the interrelationship between substance and function. Only with ample substance can the human body function in a healthy way; only when the functional processes are in good condition, can the essential substances be appropriately refreshed.

所有物体和现象与其对立面都是不断运动和变化的：一方的增加、增长和进步意味着另一方的减少、下降和后退。例如，白天为阳，夜晚为阴，而上午可以理解为阳中阳，下午则是阳中阴，傍晚到午夜是阴中阴，午夜后则为阴中阳。种子（阴）长成植物（阳）最终枯死到地里（阴），这是随季节的变化而发生的。冬季（阴）经过春天进入夏天（阳），反过来经过秋天再次变为冬天。自然现象在不断阴阳交替变迁中得以平衡，阴阳的改变和转化已被当作普遍规律。

传统中医学认为人的生命是一个不断运动和变化的生理过程。正常情况下，阴阳盈亏有一定的界限，反映了一种生理过程的动态均衡。一旦平衡被打破，疾病便会爆发。与疾病相关的阴阳不平衡的典型例子包括阴阳过剩和阴阳不足。

The opposites in all objects and phenomena are in constant motion and change: The gain, growth and advance of the one mean the loss, decline and retreat of the other. For example, day is yang and night is yin, but morning is understood as being yang within yang, afternoon is yin within yang, evening before midnight is yin within yin and the time after midnight is yang within yin. The seed (Yin) grows into the plant (Yang), which itself dies back to the earth (Yin). This takes place within the changes of the seasons. Winter (Yin) transforms through the Spring into Summer (Yang), which in turn transforms through Autumn into Winter again. Because natural phenomena are balanced in the constant flux of alternating yin and yang, the change and transformation of yin-yang has been taken as a universal law.

Traditional Chinese Medicine holds that human life is a physiological process in constant motion and change. Under normal conditions, the waxing and waning of yin and yang are kept within certain bounds, reflecting a dynamic equilibrium of the physiological processes. When the balance is broken, disease occurs. Typical cases of disease-related imbalance include excess of yin, excess of yang, deficiency of yin, and deficiency of yang.

五行理论

与阴阳理论相似，五行理论——木、火、土、金和水，是古代哲学概念，用于解释宇宙的构成和现象。中医学用五行理论来解释人体的生理、病理和自然环境之间的关系。根据这一理论，五行是不断运动和变化的，五行的相互依存和相互制约说明了物质对象之间相互联系以及人体与自然界之间的统一。

中医中的内脏器官以及其他器官和组织，具有与五行相似的属性；它们像五行一样在生理和病理上相互影响。通过相似性比较，五行的类属产生不同的现象。基于这些不同现象的特征、形式和功能，可以说明生理和病理之间的复杂联系以及人体与自然世界之间的统一。

The Theory of Five Elements

Similar to the theory of yin-yang, the theory of five elements—wood, fire, earth, metal and water, was an ancient philosophical concept used to explain the composition and phenomena of the physical universe. In Traditional Chinese Medicine the theory of five elements is used to interpret the relationship between the physiology and pathology of the human body and the natural environment. According to the theory, the five elements are in constant move and change, and the interdependence and mutual restraint of the five elements explain the complex connection between material objects as well as the unity between the human body and the natural world.

In Traditional Chinese Medicine, the visceral organs, as well as other organs and tissues, have similar properties to the five elements; they interact physiologically and pathologically as the five elements do. Through similarity comparison, different phenomena are attributed to the categories of the five elements. Based on the characteristics, forms and functions of different phenomena, the complex links between physiology and pathology as well as the interconnection between the human body and the natural world are explained.

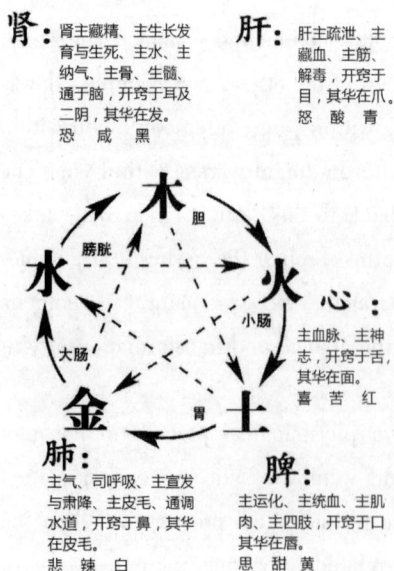

肾：肾主藏精、主生长发育与生死、主水、主纳气、主骨、生髓、通于脑，开窍于耳及二阴，其华在发。恐 咸 黑

肝：肝主疏泄、主藏血、主筋、解毒，开窍于目，其华在爪。怒 酸 青

心：主血脉、主神志，开窍于舌，其华在面。喜 苦 红

肺：主气、司呼吸、主宣发与肃降、主皮毛、通调水道，开窍于鼻，其华在皮毛。悲 辣 白

脾：主运化、主统血、主肌肉、主四肢，开窍于口，其华在唇。思 甜 黄

木 胆
水 膀胱
大肠
金 胃
土
小肠

五行是在观察各群体的动态过程、功能及特征中形成的。五行涉及如下几个方面：

火：气流、热量、燃烧、优势、运动等。

木：萌发、扩展、柔软、和谐、灵活性等。

金：强度、硬度、杀害、切割、清理等。

土：增长、变化、滋养、生产等。

水：水分、寒冷、下降、流动等。

下表根据五行对现象分类：

The five elements emerged from an observation of the various groups of dynamic processes, functions and characteristics observed in the natural world. The aspects involved in each of the five elements are as follows:

Fire: draught, heat, flaring, ascendance, movement, etc.

Wood：germination，extension，softness，harmony，flexibility，etc.

Metal：strength，firmness，killing，cutting，cleaning up，etc.

Earth：growing，changing，nourishing，producing，etc.

Water：moisture，cold，descending，flowing，etc.

五行	木	火	土	金	水
味道	酸	苦	甜	辣	咸
脏	肝	心	脾	肺	肾
腑	胆	肠	胃	肠	泌尿系统
五官	眼	舌	口	鼻	耳
组织	腱	血管	肌肉	头发/皮肤	骨
方向	东	南	中	西	北
变化	发芽	生长	转变	收获	储存
颜色	绿	红	黄	白	黑

Five Elements	Wood	Fire	Earth	Metal	Water
Flavors	sour	bitter	sweet	pungent	salty
Zang	liver	heart	spleen	lung	kidney
Fu	gall bladder	s. intestine	stomach	l. intestine	urinary
Senses	eye	tongue	mouth	nose	ear
Tissues	tendon	vessel	muscle	hair/skin	bone
Directions	east	south	center	west	north
Changes	germinate	grow	transform	reap	store
Colors	green	red	yellow	white	black

五行之间关系紧密，可以归类为在生理条件下相互促进和相互制约以及在病理条件下相互侵占和相互违反两种。通过相互促进和制约，各种系统的功能得以调整，体内得以维持平衡。通过相互侵占和违反，可以解释病理变化，预测并发症。

五行之间相互促进的顺序是木生火、火生土、土生金、金生水、水生木。五行中的每一行都与另一行有相互促进的关系，因而促进是循环的、无休止的。然而，根据相互制约的顺序，即木克土、金克木等，五行中的每一行都与另一行有相互制约的关系。相互促进和相互制约是不可分割的两个方面。要保持正常和谐的关系，没有促进，就没有产生和成长。没有限制，就没有变化和发展。因而一切事物的运动和变化都因其相互促进和制约的关系而存在。这些关系是自然五行循环的基础。

侵占和违反是正常的相互促进和制约关系的病理条件。侵占表示五行中的一行对另一行的制约超出正常水平，而违反则意味着五行中的一行制约了与正常相互制约顺序相反的另一行。

Between the five elements there exists close relationships that can be classified as mutual promoting and mutual restraining under physiological conditions，and mutual encroaching and mutual violating under pathological conditions. By mutually promoting and restraining, functions of the various systems are coordinated and homeostasis maintained. By encroaching and violating, pathological changes can be explained and complications predicted.

The order of mutual promoting among the five elements is that wood promotes fire, fire promotes earth, earth promotes metal, metal promotes water, and water promotes wood. In this way, each of the five elements has this type of mutual promoting relationship with the other, thus promoting is circular and endless. According to the order of mutual restraining, however, wood restrains earth, metal restrains wood, etc. Each of the five elements also shares this restraining relationship with the other. Mutual promoting and mutual restraining are two aspects that cannot be separated. If there is no promoting, then there is no birth and growth. If there is no restraining, then there is no change and development for maintaining normal harmonious relations. Thus the movement and change of all things exists through their mutual promoting and restraining relationships. These relationships are the basis of the circulation of natural elements.

Encroaching and violating are the pathological conditions of the normal mutual promoting and restraining relationships. Encroaching denotes that the restraining of one of the five elements to another surpasses the normal level, while violating means that one of the five elements restrains the other opposite to the normal mutual restraining order.

针灸

针灸和艾灸是基于人体的经络学说的。根据这一理论，气和血通过经络渠道系统在体内循环，使身体内部器官与外部器官或组织相连。通过针刺或艾灸刺激体表的某些穴位运行经络，可以调节气血的流通，治疗疾病。这些受刺激的部位称为针灸穴位。

穴位位于十多个主要经络两侧。有十二对有规则的经脉对称分布在身体两侧，另外两个主要经络分布在腹部和背部的中线。沿着这些经络，可以看到三百多个穴位，每个穴位都有疗治效用。例如，位于第一和第二掌骨之间的合谷穴可以减少头和嘴的疼痛；位于腕部横肌线内侧的神门穴可以安神。

在针灸诊所，医生首先根据已确定的健康问题沿不同经络选择适当穴位，然后把非常细的钢针插入这些穴位。针由不锈钢制成，从半英寸到三英寸长不等。针的选择通常是由穴位的位置和所要的效果决定的。如果穴位位置正确，达到了所需的深度，病人通常会有疼痛、沉闷、麻木和腹胀的感觉。针灸师同时也会感到针拉紧了。

Acupuncture

The practice of acupuncture and moxibustion is based on the theory of meridians. According to this theory, qi (vital energy) and blood circulate in the body through a system of channels called meridians, connecting internal organs with external organs or tissues. By stimulating certain points of the body surface reached by meridians through needling or moxibustion, the flow of qi and blood can be regulated and diseases are thus treated. These stimulation points are called acupuncture points, or acupoints.

Acupoints reside along more than a dozen of major meridians. There are 12 pairs of regular meridians that are systematically distributed over both sides of the body, and two major extra meridians running along the midlines of the abdomen and back. Along these meridians more than three hundred acupoints are identified, each having its own therapeutic action. For example, the point Hegu, located between the first and second metacarpal bones, can reduce pain in the head and mouth. The point Shenmen, located on the medial end of the transverse crease of the wrist, can induce tranquilization.

In acupuncture clinics, the practitioner first selects appropriate acupoints along different meridians based on identified health problems. Then very fine and thin needles are inserted into these acupoints. The needles are made of stainless steel and vary in length from half an inch to 3 inches. The choice of needle is usually determined by the location of the acupoint and the effects being sought. If the point is correctly located and the required depth reached, the patient will usually experience a feeling of soreness, heaviness, numbness and distention. The manipulator will simultaneously feel that the needle is tightened.

通常针留在原地15～30分钟。这段时间可以用针按压以达到补气的效果。根据疾病治疗的规定，针压法一般包括提、推、扭、旋。穴位电刺激法通常称为电针灸，即通过不同的频率和电压实现的操作过程来激活针。

治疗方案、频率和持续时间是医生与病人协商后的专业诊断问题。普通疗程最初包括10～15次治疗，大约以每周为一次间隔，再延长为每月一次的间隔。

专业医生总会提醒病人：治疗过程开始时病情可能会恶化。病人可能会发现治疗后短时间内症状实际上并没有任何改善甚至变得更糟。这是针灸治疗的共同特征。

病人应在治疗之前询问使用的针的类型。现在，大部分从业人员使用预先包装的一次性消毒针。如果使用的是再用性针头，病人应注意观察医生的消毒程序。

The needles are usually left in situ for 15–30 minutes. During this time the needles may be manipulated to achieve the effect of tonifying the qi. Needle manipulations are generally involved with lifting, thrusting, twisting and rotating, according to treatment specifications for the health problem. Needling may also be activated by electrical stimulation, a procedure usually called electro-acupuncture, in which manipulations are attained through varying frequencies and voltages.

Treatment protocols, frequency and duration are a matter of professional judgment of the practitioner, in consultation with the patient. A common course of treatment may initially involve between ten and fifteen treatments spaced at approximately weekly intervals, and spread out to monthly later in a program.

A professional practitioner will always warn the patient of the possibility of exacerbation at the start of a course of treatment. The patients may find that in the short term after treatment, the symptoms may in fact get worse before an improvement sets in. This is a quite common feature of acupuncture treatment.

Patients should inquire about types of needles used prior to treatment. Most practitioners now use pre-packed and sterilized disposable needles. If re-useable needles are being used, patients should ask to see the sterilization procedures that the practitioner adopts.

针灸的疗效取决于精确的中医诊断，医生的针法技巧也会大大地影响疗效。对很多疾病来说针灸治疗是非常有效的。但在西方，病人通常只有治疗慢性病时才会选择使用针灸。因此我们有时看到疗效很慢，而对某些病情则有边际效应。随着针灸地位的逐渐确立，很多病人开始选择针灸疗法，他们已经认识到用针灸法治疗急性和慢性病都很有效。

针灸往往是结合艾灸进行的。艾灸是把干艾叶做的艾条点燃，放在离病人皮肤一英寸的特定穴位上方。艾条可以做成松散的锥体，或者把艾条包扎在一根长棍子上，就像一支大雪茄，长 15～20 厘米，直径 1～2 厘米。这一过程的目的是温经络里的气和血。驱寒驱湿或补气补血时最常用的是艾灸。一次艾灸治疗通常持续 10～15 分钟。此方法提高了针灸的效果，并经常用于治疗慢性风湿和类风湿关节炎。

The effectiveness of an acupuncture treatment is strongly dependent upon an accurate Chinese medical diagnosis. The needling skills and techniques of the practitioner will also influence greatly the effectiveness of the outcome. Acupuncture can be remarkably effective in many conditions, but in the West, patients often use acupuncture as the last option for their long-term chronic problems. Therefore, we sometimes see the treatment as slow and in some cases of marginal benefit. With the gradual establishment of acupuncture as the treatment of choice for many people, the effectiveness of the approach with acute as well as with more chronic conditions is being recognized.

Acupuncture is often conducted in combination with Moxibustion. Moxibustion is the process where moxa sticks, made of dry moxa leaves (Artemisia vulgaris) is ignited and held about an inch above the patients' skin over specific acupuncture points. Moxa is available in a loose form that can be used for making moxa cones. Alternatively, moxa is packed and rolled in a long stick like a large cigar, 15 – 20 cm long and 1 – 2 cm in diameter. The purpose of this process is to warm the qi and blood in the channels. Moxibustion is most commonly used when there is the requirement to expel cold and damp or to tonify the qi and blood. A single treatment of moxibustion usually lasts 10 – 15 minutes. This method enhances the effects of needling and is often used to treat chronic rheumatism and rheumatoid arthritis.

中草药治疗

中草药

中草药和针灸是中医的主要支柱。《中华药典》根据它们的属性和对不和谐的帮助作用列出了 6 000 多种不同的药物。如今，常见的草药有 600 多种。

草药可分成两大类。第一类是指温性药草，即热、温、寒、平和香。第二类是指口味性药草，即酸、苦、甘、辛和咸。

温性和口味的不同组合使药草影响身体的阴阳属性。例如，酸味、苦味和咸味与阴相关，而辛辣、甜归于阳。有温药，有凉药，有补药，也有解除滞涨的药等。要明白中药不是单一品质，而总是属性和温度的组合，可作用于一个甚至多达十二个器官系统。温药可以治疗热失调，但温药必须与凉药相混合以使药的温性综合平衡偏于凉性。同样，凉药可以治疗寒失调患者，前提是该混合药的综合平衡是温性。中性草药不热不寒，所以人们认为是温和的草药。药典中中性草药不多。

Herbal Therapy

Herbal Medicine

Together with acupuncture, herbal medicine is a major pillar of Chinese medicine. The *Chinese Pharmacopoeia* lists over 6,000 different medicinal substances in terms of their properties and the disharmonies that they were helpful with. There are about 600 different herbs in common use today.

Herbs are classified in two major dimensions. The first dimension refers to the temperature characteristics of the herb, namely hot (re), warm (wen), cold (han), neutral (ping), and aromatic (xiang). The second dimension refers to the taste property of the herb, namely sour (suan), bitter (ku), sweet (gan), spicy (xin), and salty (xian).

The various combinations of temperature and taste give the herb its properties that can influence the yin and yang energy patterns of the body. For example, sour, bitter and salty tastes are related to yin, whereas acrid, sweet are attributed to yang. There are herbs that will warm, herbs that will cool, herbs that will tonify, herbs that will move stagnation and so on. It is also important to understand that herbs do not possess one quality. They are most always a combination of properties and temperatures and may reach one to as many as twelve organ systems. Warm herbs can be used with individuals suffering from Heat disorders, but the herb with warm energy must be mixed with herbs with Cool/Cold energy so that the overall balance of the mixture is on the Cool side. Likewise, Cool herbs can be used with people with Cold disorders as long as the overall balance of the mixture is warm. Neutral herbs are those that are neither hot nor cold, so they are often considered gentle herbs. There are not too many neutral herbs in the pharmacopoeia.

至于口味，酸起收缩或整合作用。酸味草药通常用来治疗流虚汗、长期咳嗽、慢性腹泻、精液和尿失禁、早泄或其他与新陈代谢有关的病症。中国传统医学中，这些病症被视为气血不足或寒性症候。

苦具有清热、清除内脏、降气、改善食欲和去除潮湿或水湿的作用。苦药常用于火热疾病，如急性传染性疾病和湿热或湿冷疾病，如关节炎或白带。

甜具有调理、改善、滋润和协调体内重要系统的功能，包括消化、呼吸、免疫和内分泌系统。甜味能纾缓紧迫感，抑制肌肉紧缩所带来的疼痛。甜药通常用于治疗内虚性疾病，如干咳，以及胃肠道功能紊乱，如脾胃不和。

As for the tastes, sour constricts or consolidates. Herbs of sour taste are often indicated for use in perspiration due to deficiency, protracted cough, chronic diarrhea, seminal and urinary incontinence, leakage or spermatic fluid, and other conditions related to hypo-metabolism (under-performance). In Traditional Chinese Medicine, they are seen as deficient or cold patterns.

Bitter possesses the function of clearing heat, purging the bowels, lowering the qi, improving appetite and drying dampness or wetness. Bitter herbs are commonly used in fire-heat patterns, such as the acute stage of infectious disease, and the patterns of damp-heat or damp-cold, such as in arthritis or leucorrhoea.

Sweet has the function of toning, improving, moistening and harmonizing many of the important systems of the body, including the digestive, respiratory, immune and endocrine systems. Sweet tastes also relieve urgency and inhibit pain due to the constrictive action of muscles. They are commonly used for treating deficiency patterns such as dry cough, and dysfunction of the gastro-intestinal tract such as spleen and stomach disharmony.

辣散气通血。这种草药能刺激汗腺出汗、通气、激活经络和器官的功能、活血以促进血液循环。总的来说，辣味药有激活和加强新陈代谢的整体效果。当经络和器官的功能减弱、血液循环受阻时，通常用辣味药来治疗外部病症（如感冒）。在中医术语中，这叫气滞血瘀症。

Spicy disperses, circulates qi and vitalizes blood. This group of herbs can stimulate the sweat glands to perspire, circulate qi, activate the function of meridians and organs and vitalize blood to promote blood circulation. As a whole, spicy herbs have the overall effect of activating and enhancing metabolism. Spicy herbs are commonly used in the treatment of external patterns (catching a cold), when the function of the meridian and organs is weakened and circulation of blood has been impeded. In traditional Chinese medical terminology, this is the stage of qi stagnation and blood cloudiness.

咸草药有软化硬块和纤维瘤的作用。咸味清理并打开肠道。咸味药剂用来治疗疮、炎性肿块、囊肿、结缔组织增生。

Salty herbs have the function of softening firm masses and fibrous adhesions. The salty taste purges and opens the bowels. Salty agents are often indicated in sores, inflammatory masses, cysts, and connective tissue proliferation.

中药方剂

中草药最独特的特点是配方量的大小。在其他草药中，特别是西方草药，常常单独配草药或合配一小份功效相同的其他草药。相比之下，中医很少用单味药治疗疾病。相反，他们发明了配方。一个配方通常包含四味到二十味草药。

草药配方可以预先做成各种形式的药。如做成药丸、片剂、胶囊、粉末、酒精提取物、水提取物等。这些配方药非常方便，因为它们不需要病人自己准备而且易服用。然而，这些产品中的药草浓度很低，医生不可以调整剂量或浓度。这些产品通常不如传统汤剂那么有效。

汤剂是预备中药的传统做法。汤剂是茶的浓缩形式。医生称出一天用的每种药草的重量，将它们混合在一个纸袋里。病人每天取一袋配好的草药服用。病人可以自己在家里熬草药。水沸腾后继续煮30~60分钟，熬出的汤一天分几次喝。

Herbal Formulas

The unique characteristic of Chinese herbal medicine is the degree to which formulation is done. In other forms of herbal medicine, especially western herbal medicine, herbs are often delivered singly or combined into very small formulas of herbs with the same function. In contrast, Chinese herbalists rarely prescribe a single herb to treat a condition. They create formulas instead. A formula usually contains at least four to twenty herbs.

Herbal formulas can be delivered in all manners of preparation. Pre-made formulas are available as pills, tablets, capsules, powders, alcohol-extracts, water-extracts, etc. Most of these formulas are very convenient as they do not necessitate patient preparation and are easily taken. However, the concentration of the herbs in these products is low and don't allow the practitioner to adjust the contents or dosages. These products are usually not as potent as the traditional preparation of decoction.

Decoction is the traditional method of preparing herbal medicine. A decoction is a concentrated form of tea. The practitioner weighs out a day's dosage of each herb and combines them in a paper bag. A patient is given a bag for each day the herbal formula will be taken. The herbs are then boiled in water by the patient at home. The boiling process takes 30 – 60 minutes and the resulting decoction will be consumed several times during the day.

草药的另一种现代做法是做成高度浓缩的粉末状提取物。这些粉末首先是通过把中药做成汤剂，然后脱水留下粉渣做成的。医生把这些粉末混合在一起，为每个病人定制配方，然后把粉末放在开水里重新做汤剂，这样病人就不需要在家里自己准备草药了，而且仍然保留了原有汤剂的功效。

Another modern way of delivering herbs is through granulated herbs, which are highly concentrated powdered extracts. These powders are made by first preparing the herbs as a traditional decoction. The decoction is then dehydrated to leave a powder residue. Practitioners can then mix these powders together for each patient into a custom formula. The powder is then placed in hot water to recreate the decoction. This eliminates the need to prepare the herbs at home, but still retains much of the original decoction's potency.

气功疗法
气的概念
与阴阳理论相似，"气"起源于中国古代哲学观点，该观点认为一切都是相关联的。中医学中的"气"被视为人体的基本物质，它的运行能说明各种生命过程。从生理意义上说，气构成、补充、滋养人的身体。气是生命之源，因为它是源于各种生命过程的基本物质的动力之源。

气往往是根据它的作用对象来分类的。例如，心气指使心脏跳动、血液循环的力量；胃气是指使胃运行，调节胃功能的力量。保持正常功能，防御疾病的气称为真气，即真正的能量或身体的抵抗力。暖身并维持正常体温的气叫阳气，类似于热能。物质和能量的新陈代谢也取决于气的运行，包括血液、体液和其他基本物质的代谢。

Qigong Therapy
The Concept of Qi
Similar to the theory of yin-yang, qi was derived from ancient Chinese philosophy, which

believes that everything is related. In Traditional Chinese Medicine, qi is treated as the fundamental substance of the human body, and its movements explain various life processes. Qi in its physiological sense constitutes, replenishes and nourishes the human body. Qi is often called vital energy because it is believed to be the motive energy derived from the essential substance for various vital processes.

Qi is often classified according to what it acts on. For example, the heart-qi refers to the force with which the heart works and the blood circulates, so it regulates the cardiac function; the stomach-qi refers to the force with which the stomach functions, so it regulates the gastric function. The qi that maintains normal functioning for resistance against disease is called zhen-qi, which means genuine energy or body resistance. The qi that warms the body and maintains normal body temperature is called yang-qi, which is similar to the heat energy. Metabolism of materials and energy also depends on the action of qi, including metabolism of blood, fluids and other essential materials.

气是吸入的氧气、膳食营养物和存储在肾脏中的先天元气形成的，它可能与基因有关。气沿经络和脉络循环。健康的身体需要气正常循环。如果气流停滞，就会有健康问题。气的流通与精神状况也密切相关。情绪不稳可能导致郁气。例如，愤怒可能会导致头晕、头痛、季肋区痛或腹胀以及食欲降低。另一方面，心智锻炼可以帮助气的流通，这就是练习气功的目的。

Qi is formed from the inhaled oxygen, the dietary nutrients, and the inborn primordial qi stored in the kidney, which may be genetically related. Qi circulates along meridians and collaterals. A healthy body requires normal circulations of qi. Health problems occur if the flow of qi is stagnated. The circulation of qi is also closely related to mental conditions. Emotional instability may cause the stagnation of qi. For example, anger may lead to dizziness, headache, distress in the hypochondriac regions, or distention in the stomach with impairment of appetite. On the other hand, the exercise of mind can help the circulation of qi, which is the purpose of qigong exercise.

气功的通用法

气功是调节意念和呼吸的运动以控制或促进气的流动。由于气在人体生命过程中起着重要作用，因此，调节气的流动可以维护健康，治疗疾病。医疗气功，即通过运气来预防和治疗疾病，不同于一般的体育锻炼。体育锻炼旨在保持健康或通过增强体质恢复身体机能，而医疗气功重点是通过意念调节来调动功能性潜能。换句话说，体育锻炼是纯粹的躯体锻炼，而气功是躯体—心理锻炼。体育锻炼和气功锻炼的另一个重要区别是体育锻炼会使肌肉绷紧，加快心脏跳动和呼吸，而气功锻炼则以轻松、缓和和调节呼吸来储存或累积体能。

医疗气功可以分为两个主要类别：内气功，即由病人自己来维护和促进自身健康；外气功，即由气功大师处理病人的健康问题。练内气功需要调节意念、身体和呼吸。内气功种类多，有些有动作，有些没有动作。可以坐着不动，直立，或仰面躺着或侧躺着练习气功，基本要求是保持舒适和放松。

General Methods of Qigong

Qigong is an exercise to regulate the mind and breathing in order to control or promote the flow of qi. Since qi plays such an important role in the vital processes of the human body, the regulation of qi flow is therefore used to preserve health and treat disease. Medical qigong, the qi exercise practiced to prevent and treat disease, is different from general physical exercise. While physical exercise is aimed at building up health or restoring physical functioning by enhancing strength, medical qigong is focused on the mobilization of functional potentialities by regulating the mind. In other words, physical exercise is purely somatic, while qigong exercise is generally psycho-somatic. Another important difference between physical exercise and qigong is that physical exercise expends energy by tensing the muscles and accelerating the heart beat and respirations, while qigong works to ease, smooth and regulate breathing to store up or accumulate energy in the body.

Medical qigong can be divided into two main categories: internal qigong, which is practiced by the patients themselves to preserve and promote their own health, and external qigong, which is performed by a qigong master on a person with health problems. Practicing internal qigong requires regulation of the mind, body and respiration. There are many kinds of internal qigong, some with motion and others without. Qigong can be practiced while sitting still, standing upright, or lying on the back or side. The basic requirement is to stay comfortable and relaxed.

拔火罐

拔火罐这种物理疗法是用玻璃杯或丙烯酸吸入杯吸附于身体的特定部位，用真空杯牢牢地吸附在皮肤上使皮肤充血治疗。通常情况下，医生点燃酒精棉，把它放在杯子里烧一会儿使杯子变为真空，然后把真空杯快速放在选好的穴位皮肤上。它主要用于治疗易引起淤塞的慢性病。

推拿

中式推拿技术旨在放松肌肉组织、刺激特定穴位，并促进气的流动。中式推拿通常令人轻松、爽快。

食疗

它是制备的药用菜肴，是从精选的食材和高级药材中获得必要的营养成分以治疗某种疾病。这种把食物和草药结合用来做药，以治疗疾病的做法称为食疗。食疗有助于定期改善健康状况，防止季节性气候等相关问题的发生，消除早期症状，对主要治疗作补充，抑制生病期间其他药物产生的不良副作用，病愈后帮助恢复活力，修复身体障碍。

Cupping

In this modality, glass or acrylic suction cups are applied to specific areas of the body. It is a congested treatment using a vacuum cup sucked firmly on the skin. Usually, the doctor fires an alcohol sponge and puts it inside the cup for a short while to make the cup a vacuum one, then he places the vacuum cup instantly over the selected spot of the skin. It is mainly used for conditions that are associated with "stagnation" which often manifests as chronic pain.

Massage

Chinese massage uses a number of techniques, which are designed to release tightness in tissues, stimulate specific points or areas, and facilitate the flow of Qi. Chinese massages are usually very relaxing, highly invigorating or both.

Diet Therapy or Food Therapy

It is the preparation of medicinal food dishes, using selected food ingredients and superior herbs, to derive the necessary nutrients to treat specific health conditions. This combination of foods and herbs to make medicinal dishes to treat sickness is food therapy. Food therapy is believed to help improve health on a regular basis, prevent seasonal climate related problems, fight early symptoms of health problems, complement the primary treatment and to combat adverse side effects of harsh drugs during sickness, revive and regain vitality after sickness and repair damages to restore health.

刮痧

治疗时，润滑背部、四肢和身体其他部位的皮肤，然后用一个圆形物（瓷勺、玉等类似的东西）按压和刮皮肤。该方法所产生的"痧"呈小红块瘀斑。刮痧可用于预防和治疗疾病，强身健体。刮痧可以去除血淤病原，促进正常循环和生理代谢。它对减轻疼痛有非常快速的效果，对内部器官的功能不协调所造成的各种疾病疗效显著。

Gua Sha

With this treatment, the skin on the back, limbs, and other parts of the body is lubricated and then pressured and scraped with a rounded object (a ceramic spoon, a piece of jade, or similar object). The method produces "sha" which are small red petechiae. Gua Sha can be used to prevent and treat diseases and strengthen the body. Raising Sha removes blood stagnation considered pathogenic, promoting normal circulation and metabolic processes. It has a very quick effect on pain and an obvious effect on various diseases caused by functional disharmony of the internal organs.

运动健身疗法

太极拳是源于中国的内功武术名。人们打太极拳可以改善身心健康。太极拳打得好可以恢复活力，改善消化系统，振奋精神，还能改善整个体内血压和能量的循环。

Exercise Therapy

Taijiquan (often Romanized as Tai Chi Chuan) is the name of an internal martial art of Chinese origin. People play Tai Chi Chuan to improve one's well being both mentally and physically. Tai Chi when correctly practiced on a regular basis is said to restore vigorous health, improve digestion and raise one's spirits. It has the ability to improve the circulation of blood and energy throughout the whole body.

口述题

1. 讲一讲你与中医药的小故事。

2. 你知道哪些中国医药文化上的名医？

Questions

1. Tell me a story about you and Chinese medicine.

2. Do you know any famous doctors in Chinese Medicine culture? Tell me something about him.

学习网站

1. 中国中医药网（http://www.cntcm.com.cn/index.htm）

2. SACREDLOTUS（https://www.sacredlotus.com/go/foundations-chinese-medicine/get/origins-history-chinese-medicine）

第九章　中国茶、酒文化

Chapter 9　Chinese Tea and Spirits Culture

第一节　茶道的形成

Section 1　The Formation of Tea Culture

茶是中国传统文化的重要组成部分。随着中国社会的发展和进步，茶叶生产在推动经济发展方面起了很大作用，且茶叶消费仍是日常生活中的一种惯例。

茶文化活动可以使人的精神生活和智慧上升到更高的层次。茶与中国文化关系密切，对它的研究涵盖范围广，内容丰富。它不仅体现了精神文明，也体现了意识形态思想。它无疑有益于提高人们的社会成就和艺术欣赏力。

茶的历史

中国茶的历史悠久。一代接一代的种植者和生产者逐渐完善了制茶方法。最初的记录是生活在 5 000 年前传说中的皇帝神农，他要求所有饮用水要煮开以作为卫生预防措施。夏日的一天，他前往领地的一个较远的地方，途中和他的皇室停下来休息。根据他的规定，仆人要煮水给皇室喝。当时，从附近灌木丛飘来的干树叶掉进沸腾的水中，水里渗入了棕色的东西。神农皇帝对新水很感兴趣，喝了点，感觉非常清爽。因此，根据这一传说，公元前 2737 年就有了茶。

Tea is an important part of traditional Chinese culture. As Chinese society developed and progressed, tea production has played a role in driving economic development while tea consumption has remained a practice of daily life.

The practice of tea culture can bring the spirit and wisdom of human beings to a higher orbit. Tea has an extremely close relationship to Chinese culture, and its study covers a wide field and has very rich content. It not only embodies the spirit of civilization, but also the spirit of ideological form. There can be no doubt that it has been beneficial in enhancing people's social accomplishments and appreciation of art.

History of Chinese Tea

The history of Chinese tea is long. Generations of growers and producers have perfected the Chinese way of manufacturing tea. The original idea is credited to the legendary Emperor Shennong, who is said to have lived 5, 000 years ago. His far-sighted edicts required, among other things, that all drinking water be boiled as a hygienic precaution. A story goes that, one summer day, while visiting a distant part of his realm, he and his court stopped to rest. In accordance with his ruling, the servants began to boil water for the court to drink. Dried leaves from a nearby bush fell into the boiling water, and a brown substance was infused into the water. Emperor Shennong was interested in the new liquid, drank some, and found it very refreshing. And so, according to legend, tea was created in 2737 BC.

茶，乃中国首创，是把从茶叶树上采摘的嫩芽烘烤后在煮沸的水中冲泡而成。茶最初是在嘴里咀嚼用于解毒。后来，人们开始在水中泡茶。也许因为茶略有苦味，在秦汉之前它被称为"荼"（即"苦涩的可食用植物"），直到汉朝才被正式命名为"茶"。

Tea, a drink pioneered by the Chinese, is brewed by infusing tender buds picked from tea trees in boiled water after baking. Tea was originally used for detoxification and meant to be chewed in the mouth. Later, people began to steep it in water. Maybe because the drink has a slightly bitter taste, it was called "tu" (meaning "a bitter edible plant") before the Qin and Han dynasties and wasn't officially named "tea" until the Han Dynasty.

早在2 000多年前的汉代，中国人对茶已经非常了解，积累了丰富的经验，包括茶的种类、茶的烘焙技能、茶的冲泡、茶水的选择、茶具及其使用等，形成了一套饮茶礼节和习俗。同时，随着中国与周边和中亚国家贸易联系的发展，中国茶由汉武帝使节通过"丝绸之路"带到世界其他地区。

In the Han Dynasty some 2,000 years ago, the Chinese already knew a lot about tea and gained a wealth of experiences, including tea species, baking skills, infusing, water selection, tea utensils and ways to use them, etc. initially forming a set of tea drinking etiquette and customs. Meanwhile, along with the development of trade links with neighboring and central Asian countries, Chinese tea was among the goods which envoys of Emperor Wu of the Han Dynasty brought to other parts of the world via "the Silk Road".

在唐代，人们积累了丰富的茶文化。约公元758年，一个名叫陆羽的人写了《茶经》，总结了唐代前后关于茶的知识和技术，包括茶的历史、产地、效果、种植、采摘、烘烤和饮用等。

In the Tang Dynasty, rich experiences in the tea culture had been accumulated. Around 758 AD, a man named Lu Yu wrote *Cha Ching* (*Classic of Tea*), in which he summarized the knowledge and techniques about tea before and after the Tang Dynasty, including the history, production places, effects, cultivation, picking, baking and drinking, etc.

在宋代，饮茶更为流行。汴梁京城到处是茶馆，那些携带水壶泡茶的人叫"茶医"。明清两代以来，不仅高官、学者和老百姓喜欢喝茶，喝茶还成了世界各地人们共享的一种高雅爱好。

In the Song Dynasty, tea drinking became more popular. Tea houses were everywhere in the capital city Bianliang and those carrying a kettle for tea making were called "tea doctors". Since the Ming and Qing dynasties, drinking tea has not only been an elegant hobby shared by high-ranking officials, scholars and ordinary people, but also been enjoyed by people across the world.

今天，世界各地的人们对中国茶特别感兴趣。显然，这不只是因为喝茶有解渴提神的功效，还因为其独特的保健功能以及茶文化艺术、礼仪和风俗的博大精深。

Today, people all over the world are showing special interest in Chinese tea. Clearly, this is not just because the drink's thirst-quenching and mind-refreshing effects, but also because its unique healthcare functions and the cultural profoundness in the art, etiquette and customs of tea.

中国茶的八大类别
作为茶的故乡，中国茶有许多种类。下面介绍中国的八种茶。
The Eight Classes of Chinese Tea
As the hometown of tea, there are many kinds of it in China. The following will offer some information about eight kinds of Chinese tea.

绿茶
绿茶是中国茶中最自然的一种。其采摘、自然烘干，然后稍煮的过程称为"杀青"，即除去青草的味道。不需要经过发酵。绿茶在所有茶类中有最好的医疗价值，咖啡因含量最少。香味中等偏高，风味淡至中等。
乌龙茶
乌龙茶在某种意义上来说是介乎绿茶和黑茶之间的。它是半发酵的茶，也叫做"青茶"。典型的乌龙茶叶子中间是绿色的，周边是红色的，这是由于做茶时软化茶叶造成的。乌龙茶在短暂的发酵过程之前让茶叶干枯、散开，然后炒、轧和烤。
黑茶
黑茶冲泡时完全呈琥珀色，做时先烘干、长时间发酵然后烘烤。黑茶叶加工后完全被氧化。黑茶味道粗野，气味芳香，是茶类中咖啡因含量最高的。
红茶
红色的叶子和红茶的颜色，是红茶发酵过程所产生的特性。红茶分三小类——"功夫红茶"、"红碎茶"和"小种红茶"。红茶淡香、中等风味。
白茶
白茶有时被认为是绿茶的一个子类。它只需烘干和烤。因采摘时叶芽呈白色而得名。咖啡因含量非常低。
黄茶
黄茶茶叶呈黄色。茶类中较少见。风味温和清爽。
Chinese Green Tea
Green Tea is the most natural of all Chinese tea classes. The process of its picking, natural drying, and then frying briefly is called "killing the green" to get rid of its grassy smell. Fermentation process is skipped. Green Tea has the most medical value and the least caffeine content of all Chinese tea classes. Aroma is medium to high, flavor is light to medium.

Chinese Oolong Tea

Oolong Tea is half way between green tea and black tea in a sense that it is half-fermented. It's also called "Qing Cha" (grass tea). Typical Oolong Tea leaves are green in the middle and red on the edges as a result of the process to soften tea leaves. Oolong Tea leaves are withered and spread before undergoing a brief fermentation process. Then Oolong Tea is fried, rolled and roasted.

Chinese Black Tea

Chinese Black Tea produces full-bodies amber when brewed. Black Tea undergoes withering (drying), left to ferment for a long while, and then roasted. The leaves become completely oxidized after processing. Black Tea has a robust taste with a mild aroma. It contains the highest amount of caffeine in Chinese Tea classes.

Chinese Red Tea

The red color is the characteristic in the fermentation process of Red Tea. There are 3 subclasses of Chinese Red Tea— "Kung Fu Red Tea", "Red Tea Bits" and "Small Species Red Tea". Chinese Red Tea has low aroma and medium flavor.

Chinese White Tea

White Tea is sometimes considered a subclass of Green Tea. It is only withered and then roasted. It gets its name from the white down on the leaf buds. It has very low caffeine content.

Chinese Yellow Tea

Yellow Tea has yellow leaves and yellow tea color. It's an uncommon class of Chinese tea. The flavor is mild and refreshing.

花茶

花茶是一种独特的茶类，可分成花茶和香茶。花茶是一个简单的概念，即用干花不怎么加工做成的茶。花茶使用绿茶和红茶作主料，混合花的香味。花茶味淡到中等，香味中等至浓。

茶砖

大多数茶砖以黑茶为主料，蒸后压缩成砖、蛋糕、柱和其他形状。茶砖有黑茶的所有特征。它可以存储几十年。久置的茶砖气味平淡，茶砖爱好者愿出高价购买。

Chinese Flower Tea

Chinese Flower Tea is a unique class of Chinese tea. It subdivides into Flower Tea and Scented Tea. Flower Tea is a simple concept that dried flowers are used, without much processing, to make tea. Scented Tea uses green tea, red tea as base and mix with scent of flowers. Chinese Flower Tea has light to medium flavor and medium to strong aroma.

Chinese Compressed Tea

Most Chinese Compressed Tea uses Black Tea as base tea. It's steamed and compressed into bricks, cakes, columns and other shapes. Compressed Tea has all the characteristics of Black Tea. It can be stored for years and decades. Aged Compressed Tea has a tamed flavor, so Compressed Tea fans would pay huge price for it.

茶的饮用方法
泡
把嫩的茶叶放在一个浅的、扁平的铁容器中，加水慢煮，然后一起倒入大茶壶中，泡茶时再倒进小茶杯或扁平的饭碗里。茶要慢慢地呷，吸入茶叶的芳香。
类型
白茶、绿茶和红茶都是从一种叫茶树的植物上采摘的。这些茶分为四种类型，取决于茶的质地、颜色和香味。白茶是初期的嫩叶，是茶树打芽时采摘的。绿茶有天然的颜色和茶树叶的芳香，因为没有经过发酵处理。

颜色和香味
在印度、马来西亚和中国等亚洲国家，红茶最受欢迎。这种茶生长在杭州农村山坡上。黑茶是红茶的分支，由于其丝质感也称为丝绿茶。最受欢迎的黑茶包括普洱和六安。乌龙茶是部分发酵的绿叶茶，经常用来做香茶。香茶是在发酵阶段混合绿茶、花瓣制成，包括玫瑰茶和茉莉花茶。

Chinese Tea Drinking Method
The Brew
The young and tender tea leaves are placed in a shallow, flat iron vessel. Water is added and boiled at a slow pace. The mixture is then drained into a large tea pot and the brew is poured into small tea cups or flat tea bowls. The tea is to be sipped slowly, inhaling the aroma of the tea leaves.

Types
White, green and black tea comes from one plant called Camellia sinensis. These tea leaves are categorized into four types depending on texture, color and aroma. White tea is made out of nascent fresh leaves, which are picked when the plant's buds are opening. Green teas acquire the natural color and aroma of the tea plant as the tea leaves are not fermented.

Color and Scent
Red tea is popular in Asian countries, such as India, Malaysia and China. This kind of tea is grown on the hillsides in the countryside of Hangzhou. An offshoot of red tea is black tea, which is also known as silky green tea owing to its silky texture. Popular black teas include Bo Lei and Luk On. Oolong teas are partially fermented green tea leaves and are often used to make scented teas. Scented teas are made by mixing green tea leaves with flower petals and scents at the fermentation stage. These include rose and jasmine tea.

对健康的好处
茶对消化有好处。它能清除结肠和肠中的毒素，可以防止胃癌的发生。茶还可以较慢速度把尼古丁冲出人体，能抵制人的吸烟欲望，帮助吸烟者在长期治疗过程中戒烟。茶还可以防止关节炎和乳腺癌。

健康饮料
茶是由维生素、矿物质、油和氟化物组成的天然保健饮料，有助于美白肌肤，提高视力。

Health Benefits

Tea has digestive benefits. It cleans the colon and intestines of toxins. This prevents the development of stomach cancer. Tea also helps nicotine to be flushed out of the human body at a slow pace. This stops smoking yearnings and helps smokers try to quit in their long-term therapy. Tea also prevents arthritis and breast cancer.

A Health Drink

Tea is a natural health drink comprised of vitamins, minerals, oils and fluoride. This composition helps skin appear white and bright and improves eyesight.

茶道精神
The Spirit of Teaism

清

清是指清洁、清廉、宁静和孤独。茶艺的艺术精华不仅追求事物外表的清洁，也追求心灵的孤独、宁静、清廉和羞耻意识。只有在宁静的气氛中喝茶，才能理解喝茶的奥妙。

敬

敬是万物之源，也是无敌的方式。人们应该尊重他人、谨慎自己。

Clearness

Clearness means cleanness, incorruptness, quietness and loneliness. The essence of tea art not only seeks the cleanness of the appearance of things, but also pursues the loneliness, tranquility, incorruptness and shame awareness of the mind. Only through drinking clear and pure tea in a still atmosphere can one appreciate the profoundness of drinking tea.

Respect

Respect is the root of everything on earth and the way of having no enemies. People should show respect for others and be cautious of themselves.

怡

怡的意义在于形式和方法，在于精神和情感的快乐。喝茶时感受的先苦后甜可以启发人们调节生活，培养宽广的胸怀和远见，与其他人之间不再有纠纷。精神上的快乐在于人们不再狂妄傲慢，而是变得和蔼有礼貌。

真

真追求真理与真知。至善至美的东西是由真理和真知结合起来的。至善至美是保留本真，去除物欲，不受利益诱惑，了解物质世界以获得知识，并不断改进。换句话说，人们应使用科学的方法寻求一切事物的至诚至善。喝茶的本质在于启发能力和良心，所以，每个人都能过简单的生活，实现自己的抱负，节俭地、合乎道德地处理日常生活中的事务，从而达到至真、至善、至美。

Joy

The meaning of joy lies in form and method and in spirit and affection. Sipping bitterness and swallowing sweetness when drinking tea can enlighten one to the spice of life and cultivate a broad mind and far-sightedness, so that disputes with others disappear. The happiness in spirit lies in that people are not pretentious and haughty, but dwell in mildness and nurture courteous conduct.

Truthfulness

Truthfulness requires truth and genuine knowledge. The supreme good is the whole that is formed by the combination of truth and genuine knowledge. The ambit of supreme good is to retain nature, to remove material desire without being tempted by advantages, to study the physical world to gain knowledge and to continually seek after improvements. In other words, people should use scientific methods to seek the complete sincerity of everything. The essence of drinking tea lies in enlightening capacity and conscience, so that everyone can live a simple life, express their ambitions and handle matters thriftily and virtuously in daily life, thus attaining the ambit of truth, kindness and beauty.

传说中品茶的最高境界

茶活动融入了哲学、伦理与道德精神。人们通过品茶培养道德和心智，尽情享受生活，从而获得精神上的愉悦。

品茶

茶的质量是根据颜色、香味、风味、水质，甚至茶具来判断的。品茶时，品尝者能尽情享受茶的味道。

茶艺

饮茶时，注重环境、气氛、音乐、泡茶艺术和人际关系。

The Highest Ambit of Tea Lore

Philosophy, ethics and morality are blended into tea activity. People cultivate their morality and mind, and savor life through tasting tea, thereby attaining joy of spirit.

Tasting Tea

The quality of the tea is judged by the color, fragrance and flavor of the tea, the water quality and even the tea set. When tasting tea, the taster should be able to savor the tea thoroughly.

Tea Art

While drinking tea, attention is paid to environment, atmosphere, music, infusing techniques and interpersonal relationships.

第二节　酒文化的特征和习俗

Section 2　The Characteristics and Customs of Spirits Culture

酒的历史

酒的历史可以追溯到中国历史的每个时期。中国酒文化有四千多年的历史，传说皇帝禹（约前 2100）的妻子仪狄发明了酿酒的方法。

在中国古代，酒被视为圣液，只有在人们把它当作祭品祭拜天地或祖先时才使用。周代以后，酒被视为九礼之一，每一个王朝都重视对酒的管理，成立了特别部门来管理酒的生产和酒宴。后来，随着发酵法和酿酒厂的发展，酒成为普通饮料。因此，与中国人的日常生活有关的酒的风俗习惯形成了，并不断演化。

在汉、唐、元期间，酒的酿造技术陆续从邻国引入。唐朝时，酒是最受欢迎的，很多著名诗人高度评价过酒。在元代，酒成为皇家祠堂的贡品。

The History of Chinese Liquor

Stories of liquor can be traced back to almost every period in Chinese history. It is believed that Chinese spirits culture has about 4,000 years of history. A legend said that Yi Di, the wife of the first dynasty's King Yu (about 2100 BC) invented the method to make alcohol.

In ancient China, since alcohol was regarded as a sacred liquid only when people made sacrificial offerings to Heaven and the Earth or ancestors was it used. After the Zhou Dynasty, alcohol was deemed as one of the Nine Rites, and every dynasty put great emphasis on alcohol administration to set up special ministries to manage alcohol production and banqueting. Later, along with the development of zymotechnics and brewery, alcohol became an ordinary drink. Thus, many customs concerning alcohol formed and evolved, which had and have various relationships with Chinese daily life.

Liquor and its brewing technology were once introduced from neighboring regions during the Han, Tang and Yuan dynasties. During the Tang Dynasty, liquor was popular and was highly praised by many famous poets. It was served as a designated offering for the Royal Ancestral Temple during the Yuan Dynasty.

开始时，小米是酿造所谓"黄酒"的主要谷物。后来稻米更受欢迎。直到 19 世纪蒸馏酒才变得更受欢迎。发酵以后，酒很香很甜，不烈。传统上，人们不单独喝蒸馏酒，而是和菜一起食用。人们第一次见面或和老朋友团聚时，酒总是就着美味菜肴一起下肚。

喝酒是中国民间风俗的一部分。在现代中国，尽管历经了许多社会变迁，酒在民间风俗中仍然保留其重要作用。它仍会出现在几乎所有的社交活动中，最常见的社交场合有长者生日、婚庆活动和祭祀，酒是这些场合的主要饮料，人们用它来传达祝福或尊重。

In the beginning, millet was the main grain to make alcohol, the so-called "yellow wine." Then rice became more popular. It was not until the 19th century that distilled drinks became more popular. After the fermentation process, Chinese alcohol has a balmy fragrance and is sweet-tasting, with no sharpness. Traditionally, Chinese distilled liquors are consumed together with food rather than drunk on their own. Alcohol always accompanies delicious dishes, either when people first meet or when old friends have a reunion.

Alcohol is part of Chinese folklore. In modern China, alcohol retains its important role in folklore despite many social vicissitudes. It still appears in almost all social activities, and the most common circumstances are birthday parties for seniors, wedding feasts and sacrificial ceremonies in which liquor is the main drink to show happiness or respect.

类别

中国白酒大致可以分为两种类型，即黄酒和白酒。

白酒或"烧酒"是蒸馏酒饮料。白酒的字面意思是"白色的酒"。白酒往往被错误地译为"wine" or "white wine"，但实际上它是蒸馏酒，一般含40%~60%酒精。人们通常在家里的饭桌上或者餐馆聚会、庆祝活动或玩乐和放松时喝酒。

Categories

Chinese liquor can be generally classified into two types, namely yellow liquors (huangjiu) or clear (white) liquors (baijiu).

Baijiu, or "shaojiu" is a Chinese distilled alcoholic beverage. The name baijiu literally means "white liquor", "white alcohol" or "white spirits". Baijiu is often mistakenly translated as "wine" or "white wine", but it is actually a distilled liquor, generally 40% – 60% alcohol by volume. It is usually served on the table of families and restaurants either for get-togethers, celebrations, or simply for fun and relaxation.

历史

当中国人的祖先们开始沿黄河流域群居的时候，种植不同种类的谷物就为制造葡萄酒和白酒奠定了基础。

一些学者认为中国酿酒技术起源于夏朝。历史记载仪狄和杜康是酒的缔造者。

History

At the time that ancestors of the Chinese people started living in communities along the Yellow River valley, the planting of various kinds of grain laid the foundation for making wines and liquors.

Some scholars believe that the technique for making Chinese liquor originated in the Xia Dynasty. Historical records credit Yi Di and Du Kang as the founding fathers of making liquor professionally.

据史料记载，仪狄用发酵的糯米酿出了醇香的酒。

According to historical records, Yi Di made great efforts to make mellow liquor with fermented glutinous rice.

生活在夏朝的杜康用高粱酿出了最好的酒。据记载，"杜康把一些高粱种子存储在空心树桩里过冬。第二年春天，芳香的气味从树桩里飘入杜康的鼻孔。之后，杜康发现是发酵的高粱种子发出诱人的香味"。这个意外的发现启发他用发酵的高粱种子酿酒。

Du Kang, who lived in the Xia Dynasty, is credited with making top-notch liquor with Chinese sorghum beans. As the story goes, "Du Kang stored some cooked Chinese sorghum seeds inside a hollow tree stump on a winter day. In the spring of the following year, a fragrant aroma wafted from the tree stump into the nostrils of Du Kang. Afterwards, Du Kang found that it was the fermented sorghum seeds which gave off the alluring fragrance." This accidental discovery inspired him to make liquor from fermented sorghum seeds.

口味

英文中有很多关于白酒的味道不好的评论，把它比做外用酒精或柴油燃料。作者蒂姆·克利索尔德经常报道中国的一些情况，他指出，"从未见过任何人，即使是在喝高了以后，会承认他们其实很喜欢酒的味道"，"喝酒后，人们都会皱着眉头，露出非情愿的痛苦表情，有些人甚至大声喊叫……"

Taste

There are a number of popular descriptions in English which comment unfavorably on the taste of baijiu, comparing it with rubbing alcohol or diesel fuel. The author Tim Clissold, who writes frequently on China, noted that he'd "never met anybody, even at the heights of alcoholic derangement, prepared to admit that they actually liked the taste," and that "after drinking it, most people screw up their faces in an involuntary expression of pain and some even yell out..."

分类

根据其香味，白酒可以分为六个不同类别。

"酱"香：豪放品质的特香蒸馏酒。西方人认为，酱香白酒很挑战人的感官。它有很浓的香味。酱香白酒加入酒精，就会释放出刺鼻的氨水味道，其气味就像臭豆腐与格拉巴酒混合在一起。一开始觉得很好喝，以为是腌渍食物的完美补充。此类酒根据最知名酒茅台酒而被命名为"茅香"。

Classification

According to its fragrance, Baijiu can be classified into 6 different categories.

"Sauce" fragrance: A highly fragrant distilled liquor of bold character. To the Western palate, sauce fragrance baijiu can be quite challenging to the senses. It has heavy aromas, with the former, in combination with the ethanol in the liquor, imparting a sharp ammonia-like note. Its smell has been described as stinky tofu crossed with grappa. To the initiated, it is quite delicious and is considered the perfect complement for fine preserved and pickled foods. This class is also referred to as "Mao xiang", after the best known liquor of this class, Maotai.

浓香：这类酒很甜、质地黏稠、醇厚。因含高酯而香味温和持久，主要是乙酸乙酯。这类酒大多数都是用曲霉菌作引子，如宜宾五粮液。

淡香：这类酒微香、燥和淡，喝后嘴里留有令人愉悦的醇香和清新的感觉。这种蒸馏酒的味道主要是由乙酸乙酯和乳酸乙酯产生的，如山西汾酒。

Heavy/thick fragrance: A class of distilled liquor that is sweet tasting, unctuous in texture, and mellow, with a gentle lasting fragrance contributed by the high levels of esters, primarily ethyl acetate. Most liquors of this class are made using Aspergillus-type starters. One example of this type of liquor is the Five Grains Liquid of Yibin.

Light fragrance：Delicate, dry, and light, leaving a delectable mellow and clean feeling in the mouth. The flavor of this distilled liquor is contributed primarily by ethyl acetate and ethyl lactate. An example of this kind of liquor is Fen Jiu of Shanxi.

稻香：这类酒是由稻米蒸馏出来的白酒，如桂林三花酒。这种酒有悠久的历史，用糖化菌作引子。喝在嘴里有一种清新的感觉，略带芳香，主要成分有乳酸乙酯和少部分乙酸乙酯。

蜜香：这类酒是有蜜香的蒸馏酒。此类白酒风味微妙，味甜。

分层的香味：这类蒸馏酒含"酱香"、浓香和淡香酒的特点。因此，此类酒的香味、在嘴里的感觉和燥热感差别很大，如产于陕西省凤翔县的西凤酒。

Rice fragrance：The character of this class of liquor is exemplified by baijiu distilled from rice, such as Tri-Flower Liquor of Guilin. This type of liquor has long history and is made using Rhizopus spp. type starters（"Small starter"）. It has a clean feeling in the mouth and is slightly aromatic aroma, dominated by ethyl lactate with lesser flavor contributions by ethyl acetate.

Honey fragrance：A class of distilled liquor with the fragrance of honey. Liquors of this class are subtle in flavor and sweet in taste.

Layered fragrance：A class of distilled liquors that contain the characteristics of "Sauce," Heavy, and Light Fragrance distilled liquors. As such, liquors of this class vary widely in their aroma, feeling in the mouth, and dryness. An example of this type of liquor is Xifeng Jiu, produced in Fengxiang County of Shaanxi.

著名的白酒

汾酒——这种酒可追溯到南北朝时期。它是由高粱制成的白酒。酒精含量：63% ~ 65%。

竹叶青——这种酒是用汾酒与十几种中草药酿造而成。竹叶是其中一种成分，颜色为绿色，该酒因此而得名。酒精含量：46%。

Famous Baijiu

Fen Jiu—the liquor dates back to the Northern and Southern dynasties. It is the original Chinese white liquor made from sorghum. Alcohol content by volume：63% ~65%.

Zhu Ye Qing Jiu—the liquor is Fen Jiu brewed with a dozen or more selected Chinese herbal medicines. One of the ingredients is bamboo leaves, which give the liquor its name and its greenish color. Alcohol content by volume：46%.

茅台酒——这种酒有200多年的历史，因起源于贵州省茅台镇而得名。它是由小麦和高粱通过一个独特的蒸馏过程，七次反复循环酿造而成。这种酒因中国政府当年国宴款待美国总统而闻名于西方世界。酒精含量：54% ~55%。

Mao Tai Jiu—the liquor has a history of over 200 years. It is named after its origin in Mao Tai town in Guizhou province. It is made from wheat and sorghum through a unique distilling process that involves seven iterations of the brewing cycle. The liquor was made famous to the western world when the Chinese government served it in state banquets entertaining US presidents. Alcohol content by volume：54% ~55%.

高粱酒——这种酒除使用高粱以外，酿造过程中还使用大麦、小麦和其他谷类。这种酒起源于明代的大直沽酒。今天，台湾有高粱酒大型生产商。酒精含量：61% ~63%。

玫瑰露酒（玫瑰精华酒）——由各种高粱酒与特种玫瑰和冰糖蒸馏而成。酒精含量：54% ~55%。

五加皮酒——由各种高粱酒与精选的中草药酿造而成。酒精含量：54% ~55%。

大曲酒——起源于四川，有300年的历史。这种酒是用高粱和小麦在地窖里长时间发酵酿成。酒精含量：52%。

玉冰烧酒——是有100多年历史的米酒。它是由蒸米饭做成。蒸馏后可以存储很长时间。酒精含量：30%。

Gao Liang Jiu—Gao Liang is the Chinese name for sorghum. Besides sorghum, the brewing process also uses barley, wheat, and other ingredients. The liquor originated from Da Zhi Gu in the Ming Dynasty. Today, Taiwan is a large producer of Gao Liang Jiu. Alcohol content by volume：61% ~63%.

Mei Gui Lu Jiu (rose essence wine) —a variety of Gao Liang Jiu with distill from a special species of rose and crystal sugar. Alcohol content by volume：54% ~55%.

Wu Jia Pi Jiu—a variety of Gao Liang Jiu with a unique selection of Chinese herbal medicines added to the brew. Alcohol content by volume：54% ~55%.

Da Qu Jiu—originated from Sichuan with 300 years of history. The liquor is made of sorghum and wheat by fermenting in a unique process for a long period in the cellar. Alcohol content by volume：52%.

Yuk Bing Shiu Jiu—a rice liquor with over 100 years history. It is made of steamed rice. It is stored a long period after distillation. Alcohol content by volume：30%.

双井酒和三井酒——是分别经过两次和三次蒸馏的酒。酒精含量分别为32%和38% ~39%。

三花酒——桂林产的米酒，据称有一千年以上的历史。因加了香草药和象山泉水而著名。酒精含量：55% ~57%。

Sheung Jing (double distill) and San Jing (triple distill) Jiu—two varieties of rice liquor by distilling twice and three times respectively. Alcohol content by volume：32% and 38% ~39% respectively.

San Hua (three flowers) Jiu—a rice liquor made in Guilin with allegedly over a thousand years history. It is famous for the fragrant herbal addition and the use of spring water from Mount Elephant in the region. Alcohol content by volume：55% ~57%.

黄酒

不要被它的名称愚弄。黄酒并不是黄色的。它通常用大米、小米或小麦酿造而成，为中医所用。

Huangjiu of Chinese Liquor（Yellow Liquor）

Don't be fooled by its name. Yellow Liquor is not really yellow. It's usually brewed with rice, millet or wheat, and is often used as a kind of Chinese traditional medicine.

与白酒不同，黄酒不是蒸馏酒，酒精含量不到20%，该浓度是乙醇发酵的抑制作用造成的。这些酒传统上要进行巴氏灭菌、囤放、过滤之后再装瓶卖给消费者。各种风格的黄酒颜色各不相同，有透明、米色、黄棕色或红棕色。

Unlike Baijiu, such liquors are not distilled, and contain less than 20% alcohol, due to the inhibition of fermentation by ethanol at that concentration. These liquors are traditionally pasteurized, aged, and filtered before their final bottling for sale to consumers. The various styles of Huangjiu may vary in color from clear to beige, yellowish-brown, or reddish-brown.

酒和社交

在中国，酒与社交有着内部联系。喝酒便有了交朋友的机会。酒也有助于深化和加强友谊，因为它代表友谊。无论误解和仇恨有多深，喝酒常能缓和。

酒的使用

祭祀仪式——用酒拜神祭祖以表示尊重。

战士饯行宴会——中国人通常在战士们离境前为他们的胜利祝酒干杯。

庆祝胜利——胜利后举行的军队传统庆功会。

宴会——酒常出现在国宴、商务宴会和家庭盛宴上。

御寒——数千年来中国人爱喝酒抵御寒冷的天气。

Liquor and Sociality

In China, liquor has internal connection with sociality. Drinking provides more chances for one to make more friends. Moreover, liquor also serves effectively to deepen and strengthen friendship because it shows friendliness. Liquor is always used to relieve misunderstanding and hatred which no matter how strong is.

Liquor and Its Use in China

Sacrificial ceremony—first and still observed use of liquor to show respect to ancestors and gods.

Warrior foy—The Chinese usually toast to their warriors' victory before their departure.

Triumph celebration—military tradition held after victory.

Banquet—liquor appears on the state banquet, business banquet and family feast.

Cold resisting—Chinese people have used it to resist cold for thousands of years.

喝酒游戏（酒令）

喝酒游戏（酒令）是一种非常传统的游戏。开始时，酒是礼仪活动的主要饮料。喝酒游戏，即酒令，只是助酒兴的。当然还有其他助酒的游戏，如箭术、下棋和射箭。为了使饮酒者保持绅士风度和守礼节，甚至特派官员来管理这些助酒法。后来，这些用于娱乐的喝酒游戏逐渐简化成一种计谋来说服、打赌、迫使对方过量饮酒。酒令是中国文化独特的一部分。

Drinking Game（Jiuling）

Drinking game（Jiuling）is a very traditional Chinese game. At the very beginning, liquor was mainly a beverage for ceremonial rites. The drinking games, called "Jiuling" in Chinese, were just aids for drinking. Certainly there were other aids for drinking, such as archery, chess playing and arrow pitching. Aimed to make drinkers stay gentlemen and preserve courtesy of the time, there were even special designated officials to manage these aids for drinking. Later, drinking games which added entertainment to rites gradually degenerated into a kind of artifice to persuade, wager and force overdrinking. Jiuling is a unique part of Chinese culture.

现在酒令有多种形式，根据饮酒者的社会地位、文化程度和兴趣爱好，可以分为三类——一般游戏、竞赛游戏和文字游戏。

Now Jiuling has many forms, depending on the drinker's social status, literacy status and interests, which can be classified into three categories—general games, contest games and literary games.

一般游戏人人都能玩，如讲笑话、猜谜和传递鲜花。女士们在宴会上常玩这种游戏。

竞赛游戏包括箭术、射箭、玩象棋、玩骰子、猜手指和赌动物。其中后两种最常见。猜手指游戏中，两个玩家伸出右手，把几个手指伸出，而其他几个手指弯在手掌中。通常他们每个人都大声从零数到十。如果伸出的手指加起来等于玩家的数字，他就赢了，而输了的人得喝酒。

General games include those games everybody can play, such as joke telling, riddling and Chuanhua（passing flowers one by one）. This category usually appears at banquets for ladies.

Contest games consist of archery, arrow pitching, chess playing, playing dice, finger guessing and animal betting. Among these, the latter two are most common. In finger guessing, two players stretch out their right hands with a few fingers sticking out while the others are closed in their palms. Each of them usually roars a number from zero to ten. If the fingers sticking out add up to a player's number, then he wins and the loser will have to drink.

饮酒习俗

大口喝完整杯酒意味着有魄力。

在中国，喝酒不只是一种乐趣，它与尊重、自我肯定、友谊和保持传统等相关。在中国，新娘和新郎要喝完传统的交杯酒以后婚礼仪式才算完成，夫妇俩交臂喝完自己酒杯的酒而不能溅出来。交杯酒后举杯向新人的父母祝酒。

喝酒习俗深深植根于中国文化之中，这使专门从事酒精滥用研究的博士们担忧，他们于是呼吁改变饮酒习俗。

Drinking Customs

Drinking one's entire glass in a single gulp is a sign of boldness.

Drinking in China is not only about pleasure; it has much to do with respect, self-affirmation, friendship and the perpetuation of tradition. In China, no wedding ceremony is complete unless the bride and groom perform the traditional jiaobeijiu, which requires the couple to drink from their respective glasses while intertwining their arms, without spilling alcohol. The jiaobeijiu is followed by a dutiful toast to each of the newlyweds' parents.

The fact that drinking is so deeply rooted in Chinese culture worries doctors who specialize in alcohol abuse, and some are calling for changes in drinking practices.

饮酒礼仪

中国有句古话，"酒逢知己千杯少"。事实上，一起喝酒是应酬和交友的重要组成部分。因此，与社会行为的任何准则一样，喝酒也必须恪守规则：

Drinking Etiquette

"A thousand cups of wine is not too much when bosom friends meet," according to an old Chinese saying. In fact, drinking together is an essential part of socializing and camaraderie. Thus, like any code of social conduct, drinking adheres to strict rules：

（1）必须一起举杯祝酒，否则被视为不礼貌。坐在同一张桌子旁的所有人必须都站起来，按照客人的提议举杯祝酒。

（2）应先给老人和尊长斟酒。自己的酒杯不要高于他们的酒杯。

（3）如果有人说"干杯"，饮酒者必须喝完酒杯中的酒，然后给客人看自己已经喝完。

（1）One should never refuse to participate in a toast, as that could be interpreted as being impolite. All people sitting at the same table must stand up, upon the initiative of one of the guests, and toast in succession.

（2）Elderly people and superiors should be served first. One should make sure not to raise his/her glass higher than those of the respected elders.

（3）If "ganbei" is called, the drinkers must drink all the contents of their glasses, and then show the other guests their glasses are empty.

口述题

1. 中国八种茶类中你最喜欢的是哪一种？为什么？
2. 你知道饮酒时有什么习俗需要注意的吗？

Questions

1. Which of the eight classes of Chinese tea do you like best? Why?
2. Do you know any customs to pay attention to when drinking?

学习网站

1. CHINA CULTURE TOUR（https：//www. chinaculturetour. com/culture/wine. htm）
2. CHINA CULTURE TOUR（https://www. chinaculturetour. com/culture/tea. htm）

第十章　中国服饰文化

Chapter 10　Chinese Clothing Culture

第一节　中国传统服饰及其流变

Section 1　Traditional Chinese Clothing and the Changes

新石器时代中国人发明了骨针。他们开始用骨针缝树叶和兽皮做冬天的衣服。后来他们开始用亚麻编织大衣。

服装是中国古代阶层的象征。衣服的面料、颜色和装饰表明着衣者的社会地位。

中国历史上出现过许多朝代，每个朝代都有其独特风格的衣服。朝代更改、衰落或被替代后每款衣服的样式会改变或消失。随着每个新王朝的来临和时间的推移，服装发生着革命性的变化。

秦汉时期，服饰风格变化极大。

It was the new Stone Age when the Chinese people invented a needle made of bone. They began to sew winter clothes made of leaves and animal skins. Later on they began to spin and weave coats made with linen.

Clothing was a show of class in ancient China. The fabric, color, and decorations on their clothing told about the wearer's position in society.

There were many dynasties throughout China's history, each having its own unique style of dress. And each style would change or disappear as its dynasty changed, declined, or was replaced. With the advent of each new dynasty and the progression of time, costumes were revolutionized.

During the Qin and Han dynasties, changes in the style of dress were dramatic.

秦始皇受阴阳概念和五行论的影响，认为秦朝将征服周朝，就像水灭火一样。因为周朝认为"火优于金，颜色是红色"，所以秦王朝最喜欢的颜色便是黑色，而黑色与水相关。

西汉实行深衣（长外套）制度。

衣：开敞的一字领服装，男女都穿。

袍：封闭的全身服装，只有男子穿汉服时穿。

襦：开敞的一字领衬衫。

衫：穿在衣上面的开敞一字领衬衫或短上装。

裙或裳：妇女和男子穿的裙子。

裤：长裤或短裤。

人们可以在服饰的皮带或腰带上佩一些流苏和玉石吊坠或各种饰品，称为珮。

The Emperor Qin Shi Huang, who was influenced by the concept of Yin and Yang as well as the theory of the Five Elements, believed that the Qin Dynasty would subdue the Zhou Dynasty like water extinguishes fire. Because the Zhou Dynasty was "fire superior to gold, its colour being red," the favourite colour of the Qin Dynasty was black, since the colour black was associated with water.

The Western Han Dynasty implemented the Shenyi (long coat) system.

Yi：Any open cross-collar garment, and worn by both sexes.

Pao：Any closed full-body garment, worn only by men in Hanfu.

Ru：Open cross-collar shirt.

Shan：Open cross-collar shirt or jacket that is worn over the yi.

Qun or chang：Skirt for women and men.

Ku：Trousers or pants.

People are also able to accessorize with tassels and jade pendants or various ornaments hung from the belt or sash, known as pei.

中国完整的服制是汉朝确立的。汉代染织工艺、刺绣工艺和金属工艺发展较快，推动了服装和服饰的发展。

西汉服制基本上沿用了秦朝的服制。东汉时期人们穿黑色衣服必配紫色丝织装饰物。祭祀神灵或祖先的大典上人们通常穿"长冠服"。皇后的祭祀服是：上身用深紫色长衣，下身用黑色长裤。

西汉时期服饰实行"深衣制"，它的特点是蝉一样的头冠（帽子）、红色的衣服、"田"字状的领子，戴玉饰，穿红鞋。深衣制把上衣下裳缝在一起，做成祭服的中衣，要用黑色边；作为朝服的中衣，需用红色边。服饰总称为"禅衣"。

China's complete code of costume and trappings was established in the Han Dynasty. The yarn-dyeing, embroidering and metal-processing technologies developed rapidly in the period, spurring changes in costume and adornments.

The costume code of the Western Han Dynasty followed the one established in the Qin Dynasty. In the Eastern Han Dynasty, people in black had to wear purple silk adornments to match their clothes. People usually wore costume with a long hat at grand ceremonies offering sacrifices to gods or ancestors. The dress of the queen in these ceremonies consisted of dark-purple frock and black trousers.

The Western Han Dynasty implemented the Shenyi (long coat) system, which featured a cicada-shaped hat, red clothes and "田"—shaped collar. In addition, people of that time wore jade articles and red shoes. The frock and skirt were sewn together in the Shenyi system. Underpants for memorial ceremonies were decorated with black brims, and those for court dress in feudal China were decorated with red brims. All the garments were collectively called as Chanyi （unlined garment）.

汉衣款式以衣襟分类，可以划分为两种：一为"曲裾禅衣"，即开襟是从领曲斜至腋下；一为直裾禅衣，开襟从领向下垂直。曲裾是战国时期流行的深衣，汉代仍然沿用。到东汉时期，男子穿深衣的已经不多了。

Costumes in the Han Dynasty fell into two categories according to Yijin（one or two pieces making up the front of a Chinese jacket or grown）. There were two types of garments：the curving-front unlined garment with buttons was deviously down from the collar to the axilla; the straight-front unlined garment with buttons was straightly down from the collar to the lower part. Curving-front garment originated from the Shenyi（long coat）prevalent in the Warring States Period, and was still in use in the Han Dynasty. But few people wore the Shenyi garments during the Eastern Han Dynasty.

汉代朝服的颜色有具体规定，官员一年四季按五时着服，即春季用青色，夏季前两个月用红色，夏季最后一月用黄色，秋季用白色，冬季用黑色。

There were specific stipulations on colors of court garments in the Han Dynasty. Officers must wear garments according to the five time periods, i. e. cyan garments in the spring, red in the first two months of the summer, yellow in the last month of the summer, white in the autumn and black in the winter.

汉代着衣有七个特点：
（1）穿外衣时，由于领大而且弯曲，穿衣时必须暴露中衣的领型；
（2）穿衣必用白色面料做里；
（3）袖宽为一尺二寸（40 厘米）；
（4）衫无袖；
（5）穿皮毛服装时裘毛朝外；
（6）腰带极为考究，所用带钩以金制成各种兽形；
（7）男子保持佩刀习俗，但所佩之刀有形无刃，只作装饰用。

Costumes of the Han Dynasty had 7 features：
（1）Wearers must expose underpants' collar form, as the collar was big and curving;
（2）Clothes must use white cloth as lining;
（3）The width of sleeve was 0. 4 meter;
（4）The blouse had no sleeve;
（5）Wearers of fur clothes should have the fur facing outside;
（6）Waistband was very exquisite; belt hook was made of gold in various lively and interesting animal figures;
（7）The male kept the habitude of wearing walking sabres without blades for decoration only.

汉代女性劳工总是上穿短襦，下穿长裙，膝上装饰长长垂下的腰带。男性劳工常服是上身穿襦，下身穿犊鼻裤，并在衣外围罩布裙。工奴、农奴、商贾、士人都这样穿。

Female laborers of the Han Dynasty always wore short jackets and long skirts, and their knees were always decorated with long hanging waistbands. Male laborers often wore jackets and calf-nose trousers with aprons around the garments. Farmers, workers, businessmen and scholars were all in the same dressing style at that time.

唐代是文化和经济蓬勃发展的黄金时代。

唐朝服装是中国历史上的一朵奇葩。

唐朝和很多地方之间的交通和贸易非常发达，人们改变了老习俗中的陈旧思想和观念。

前唐时期，中国妇女受旧儒家准则的限制，地位低，衣服穿得保守。然而在唐朝期间，妇女的服装逐渐变得宽松。有些人认为唐装是汉服的另一个转折点。

Tang Dynasty was a period of golden age for the people where culture and economy were thriving.

The costumes of the Tang Dynasty are like exotic flowers in Chinese history.

Communications and trades were flourishing between the Tang and many places and it has changed the thoughts and concepts of the old practices.

Before the Tang, Chinese women were restricted by the old Confucian code where a woman's status was low and her clothing had to be concealed. However, during the Tang, women's clothing gradually became broad and loose. Tang Dynasty was considered by some as another turning point for Hanfu.

唐高宗统治以后，以紫色为三品官的服色，浅绯色为五品官服色，深绿色为六品官服色，浅绿色为七品官服色，深青色为八品官服色，浅青色为九品官服色，黄色为宫外之人及庶民服色。

唐装对邻国有很大影响。比如日本和服从色彩上大大吸取了唐装的精华，朝鲜服也从形式上承继了唐装的长处。唐装襦裙线条柔长，十分优美自如，用料主要是丝织品，因此它的衣物以"软"和"轻柔"著称。

After the reign of Tang Emperor Gaozong, purple was used as the garment color for officials above the third grade; light red, officials above the fifth grade; dark green, officials above the sixth grade; light green, officials above the seventh grade; dark cyan, officials above the eighth grade; light cyan, officials above the ninth grade; and yellow, ordinary people and those who did not live in the palace.

The garments in the Tang Dynasty also greatly affected the garments of neighboring countries. For instance, Japanese kimono adopted the elites of the dresses of the Tang Dynasty in terms of colors, and the Hanbok (traditional Korean clothing) also adopted the advantages of the dresses of the Tang Dynasty. The dresses of the Tang Dynasty were mainly made of silk, so dresses were famous for softness and lightness.

唐朝还流行女子穿"胡服"。高唐以后，胡服的影响逐渐削弱，妇女的服装越来越宽松。普通妇女的服装袖子的宽度为1.3米以上。

It was a fashion for women to wear Hufu. After the High Tang, the influences of Hufu were gradually weakened and women's garments became broad and loose day by day. As to ordinary women's garments, the width of sleeves was always more than 1.3 meters.

宋代服装可以分为三类样式。

其中一类是为皇后、妃嫔和各级官方女性设计的；一类是为普通百姓设计的"正服"；还有一类是日常穿的便服。

Song Dynasty clothing can be divided into three categories of style.

One was designed for the empress, the noble concubines, and females of all levels of "government uses"; another style called "formal clothes" was for ordinary people; and one style was casual for daily use.

妇女的服饰主要包括衬衫、短上装、外套、裙子、长袍、短袍和长大衣。大多数没有皮带和扣子的服装是立领，沿着前页系扣领，领口外沿上缝了保护性衣领。所有衣服袖子边缘和衣领边缘饰有花边或刺绣图案，常饰的图案有牡丹、山茶、梅花和百合等。

总的来说，宋代官员的等级制度沿袭了唐代官员的等级制度，所以两个朝代的宫廷官员服装很相似，都可分为以下几类：朝服（宫廷服饰）、祭服（礼仪服装）、公服（正式长袍）、戎服（军用制服）、丧服（葬礼服饰）和时服（季节性服装）。

Women's costume mainly included blouses, jackets, coats, skirts, robes, short gowns and long coats. Most garments without belt and buckle had an erect collar and were buttoned down the front, and protective collar was sewn on the outer edge at the neckline. Collar edges and sleeve edges of all clothes were decorated with laces or embroidered patterns. Such clothes were decorated with patterns of peony, camellia, plum blossom, and lily, etc.

By and large, the rank system of officials of the Song Dynasty followed that of the Tang Dynasty, so official costumes in the palace during the two dynasties were similar, both falling into the following categories, Chaofu (court costumes), Jifu (ceremonial costumes), Gongfu (formal robes), Rongfu (military uniforms), Sangfu (funeral costumes) and Shifu (seasonal costumes).

袍分成两种类型：宽袖袍和窄袖袍。

襦和袄是老百姓日常生活中必穿的服装。

蓝衫是男子穿的一种长袍，下摆有侧带。

衫继承了古时上层服装（短上装和上衣）和下层服装（裙子），有冕服、朝服和私居服的样式。

直掇是下部没有剪开的宽松长袍（但后面有后踵中央接缝）。

鹤氅（鹤的绒毛制成的斗篷）又长又宽松。

因为旗装方便穿着，花费布料少，它们取代了古代复杂的衬衣和裙子。这是后代容易接受旗装着装风格的主要原因。

Pao (gown) fell into two types: with broad sleeves and with narrow sleeves.

Ru (jacket) and Ao (coat) were the necessary costumes for common people in their daily life.

Lanshan (scholar's blouse) was a kind of men's long robes with a lateral ribbon attached to the lower hem.

Shan (lower garment) followed the ancient code of upper garment (jacket and blouse) and lower garment (skirt), and it was the style of Mianfu (mitral garment), Chaofu (court robe) or Sijufu (private garment).

Zhiduo (straight long robe) was a long loose robe without split at the lower part (but there was central seam on the back part).

Hechang (cloak made of cranes' down) was long and loose.

Since Qizhuang (costumes of bannermen) were convenient for dressing and cost fewer materials, they replaced the complicated ancient blouses and skirts. This was the main reason that later generations easily accepted the dressing style of Qizhuang.

宫廷服饰严格规定为皇后和七级官员的妻子或母亲制特定的衣服。礼服是吉兆和哀悼服装。妇女按其等级穿婚礼、葬礼和生日所规定的服装。便服有各种样式。

对妇女穿的日常服饰和样式也有严格规定。

男士服装主要包括长衫和马褂，袖子末端首次改为马蹄形。

The code of court costume was prescribed as specific dresses for women from the queen to wives or mothers of the seven-rank officials. Ceremonial costume referred to auspicious dresses and mourning apparels. Women's dress for wedding, funeral and birthday were prescribed according to their ranks. Casual costume had various styles.

There was strict stipulation governing women's daily costume and the dressing styles were bound by laws.

Men's costume mainly included long gowns and mandarin jackets, and the sleeve ends employed the horse-hoof shape for the first time.

短上装是男子服饰中最受欢迎的。马褂是满族男子四大服装（即礼服、休闲袍、防雨上衣和马褂）之一，分为几种类型：无衬里单层、衬布和棉布。通常是石青色、暗紫色或黑色。

旗袍是具有中国特色的女裙，在国际高级时装中日益普及。

"旗袍"的意思是"长裙"，来自广东方言，已进入英语词汇。

Jackets were the most popular dress among men's costumes, and mandarin jackets were one of the four costumes of Manchu men, namely ceremonial robes, casual gowns, rain jackets and mandarin jackets which fell into several types: unlined single-layer, interlining and cotton. They were usually azurite, dark purple or black.

The cheongsam is a female dress with distinctive Chinese features and enjoys a growing popularity in the international world of high fashion.

The name "cheongsam," meaning simply "long dress", entered the English vocabulary from the dialect of China's Guangdong Province.

旗袍是从满族古老的服装演变而来的。古时泛指满洲、蒙古、汉军八旗男女穿的长衣袍。

清初衣袍式样有几大特点：无领、箭袖、左衽、四开衩、束腰。箭袖，是窄袖口，上加一块半圆形袖头，形似马蹄，又称"马蹄袖"。马蹄袖平日绾起，出猎作战时则放下，覆盖手背，冬季可御寒。四开衩，即袍下摆前后左右，开衩至膝。左衽和束腰，紧身保暖，腰带一束，行猎时，可将干粮、用具装进前襟。男子的长袍多是蓝、灰、青色，女子的旗装多为白色。

Chinese Cheongsam

The cheongsam, or Qipao in Chinese, is evolved from a kind of ancient clothing of Manchu ethnic minority. In ancient times, it generally referred to long gowns worn by the people of Manchuria, Mongolia and the Eight-Banner.

In the early years of the Qing Dynasty, long gowns featured collarless, narrow cuff in the shape of a horse's hoof, buttons down the left front, four slits and a fitting waist. Wearers usually coiled up their cuff, and put it down when hunting or battling to cover the back of hand. In winter, the cuff could serve to prevent cold. The gown had four slits, with one on the left, right, front and back, which reached the knees. It was fitted to the body and rather warm. Fastened with a waistband, the long gown could hold solid food and utensils when people went out hunting. Men's long gowns were mostly blue, gray or green; and women's, white.

满族旗袍还有一个特点，就是在旗袍外套上坎肩。坎肩有对襟、捻襟、一字襟等。

清世祖入关，迁都北京，旗袍开始在中原流行。清统一中国，也统一全国服饰，男人穿长袍马褂，女人穿旗袍。虽然1911年辛亥革命推翻了清朝的统治，女性服饰却从这场政治变革中幸存下来，并经过后来的改进，就成为中国妇女的传统服饰。

Another feature of Manchu cheongsam was that people generally wore it plus a waistcoat that was either with buttons down the front, a twisted front, or a front in the shape of lute, etc.

When the early Manchu rulers came to China proper, they moved their capital to Beijing and cheongsam began to spread in the Central Plains. The Qing Dynasty unified China, and unified the nationwide costume as well. At that time, men wore a long gown and a mandarin jacket over the gown, while women wore cheongsam. Although the 1911 Revolution toppled the rule of the Qing (Manchu) Dynasty, the female dress survived the political change and, with succeeding improvements, has become the traditional dress for Chinese women.

自20世纪30年代起，旗袍几乎成了中国妇女的标准服装，民间妇女、学生、工人、达官显贵的太太，无不穿着。旗袍甚至成了交际场合和外交活动的礼服。后来，旗袍还传至国外，为他国女子效仿穿着。

至 20 世纪 30 年代，满族男女都穿直筒式的宽襟大袖长袍。女性旗袍下摆至小腿，有绣花卉纹饰。男性旗袍下摆及踝，无纹饰。

From the 1930s, cheongsam almost became the uniform for women. Folk women, students, workers and highest-tone women all dressed themselves in cheongsam, which even became a formal suit for occasions of social intercourses or diplomatic activities. Later, cheongsam even spread to foreign countries and became the favorite of foreign females.

Till the 1930s, Manchu people, no matter male or female, all wore loose-fitting and straight-bottomed broad-sleeved long gowns with a wide front. The lower hem of women's cheongsam reached the calves with embroidered flower patterns on it, while that of men's cheongsam reached the ankles and had no decorative patterns.

20 世纪 40 年代后，受国内外新式服饰新潮的冲击，满族男性旗袍已废弃，女性旗袍由宽袖变窄袖，直筒变紧身贴腰，臀部略大，下摆回收，长及踝，逐渐形成今日各色各样讲究色彩装饰和人体线条美的旗袍样式。

汉族妇女为啥喜爱穿旗袍？主要因为旗袍的造型与妇女的体态相吻合，线条简便，优美大方。而且，旗袍老少宜穿，四季相宜。

旗袍可长可短，可做单旗袍、夹旗袍，也可做衬绒短袍、丝棉旗袍，并且选料不同，可展现出不同风格。选用小花、素格、细条丝绸制作，可显示出温和、稳重的风韵；选用织锦类衣料制作，可当迎宾、赴宴的华贵服饰。

中国旗袍在日本、法国等地展销时，很受当地妇女欢迎。她们不惜重金，争购旗袍，特别是黑丝绒夹金花、簍金花的高档旗袍最为抢手。旗袍以浓郁的民族风格体现了中华民族传统的服饰美。它不仅成为中国女装的代表，同时也被公认为东方传统女装的象征。

After the 1940s, influenced by new fashion home and abroad, Manchu men's cheongsam was phased out, while women's cheongsam became narrow-sleeved and fitted to the waist and had a relatively loose hip part, and its lower hem reached the ankles. Then there emerge various forms of cheongsams we see today that emphasize color decoration and set off the beauty of the female shape.

Why do Han people like to wear the cheongsam? The main reason is that it fits well the Chinese female figure, has simple lines and looks elegant. What's more, it is suitable for wearing in all seasons by old and young.

The cheongsam can either be long or short, unlined or interlined, woolen or made of silk floss. Besides, with different materials, the cheongsam presents different styles. Cheongsams made of silk with patterns of flowerlet, plain lattices or thin lines demonstrate charm of femininity and staidness; those made of brocade are eye-catching and magnificent and suitable for occasions of greeting guests and attending banquets.

When Chinese cheongsams were exhibited for sales in countries like Japan and France, they received warm welcome from local women, who did not hesitate to buy Chinese cheongsams especially those top-notch ones made of black velour interlined with or carved with golden flowers. Cheongsam features strong national flavor and embodies beauty of Chinese traditional costume. It not only represents Chinese female costume but also becomes a symbol of the oriental traditional costume.

第二节 中国服饰与西方服饰的差异

Section 2　Differences Between Chinese and Western Clothing

服装、食品和饮料始终是人们的生活必需品，人们必须着装而且着装日新月异。另一方面，作为社会和文化形态，服装不仅揭示了一个国家的物质文明和精神文明，也反映了人们的精神和情感活动正渗透到我们日常生活中。

事实上，中国和西方服饰文化在自身社会环境中形成了自己的服装体系。现在，由于经济和技术的发展以及全球商贸一体化，中西生活方式变得越来越相似。服装也遵循这一趋势。西方人受到正在崛起的中国的深刻影响。这种影响很容易在结合了西方设计的中国服饰文化中找到答案，也给人们带来一系列的思考：中国和西方服饰文化之间的区别是什么？两种服饰文化之间有什么相同吗？中国服装应参考更多的西方服饰文化还是更多的中国服饰文化呢？

Clothing has always been a necessity as well as food and beverages, because you will see the ever-changing attire instead of a person who never wears clothes. On the other hand, as a social and cultural pattern, clothes not only reveal a nation's material and spiritual civilization, but also reflect the people's mental and emotional activities, being permeating in our daily life.

As a fact, Chinese and Western clothing cultures have formed their own clothing system in their own social environment. By now, life style is becoming more and more similar due to the development of economy and technology, as well as the global integration of commercial trade. Fashion is also following this trend. Western people are deeply impressed by rising China. This influence is easy to be found in Chinese clothing culture combined in Western designs. This brings us a series of thought: What are differences between Chinese and Western clothing cultures? Is there anything same between the two cultures? Should Chinese clothing refer more Western clothing culture or more Chinese clothing culture?

有这样一个说法："人靠衣装，美靠靓妆。"这一点中国和西方是相同的，但具体表现却不尽相同。

首先，中国人和西方人之间的服装概念有明显的差异。中国人由于受儒家思想和道德功能的影响，一直保持东方的保守风格。衣服紧裹着皮肤。从某种程度上说，中国服装文化是一种"裹"文化；人们不应"露出"体形甚至皮肤。这使衣服在形式上的变化相对稳定，而演变更多的是外表装饰、图案、颜色、材料质地和装饰风格。除了一些男士大袖衫服饰以外，这些演变严格遵循中国服饰的形式。

As the saying goes, "people rely on apparel, beauty relies on good make-up". This is the same between China and the West, but for the specific performance—it will be different.

Firstly, there are obvious differences on clothing concepts between Chinese and Western people. Influenced by Confucian thought and Ethical Function, Chinese people have always maintained an eastern style conservative. Skin is closely covered and concealed. To some extent, Chinese clothing culture is a kind of "cover" culture. People should not "reveal" body shape and even skin. This kept clothing relative stable in change on form, but to develop more surface decoration, patterns, colors, material textures and decoration styles. These developments have always kept Chinese clothing in strict form, except for some men's clothing.

在西方文化中，除了人们受基督教的影响那段时期之外，情况完全不同。西方服饰无视人与人的身体的存在，用非常现实甚至夸张的方式来呈现身体的形状。这可以从古代"宽松衣服"文化和自文艺复兴时期以来"紧身衣物"文化中反映出来。服装已用于"突出"甚至"强调"男性和女性之间的不同性别特征，皮肤越来越裸露（特别是女性服装）。

It is different in Western culture, except for a period when people are influenced by the Christianity. Denied the existence of human and human body's performance, Western clothing was used to present body shape in a very realistic and even exaggerated way. This is reflected both in ancient "loose clothing" culture and "close-fitting clothing" culture since the Renaissance. Clothing has been used to "stand out" and even "intensify" different sex characteristics between male and female, and skin is more and more exposed (especially for women's clothing).

其次，中国与西方服饰文化之间在功能意识上有差异。中国人自古以来非常重视服装的社会伦理功能。他们定义服装的功能不仅用于保暖和装饰，更与社会地位相关。从夏、商、西周时期开始，这一观念在礼仪服饰的改进方面从未中断过。每个朝代的每个统治者都高度重视通过穿戴和着装统一人们的思想。

西方服饰文化远远落后于中国服饰文化。只有罗马人极为重视服装的身份功能，引入过封建时代各式各样的服装禁令。大多数西方文化主要侧重服装的富贵身份和审美功能。

再次，自原始社会末期以来，不同环境的人类已创建他们自己的物质文化。很久以前，中国人已经开始使用植物纤维如亚麻、苎麻等和动物纤维如羊毛来编织衣物，也已经开始养蚕织丝绸。丝绸是中国人对人类生活的一大贡献，所以每谈中国服饰文化无不谈丝绸。

与中国丝绸文化不同，亚麻文化盛行于古埃及，羊毛文化盛行于美索不达米亚，棉文化盛行于印度。古希腊和古罗马对衣服布料没有什么开创性，他们从地中海海岸和上古文明进口亚麻和羊毛。至于丝绸，虽然在公元前古罗马已从远东地区通过丝绸之路进口，但是古罗马人永远不懂得这种漂亮织物的奥秘。后来，拜占庭帝国派出两个传教士到中国了解丝绸的秘密。一个世纪以后，拜占庭帝国生产出第一批丝绸，但欧洲人直到13世纪~14世纪意大利文艺复兴时期才生产第一批丝绸。

Secondly, there are differences on function awareness of clothing between Chinese and

Western culture. Chinese people attach great importance on social ethics function of clothing since ancient times. They defined the function not only concerning warm and decorative features, but more concerning social status. From the Xia, Shang to the Zhou Dynasty, this concept has never been given up in the improvement of ceremonial costume. Every ruler in every dynasty has attached great importance to unify people's thought by wearing and clothing.

The West is far behind from China in this culture. The Romans attached great importance to identity function of clothing, and have introduced a variety of apparel ban in feudal times. Most of them focused mainly on wealth and aesthetic functions of clothing.

Thirdly, the human beings in different environments have created their own material culture since the end of Primitive Society. From long time ago, Chinese people have begun to use plant fiber, such as linen, ramie, etc. and animal fibers, such as wool to weave, and they have begun to weave silk sericulture. Silk is a great contribution to human life from Chinese people, so it is impossible to talk Chinese clothing culture without silk.

Different from silk culture in China, flax culture prevails in ancient Egypt, wool culture prevails in the Mesopotamia and cotton culture prevails in India. Ancient Greece and Ancient Rome had no pioneering work in materials, and they imported flax and wool cultures from Mediterranean coasts and Upper Paleozoic civilizations. As for silk, although ancient Rome had touched silk from Far East through Silk Road in BC, they were never able to understand the mysteries of this beautiful fabric. Lately, they had known the secrets of silk from two missionaries sent to China by the Byzantine Empire. Then one century later, the first silk was produced in Byzantine Empire, but Europeans produced first silk until the Italian Renaissance in 13 – 14 century.

最后，中西方服装的颜色也不同。我们都知道"红"被称为中国元素，代表着幸福，所以举行婚礼仪式时，人人都穿红色衣服。黄色是一种特殊颜色，以前仅为皇帝所用。在西方，红色是不吉利的颜色。西方人更喜欢白色，代表纯洁和正直，他们还喜欢黑色，代表高贵和神秘。

虽然中国人和西方人在不同的地理环境中创建了不同的文化、世界观、价值观、审美标准和服饰文化，作为生活在一个地球的人类，面临生存问题时，仍然有一些共同的文化形态。因此，中西服饰文化虽有以上差异，但还是有一些共同点。

目前，中国服饰的发展应学习西方先进的技术和文化，并坚持中国独特的文化。这样，中国服饰将得以改善并作为一种新的东方艺术形式被世界各地人民认可，并因此而走向世界舞台。

Lastly, the color of clothing is also different, we all know that red is known as the Chinese element, which represents happiness, so when holding wedding ceremony, everyone is supposed to wear red clothes. And yellow is considered as a kind of special color, only used by emperors. In the West, red is the unlucky color. They prefer white, on behalf of purity, integrity, or black, representing the noble and mysterious.

Although the Chinese and Westerners have established their own cultures, world view, sense of value, aesthetic standard and clothing cultures in different geographical environments, as the human beings living together in the Earth, there are still some cultural patterns in common when facing survival issues. Therefore, in addition to the differences in clothing culture mentioned above, there is something in common.

At present, the development of Chinese clothing should take on the path of both learning the advanced technology and culture from the West, and maintaining the unique culture of Chinese people. In so doing, China clothing will be improved and recognized as a new Oriental art form by people around the world, and thus it will make its way to the world stage.

口述题

1. 根据本章节内容，请告诉我为什么汉族妇女喜欢穿旗袍。
2. 你最喜欢的中国传统服饰是哪一种？讲出你的理由。

Questions

1. According to the content of this chapter, please tell me why Han women liked to wear cheongsam.
2. What is your favorite traditional Chinese clothing? Give me your reasons.

学习网站

1. 汉服网（https://www.hanfuwang.com/）
2. Travel China Guide（https://www.travelchinaguide.com/intro/clothing/）

第十一章　中国建筑文化

Chapter 11　Chinese Architecture Culture

第一节　中国古代建筑的历史和特点

Section 1　History and Characteristic of Ancient Chinese Architecture

中国古代建筑是中国悠久历史和文化的缩影。它有明显的区域、民族和时代特征。中国古代建筑在单体建筑、综合建筑和建筑艺术方面具有鲜明的特征，是古代东方建筑的杰出范例。

中国古代建筑史

从原始社会到汉代，木结构建筑技术逐步改进和完善。建设者已掌握了土夯技能。他们也知道如何烧火砖和用石头建房。建筑技术在魏晋南北朝时期发展很快，生产砖、瓦的质量以及木材结构技术得到了改进。之后建了许多佛教建筑。

中国古代建筑的特点

中国古代建筑的特点是结构灵活、外观美妙优雅、布局整齐、装饰华丽。

Ancient Chinese architecture is a miniature of the long-standing history and culture of China. It is obviously characterized by the region, nationality and times. Ancient Chinese architecture, which has distinctive features in single building, building complex and architectural art, is an outstanding example of the ancient oriental architectures.

History of Ancient Chinese Architecture

From Primitive Society to the Han Dynasty, the technique on timber structure buildings were gradually improved and perfected. Builders had mastered earth ramming skills. They also knew how to fire tiles and build with stones. Architecture technology developed significantly during the Wei, Jin, Southern and Northern Dynasties. The output and quality of the bricks and tiles were improved, as well as the techniques on timber structure. Many Buddhist architectures were built then.

Features of Ancient Chinese Architecture

Ancient Chinese architecture features flexible structure, wonderful and elegant appearance, regular layout and gorgeous ornaments.

古代中国建造了许多陵墓、寺庙、宝塔、城墙和富丽堂皇的皇家宫殿和住宅，这些都是丰富的遗产。

现代中国建筑

从 1840 年鸦片战争爆发到 1949 年中华人民共和国成立，中国建筑见证了中式和西式建筑的结合。虽然传统中国建筑系统仍然起主导作用，但娱乐行业的建筑，如电影院、餐馆和酒店，以及商业建筑，如百货公司、食品市场等，也取得了传统建筑风格上的突破。

中国建筑的基本特征是连成整体的空间矩形单位。古希腊的寺庙采用过矩形空间，但整体效果往往紧缩。相比之下，中国建筑根据大小和位置的重要性把矩形整合成一个有机的整体，每一层级和结构区分明确。因此，传统中国建筑外观很壮观、动态、耐人寻味。

Ancient Chinese built many mausoleums, temples, pagodas, city walls and magnificent imperial palaces and residences, which are considered rich heritages.

Modern Chinese Architecture

During the period from the broke out of Opium War in 1840 to establishment of People's Republic of China in 1949, Chinese architecture witnessed a blend in Chinese style and Western style. Although the traditional Chinese architectural system still took the dominant role, buildings serving for entertainment industry, such as theaters, restaurants, and hotels, as well as the business buildings, such as department stores, food market and so on, all made breakthrough in the traditional architecture style.

The basic feature of Chinese architecture is rectangular-shaped units of space joined together into a whole. Temples in ancient Greece also employed rectangular spaces, but the overall effect tended to austerity. The Chinese style, by contrast, combines rectangular shapes varying in size and position according to importance into an organic whole, with each level and component clearly distinguished. As a result, traditional Chinese style buildings have an imposing yet dynamic and intriguing exterior.

中国传统建筑中的空间单位组合遵循平衡和对称原则。主要结构是轴，次级结构定位在两侧的翼，形成主卧和院子。住宅、官方建筑、寺庙和宫殿都遵循这些基本原则。室内空间的分布反映了中国的社会和道德价值观。例如，在传统的住宅建筑中，家庭成员是根据家人等级分配卧室的。房子的主人住主卧，主人家的长者住后边大院，年轻家庭成员住在两翼的左右厢房，年纪大点的住左边厢房，其他人住右边厢房。

中国建筑的另一个特点是柱和梁使用木结构框架，用土墙围着建筑的三面。主门和窗户在前面。中国用木材作主要建筑材料已有上千年的历史，对中国人来说木代表生命。

传统的中国矩形建筑根据木梁和支柱结构分成几个房间。为了把悬挂的屋顶置于结构的顶部，中国人发明了特殊的支架，称为斗栱。从每个支柱上一层接一层升起。这些支架支撑着房屋结构，成为独特而好看的建筑装饰。这种建筑风格后来被韩国和日本等国采用。

The combination of units of space in traditional Chinese architecture abides by the principles of balance and symmetry. The main structure is the axis, and the secondary structures are positioned as two wings on either side to form the main rooms and yard. Residences, official buildings, temples, and palaces all follow these same basic principles. The distribution of interior space reflects Chinese social and ethical values. In traditional residential buildings, for example, members of a family are assigned living quarters based on the family hierarchy. The master of the house occupies the main room, the elder members of the master's family live in the compound in back, and the younger members of the family live in the wings to the left and right; those with seniority on the left, and the others on the right.

Another characteristic of Chinese architecture is its use of a wooden structural frame with pillars and beams, and earthen walls surrounding the building on three sides. The main door and windows are in front. Chinese have used wood as a main construction material for thousands of years; wood to the Chinese represents life.

Traditional rectangular Chinese buildings are divided into several rooms, based on the structure of the wooden beams and pillars. In order to top the structure with a deep and over hanging roof, the Chinese invented their own particular type of support brackets, called tou-kung, which rises up level by level from each pillar. These brackets both support the structure and are also a distinctive and attractive ornamentation. This architectural style was later adopted by such countries as Korea and Japan.

木头的使用使建筑有了特别之处。第一是室内空间的深度和宽度是由木结构框架决定的。第二是用亮漆涂在结构上以保护木材的技术得以发展。这些漆的颜色鲜艳、大胆，成为辨别传统中国建筑的关键特征之一。第三是在平台上建筑房屋防止其受潮而损坏的技巧。平台的高度能说明建筑物的重要性。高的平台使大型建筑物显得有气势、高雅和庄严。

在中国传统建筑物上发现的色彩多变的壁画具有象征意义和美学意义，壁画有龙凤画，也有神话描写、风景画、花卉画和鸟画。在我国南方，特别是台湾，一个明显的建筑特点是细纹木雕塑。这些雕塑和壁画使建筑结构看起来典雅，赏心悦目。

Some special architectural features resulted from the use of wood. The first is that the depth and breadth of interior space is determined by the wooden structural frame. The second is the development of the technique of applying color lacquers to the structure to preserve the wood. These lacquers were made in brilliant, bold colors, and became one of the key identifying features of traditional Chinese architecture. The third is the technique of building a structure on a platform, to prevent damage from moisture. The height of the platform corresponds to the importance of the building. A high platform adds strength, sophistication, and stateliness to large buildings.

The highly varied color murals found on a traditional Chinese building have both symbolic and aesthetic significance, and may range from outlines of dragons and phoenixes and depictions of myths to paintings of landscapes, flowers, and birds. One notable architectural development in southern China, particularly in Taiwan, is fine wood sculpture. Such sculptures, together with the murals, give the structure an elegant and pleasing ornamental effect.

植根于一个长期的宗法社会国家，中国建筑在宫殿建造和首都城市建设方面取得了最辉煌的成就。中国建筑突出权力者的主权地位和严格的等级制度，这一点明显不同于欧洲、伊斯兰教国家或古代印度建筑在寺庙、教堂、清真寺和其他宗教的建筑物中所取得的更高成就。宫殿建筑起源于夏朝，隋唐时期达到顶峰，到清代建得更为精致。西周时期形成了完整的首都城市规划建设模式，注重标准规则和对称，突出皇家宫殿模式。春秋战国时期"礼崩乐毁"，这种标准化模式也变得有些不完整，但汉代开始恢复标准规则，隋唐时期完全恢复，元明清时期得以丰富。隋唐时期的长安（现在的西安），元朝时期的大都和明清时期的北京是中国历史上享有皇家宫殿最高声誉的三个都城。

Based on the soil of China's long-term patriarchal society, China's architecture has gained the greatest achievements in palatial and capital city plans, giving prominence to the supremacy of authoritarianism and strict obsession of hierarchy, which are obviously different from the still higher achievements gained by European, Islamic or ancient Indian architecture in temple, church, mosque and other religious structures. The palace had its roots in the Xia Dynasty and reached its pinnacle in the Sui and Tang dynasties and became even more exquisite in the Qing Dynasty. The pattern of the complete capital city plan had been formed in the Western Zhou Dynasty. Importance was paid to standard rule and symmetry, giving prominence to the pattern of the imperial palace. In the Spring and Autumn Warring States Period when "courtesy disintegrated and music destroyed", the standardized pattern was somewhat damaged. But the Han Dynasty began to restore the standard rule and this process was completed in the Sui and Tang dynasties, and was enriched during the Yuan, Ming and Qing dynasties. Chang'an (present Xi'an), capital of the Sui and Tang dynasties, Dadu of Yuan Dynasty and Beijing of the Ming and Qing dynasties are the three capitals enjoying the highest reputation in Chinese history.

中国的族长制和伦理观念也影响了几乎所有的建筑结构类型。例如，供奉神灵、哲人和圣贤的半宗教建筑祭坛和寺庙以及皇陵是逆文化发展的，这些建筑特别重视血缘和宗族关系，强调"视死如生"等观念的重要性。它们成为中国独特的建筑类型，其盛大的规模和肃穆的气氛成为人们关注的焦点。

从印度传来的佛教成为盛行于中国的主要宗教，出现了佛教寺庙和佛塔等建筑。虽然早期受印度建筑的影响，但它们很快成为中式建筑，表现出中国人的审美标准和文化特征，充满宁静、和平和内向的氛围，完全不同于西方宗教建筑的外向、紊动的氛围。道教是中国的土著宗教。道教寺庙和佛教寺庙一样有一种安详宁静的魅力。佛塔在中国建筑艺术史上占有重要位置。

China's patriarchal and ethical concepts also influenced almost all structural types. For instance, the quasi-religious architectural altars and temples for worshipping deity and wise men and sages, as well as imperial mausoleums developed against the cultural backgrounds where in particular emphasis was placed on blood and clan relationship, and importance was attached to such concepts as "taking death as life". They were structural types almost unique to China, their grand scale and their solemn and respectful atmosphere became the focus of attention.

Buddhism from India was the main religion prevailing in China, and Buddhist structures such as temples and pagodas emerged. Although subjected to Indian influence in the early stages, they quickly began the process of becoming Chinese-style structures, giving expression to the esthetic standards and cultural character of the Chinese, filled with the atmosphere of tranquility, peace and introversion, completely different from the extroverted, turbulent atmosphere of Western religious structures. Taoism is the indigenous religion of China, and Taoist temples, like Buddhist ones, have a serene charm. The pagoda occupies an important position in the history of China's architectural art.

基于与自然高度协调的中国文化精神，显示出对大自然炽热的爱和尊重。中国建筑似乎成为大自然的有机组成部分，不同于那些重视人工和自然之间的对照的建筑系统。这一点可以从中国建筑的各种类型反映出来，例如，城市、村庄、城镇、墓葬或住宅的地点选择和布局。中国的花园沙洲自然型建筑园林，不同于欧洲或伊斯兰几何图形的花园建筑，中国园林主要有皇室花园和私人花园。皇室花园主要集中在北京地区，规模庞大，样式别致。私人花园更多地表达了文人、学者的审美心理状态，现有花园最高成就是江南水乡的清新、美丽和精致的风格和巧妙的建筑艺术。中国园林在世界享有盛誉，被欧洲人誉为"世界园林之母"。

The Chinese cultural spirit, basing on its high coordination with nature, shows ardent love and respect for nature. Structures seem to be an organic component of nature and are different from other architectural systems which place more emphasis on the contrast between artificiality and nature. This finds visible reflection in various types of Chinese structures, such as the selection and layout of sites for cities, villages, towns, tombs or residences. They find outstanding expression in garden sand belong to a natural type, different from European or Islamic geometric gardens. Chinese gardens are mainly imperial and private gardens. The former of the largest existing concentration is in the Beijing area, which is huge in scale and has a beautiful style. The latter gives more expressions to the esthetic state of mind of literati and scholars. Existing gardens have the highest accomplishments in regions south of the Yangtze River, a fresh, beautiful and refined style and exquisite and ingenious technique. Chinese gardens enjoy a high reputation in the world and are acclaimed as "mother of world gardens" by Europeans.

各式各样的民间公共建筑如祠堂、圣人庙、神庙、会馆、经学书院、景观塔和亭子等，现存的大多是明清时期的建筑，无一例外都深受传统文化精神的影响。特别值得一提的是住宅，它们不仅类型多变、形式多样，还可以更直接生动地反映平凡的生活。它们所体现的群体文化和心态特别真挚淳朴。它们反映的区域特点更加显著。有时它们的独特在于简约之美而不在于其辉煌的建筑。

A variety of folk public structures, such as ancestral halls, temples of wise men, temples of gods, guild halls, academies of classical learning and landscape towers and pavilions are mostly extant structures from Ming and Qing dynasties and are all, without exception, deeply influenced by the traditional cultural spirit. Residences are especially noteworthy. They not only vary in types and are diverse in forms, but can also face ordinary life more directly and vividly. The group culture and state of mind embodied in them are particularly sincere and simple. The regional features reflected in them are more outstanding. The beauty of their unique simplicity sometimes does not lie in the brilliant structure.

自然山水的模仿

较早时期的古代中国园林是真正的山水形成的围墙花园。自魏、晋、南北朝以来，对自然山水的模仿应运而生。宋朝时期，被称为"寿山艮岳"的皇家园林始建于东部首都汴梁，宋徽宗要求建筑能呈现中国五岳的壮美和四川山径的险峻，他领创人工山水园林建筑达到最高点。到明清时期，模仿自然已成为私家花园建设的重要工艺。

从外表看，自然山水往往高低绵延起伏，总是有主峰和次峰。山坡上常常覆盖着茂密的植被。在花园里造山最不可取的是山峰并排立着或有几个山峰齐排成画笔架子似的。山峰的排列方式取决于场景。场景的空旷宽敞或深邃安静决定着山峰的数量、大小和高度。山是用土、石头建成的，用湖石建的山看起来自然雄伟。山上种植些鲜花和植物，看起来才繁茂，石头应分散在土里，这样看起来才像是从地面冒出来的。石头山应盖满土，岩石之间要种上花卉和植物，这样显得自然活泼。自然山水中有沟渠、山径和石窟，人工山也应遵循这一规则。

Imitation of Natural Mountains and Waters

The ancient Chinese gardens and parks of earlier periods were enclosure gardens formed with real mountains and waters. Ever since the Wei, the Jin and the Southern and Northern Dynasties, the practice of simulating natural mountains and waters came into being. In the Song Dynasty, an imperial garden called Gen Yue was built in the eastern capital Bianliang, and Emperor Huizong demanded that the magnificence of the Five Mounts in China be represented and the precipitous Sichuan mountain paths reproduces, leading the craft of creating artificial mountains and waters to its peak. By the Ming and Qing dynasties, imitating nature had already become an important craft in garden construction among private gardens.

From appearance, natural mountains are often high and low in their rolling hills, and there are always the main peak and the subsidiary peaks. The hillsides are often covered with lush vegetation. As to build mountains in the garden, it is most undesirable for mountain peaks to lie side by side or to have several peaks lined up like a paintbrush stand. The way peaks are organized depends on the requirement of the scenes. Whether the scene is to be open and spacious or deep and quiet determines the number, the size and the arrangement in height of the peaks. Mountains are built using earth, stone or both. Built with lake stones, the mountain looks natural and majestic. Mountains of earth should be covered with flowers and plants for a lush appearance, and stones should be scattered among the earth as if they appear out of the ground. Stone mountains should also be filled with earth in between rocks, and flowers and plants should be planted in there for a natural lively look. Within natural mountains there should be no lack of gullies, mountain paths and stone caves, and artificial mountains should follow this rule as well.

再看看水的管理。私家花园通常建在城市，因此即使在南方水资源丰富的地方，大多数花园池塘都是人工的。自然界中长流不息的河流迂回曲折，湖泊和池塘延伸很远，因此人工池塘不应造成矩形和方形，而要弯曲自然。水面要宽，应建小桥把水面分隔成大小不一的水上景观。池塘的尽头往往形成一个小水湾，与房子的拐角或凉亭相接，塘水似乎在此突然消失，静水的池塘因而有了生气。水上应种些植物，使水有鲜活的感觉，但不能种满整个水面空间，因为它们会遮挡建筑物在水中的倒影。在池塘起伏的两岸可以放置黄色石头或湖石。石头堆放的高度不一。站在石头的最高处，可以看到四周的景色；站在石头的最低点，可以轻松玩水。

Now let us look at the management of water. Private gardens are often built within the city, and for this reason even in the south where water abounds, most garden ponds are dug by men. In nature the ever-flowing rivers twist and turn, the lakes and ponds extend into the distance, and for this reason artificial ponds should never be regular and square in shape, but need to be crooked and natural. Where there is a large water surface, small bridges should be placed to break up the pond into large and small water areas for a gradation of the water scene. The end of the pond often turns into a small bay, stopping at the corner of the house or underneath the water pavilion, where the water seems to disappear. A pond of still water is thus brought to life. Water plants should be planted to create a sense of liveliness to the water but not to fill up the entire water space, because they should not block the shadow of buildings in the water. It is appropriate to place yellow stones or lake stones among twining banks of the pond. Stones are placed at different heights. Standing on the high points one can see the scenery on all four sides, whereas standing on the low points one can easily play with the water.

天然环境中常见山和水共存。当大山里有山洞和长流水时，人们会称之为奇观。私家花园也有斗胆模仿这一奇观的。扬州市个园的夏山建在池塘边，山洞曲折延伸入小山，水从池塘流入山洞，带来凉爽的感觉，给夏山增添了一个新维度。

山水是天然环境园林的灵魂。山给风景增添精神，水给风景注入活力。只有深入了解自然山水，才能准确地浓缩和提取精华，在花园建筑中忠实地呈现。

In a natural environment it is common for mountains and waters to coexist. But when there is a cave in the mountain and endlessly-flowing water in the cave, it is then considered a scene of wonders. And the private gardens venture to imitate the scene. The Summer Hill of the Yangzhou Geyuan Garden is built by the pond, with stone caves winding deep into the hill. Water from the pond twists into the cave, brings a sense of coolness and adds a new dimension to the name Summer Hill.

Mountains and water can be regarded as the soul of the natural environment gardens. Mountain adds spirit and water adds liveliness to the scenery. It is only through a profound understanding of the natural mountains and waters that one can accurately condense and extract their real essence, and represent them faithfully in the construction of gardens.

第二节　中国建筑艺术成就

Section 2　Achievements of Chinese Architecture

亭阁

中国的亭阁常用木头、石头或竹做成各种形状——正方形、三角形、六角形、八角形、五瓣花形、扇形等。所有的亭阁都有柱无墙。在公园或一些风景优美的地方，亭子建在斜坡上以眺望全景，或者建在湖畔以营造迷人的水上倒影。

Pavilion

A common sight in the country, the Chinese pavilion (ting, which also means a kiosk) is built normally either of wood or stone or bamboo with any of several shapes—square, triangle, hexagon, octagon, a five-petal flower, a fan and more. But all pavilions have columns for support without walls. In parks or some scenic places, pavilions are built on slopes to command the panorama or are built by the lakeside to create intriguing images by water.

阁

阁与楼类似，都是两层或多层建筑物。他们之间的区别是阁只在前面有一扇门和窗户而其他三面都是实心墙。此外，阁通常是木楼梯栏杆或全部用木板装饰。

阁的作用：

——古代用于储存重要文章或文献；

——受过教育的人聚在一起写文章，并举行宴会的地方；

——用于观赏风景。

Storeyed Pavilions

The Chinese Ge is similar to the Lou in that both are of two or more storeyed buildings. The difference between them is that the Ge has a door and windows only on the front side with the other three sides being solid walls. Moreover, Ge is usually enclosed by wooden balustrades or decorated with boards all around.

Functions of storeyed pavilions:

—used in ancient times for the storage of important articles and documents;

—a place where educated men used to gather to write articles and hold banquets;

—used for enjoying the sights.

台

台作为中国古代建筑结构，是抬高的平台，顶部平坦，一般用土和石头建成，表面铺上砖。

台的作用：

——作观象台；

——长城沿线的烽火台；

——为纪念诚挚的友谊。

Terraces

As an ancient architectural structure of Chinese, the Tai was a very much elevated terrace with a flat top, generally built of earth and stone and surfaced with brick.

Functions of terraces：

—as an observatory;

—as beacon towers along the Great Wall;

—in honor of the sincere friendship.

楼

楼是指有地平线主屋脊的两层或多层的建筑物。

楼的作用：

——军事用途；

——作私人住宅；

——作望景楼；

——作钟塔和鼓塔。

塔

佛教在东汉或后汉时期传到中国。中国最古老的寺院是洛阳白马寺。塔也可以被视为佛教修道院的象征。"塔"一词源自梵文 bhagavat，意为"圣洁"。

Storeyed Building

A Lou can refer to any building of two or more storeys with a horizontal main ridge.

Functions of multi-storey buildings：

—for military use;

—as private homes;

—as belvederes;

—as bell and drum towers.

Pagoda（Ta）

Buddhism came to China during the Eastern or Later Han period. The oldest monastery (siyuan) on Chinese ground is the White Horse Monastery (Baimasi) in Luoyang. A pagoda can also be seen as a symbol for a monastery. The word "pagoda" derives from the Sanskrit word bhagavat meaning "holy".

宗教建筑

道教庙宇建筑

中国的道教寺庙，一般称为宫或观，是道家在其中做宗教仪式的神圣大厅。

佛教寺庙建筑

中国佛教寺庙建筑包括佛庙、寺院、佛塔、佛殿和石窟。

伊斯兰清真寺

清真寺是伊斯兰教信徒礼拜的场所。

陵墓建筑

所有社会阶层的人都有陵墓。几百年来，墓施工艺逐步融合了绘画、书法和雕塑艺术。它最终有了自己的艺术形式。

Religious Structures

Taoist Temple Constructions

Chinese Taoist temple, generally called *gong* or *guan* in Chinese, is the holy hall where Taoists perform their religious ceremonies.

Buddhist Temple Constructions

Buddhist Temple Constructions in China include Buddhist temples, monasteries, pagodas, Buddhist halls and grottoes.

Islamic Mosques

A mosque is a place of worship for followers of Islam.

Tombs and Mausoleums

People of all social classes had their tombs carefully built. Over the centuries, the craft of tomb construction gradually merged with arts like painting, calligraphy and sculpture. It eventually became its own art form.

院落式民居

院落式民居是几栋建筑物围绕一个中央庭院而建的建筑。

四合院

四合院是一种带院子的住宅。它是遍布整个中国的历史性住宅，以北京的四合院最著名。四合院字面意思是被四个建筑物包围的庭院。你知道为什么这些房子通常都朝南吗？

Courtyard House

A courtyard house is a type of house where several buildings are disposed around a central courtyard.

Siheyuan

A *siheyuan* is a style of Chinese courtyard house. It is a historical type of residence that was commonly found throughout China, most famously in Beijing. The name literally means a courtyard surrounded by four buildings. Do you know why these houses usually face south?

这些房子朝南通常是为了在冬天能获得更多的阳光。

而且，人们认为朝南会带来好风水。

These houses usually face south in order to get more sunlight during winter.

People believe that facing south will bring good *feng shui*.

碉房

碉房主要分布在西藏、新疆和云南。他们通常有三到四层楼高，一座碉房住一家人。外墙是石头做的，方形平面。屋顶是平的。房子依山的轮廓而建。典型的四层碉房，最底层是饲养牲畜的地方；第二层是人们做饭和储存食品和干草的地方；第三层包括一间起居室、卧室和迷你库房；顶层为干燥的甲板和拜神大厅，装饰精美。

随着中国经济的快速发展，很多摩天大楼拔地而起。其中一些大楼绝世无双，成为城市的地标。

Flat-roof House

These houses are found mainly in Tibet, Xinjiang and Yunnan. They are usually three to four storeys tall, each occupied by one single household. The external walls are made of stone and are flat and square. The roofs are flat. The houses blend in with the contours of the mountain. In a typical four-storey house, the lowest storey is for keeping livestock; the second storey is where people cook and store food and hay; the third storey consists of a living room, bedroom and mini storeroom; and the top storey serves as a drying deck and worship hall which is beautifully decorated.

With the rapid development of China's economy, many skyscrapers were built. Some of them are regarded as masterpieces and became landmarks of the city.

中国风景园林

中国园林是中国传统文化和艺术特殊的一面。它不是一片陪衬于大厦的广阔的绿色，而是和谐地把人造景观与自然风光、建筑、绘画、书法和园艺混搭在一起。整个大院用墙围起来，表明院内所有财产为主人私人享有。

Chinese Landscape Gardens

Chinese Gardens are a special aspect of traditional Chinese culture and art. It is not an expanse of green with accompanying buildings, but more of an area harmoniously mixing man-made landscape with natural scenery, architecture, painting, calligraphy and horticulture. The entire compound is enclosed by walls, which mark the property off as a special place for the owner's private enjoyment.

中国园林的历史

古代中国园林，也称为传统中国园林或古典中国园林，有悠久的历史、丰富的文化和独特的特点。类型丰富、充满艺术魅力的古代中国园林被认为是世界三大园林建设系统中最好的。在近 5 000 年的历史中，中国园林有了一定的地位，为世界文化遗产宝库增添了一颗璀璨辉煌的东方明珠。

中国园林的特点

典型的中国园林建筑与自然相结合，由假山、水、植物和建筑组成。

著名的中国园林

古代中国园林可以分为皇家园林和私家花园。中国南方风景园林，特别是长江三角洲周围景观花园被认为是最美丽、最典型的中国园林。苏州园林被教科文组织列为世界文化遗产之一。

History of Chinese Gardens

The ancient Chinese gardens, also known as traditional Chinese gardens or classical Chinese gardens, have centuries-old history, rich culture and unique features. Rich in various types and full of artistic charm, ancient Chinese gardens are considered to be the best among three systems of garden building in the world. In the history of nearly 5,000 years, the gardens found their places and also add a lustrous and brilliant oriental pearl to the world heritage treasure-house.

Features of Chinese Gardens

Following the principle of integrating buildings with nature, a typical Chinese garden consists of rockery, water, plants and buildings.

Famous Chinese Gardens

Ancient Chinese gardens can be categorized into royal gardens and private gardens. Landscape gardens in south China, especially around the Yangtze River Delta are considered to be the most beautiful and typical of Chinese landscape gardens. Gardens in Suzhou were listed as one of the World Cultural Heritages by UNESCO.

口述题

1. 中国古代建筑有什么特点？
2. 你最喜欢的中国建筑是什么？给出你的理由。

Questions

1. What are the characteristics of ancient Chinese architecture?
2. What's your favorite Chinese architecture? Give your reasons.

学习网站

1. 古建筑网（https://www.gujianw.com/）
2. TOP CHINA TRAVEL（https://www.topchinatravel.com/china-guide/chinese-architecture/）

第十二章　中国旅游文化

Chapter 12　Chinese Attractions Culture

第一节　旅游文化的发展历程

Section 1　The Development of Chinese Attractions Culture

中国旅游景观一般可分为三种类型：自然景观、人文景观和历史景观。自然景观突出自然风景，如中国很多世界级地质公园和以玉龙雪山为代表的大山。人文景观和历史景观是主要组成部分。由于中国特殊的文化和传统生活方式，几乎所有的景观可以归类为人文景观和历史景观。与西方不同的是，中国景观不能描述为纯自然或纯人文景观。在中国传统中，自然与人文始终是完美融合，这是绝对独特之处。

中国旅游景观还有一个独特的部分，即无形的景观。这是触摸不到的景观，但可以根据中国传统所强调的固定意象在头脑里想象和描绘。例如，中国生活方式、中国民俗、中国书法、中国传统音乐、中国抽象画和中国篆刻，都具有这一方面的特点。因此，不理解中国传统文化和中国历史，则无法理解这些特殊景观的重要性和伟大之处。这也是很多西方人不能理解为什么中国人或东亚人那么喜欢杭州西湖，不知道怎么理解杭州和苏州的魅力的重要原因之一。

In general, category of Chinese Attractions is comprised of natural attractions, cultural and historic attractions. Natural attractions are basically highlighted with the featured natural beauty and landscape like many Chinese world-class geoparks and mountains represented by Jade Dragon Snow Mountain. Cultural and historical attractions in China are the main part. Nearly all the attractions can be classified into this part thanks to China's special culture and traditional lifestyle. Different from western world, Chinese attractions are hardly depicted to be a pure natural or cultural landscape. In Chinese tradition, nature and humanity are always considered to be a perfect integration. That is absolutely distinctive.

What is more, Chinese attractions also include a unique part: intangible attractions. This is hardly touchable but can be imagined and portrayed in mind on the basis of its fixed image of Chinese traditional highlights. For instance, Chinese lifestyle, Chinese folk custom, Chinese calligraphy, traditional Chinese music, Chinese abstract painting and Chinese seal are all featured of this aspect. Hence without any understanding to traditional Chinese culture and Chinese history, it is impossible to understand the importance and greatness of these special attractions. That is also one of important reasons that plenty of westerners cannot understand why Chinese people or east-Asian like the West Lake or Xi Hu of Hangzhou so much, and majority of westerners cannot know how to see the charm of Hangzhou and Suzhou.

中国景观主要由中国最著名景点（如长城、紫禁城、西安兵马俑、三峡等）、中国世界遗产（包括世界文化和历史遗产、世界自然遗产、世界文化和自然遗产和世界非物质文化遗产），中国江南美景（也被称为中国江南文化景点）以及北京和上海等典型的旅游景点组成。中国不知名的景点，特别是那些西方游客少知的景点，实际上也是游客不错的选择。像扬州瘦西湖、无锡锡惠公园、大同悬空寺、沈阳故宫和池州九华山，都非常独特迷人。这些景点由于推广不足，不为国内和国外游客所知。如果进一步广泛推广，毫无疑问，它们将会受到来自世界各地更多游客的欢迎。

Chinese Attractions is mainly comprised of Chinese Top Attractions (the highlighted tourist attractions of China such as Chinese Great Wall, Beijing Forbidden City, Terracotta Army of Xi'an and Three-Gorges Area Tourist Resources), World Heritage in China (including World Cultural and Historical Heritage Sites, World Natural Heritage Site, World Cultural and Natural Heritage Site and World Intangible Cultural Heritage), China Jiangnan Attractions (also widely called China Jiangnan Cultural Attractions) as well as Shanghai and Beijing as the typical tourist destinations. Chinese Unknown Attractions, specifically less internationally known by western tourists, is not actually low quality. Majority of them like Slender West Lake of Yangzhou, Xihui Classical Garden of Wuxi, Hanging Temple of Datong, Shenyang Imperial Palace and Jiuhua Buddhist Mountain of Chizhou, are unique and fascinating. Due to the insufficiency of wide promotion, they are not extensively known and accepted by tourists at home and abroad. As the further and broader promotion, they, no doubt, will be welcomed by more and more tourists throughout the world.

世界文化遗产和自然遗产是由自然和人类共同创造的经典杰作。有效保护世界文化遗产和自然遗产等同于保护人类和人类文明赖以生存的环境。1972 年 11 月 16 日，世界教科文组织第 17 届会议通过了《关于保护世界文化遗产和自然遗产公约》。此外，文化遗产和自然遗产的定义也确定下来了。

World Cultural Heritage and Natural Heritage are both the classic masterpieces created by nature and humankind. Effectively protecting the world cultural heritage and natural heritage sites equates protecting the existent environment that human and humankind's civilization exist in. On November 16, 1972, in the 17th conference of UNESCO, *Convention Concerning the Protection of the World Cultural and Natural Heritage* was approved; additionally, the definitions of cultural heritage and natural heritage were also fixed.

文化遗产：从历史、艺术和科学方面来看，文化遗产包括有突出和广泛价值的建筑、雕塑和绘画作品、有考古意义的结构和建筑，以及铭文、石窟、住宅区和多样化建筑群。从历史、艺术和科学方面来看，应突出和广泛重视单一或相互关联的有特殊形状、相容性和在风景区中有独特地位的建筑群。从历史、美学、民族学与人类学方面来看，应突出和广泛重视人工景点、人和自然共同创造的景点以及考古遗址区。

自然遗产：从美学和科学方面来看，自然遗产是生态和生物结构以及由生态和生物结构构成的几个建筑群组成的有突出和普遍价值的自然景观。从保护性和科学方面来看，自然遗产突出和广泛重视地质结构和自然地理学以及濒临灭绝的野生动植物生态区。从保护性、科学和自然之美方面来看，自然遗产突出和广泛重视自然名胜古迹以及明确规划的自然区。

Cultural Heritage：Cultural relics seen in the aspect of history, art and science consist of highlighted and extensively valued architecture, sculptures and paintings, segments and construction with the significance of archeology as well as the engraved inscriptions, grottos, residential areas and the complex of diversity of cultural relics. Architectural complex seen from the aspect of history, art and science should be highlighted and widely valued single or interrelated architectural complex with the special shape, consistency and the unique status in sights. Site seen from the aspect of history, aesthetics, ethnology and anthropology is the highlighted and widely-valued artificial project, the masterpieces jointly created by human and nature as well as zone of archeological sites.

Natural Heritage：Seen from aesthetics and science, natural heritage is the ecological and biological configurations as well as the highlighted and widely valued natural visage composed by several complexes of ecological and biological configurations. Seen from protection and science, natural heritage is highlighted and widely valued configurations of geology and physical geography as well as the eco-zone of wildlife on the verge of depopulation. Seen from the aspect of protection, science and natural beauty, natural heritage is highlighted and widely-valued natural places of interest as well as the definitely designed natural zone.

人文景观：精心设计的建筑景观指基于某些审美标准而建的花园和公园，通常与宗教和其他纪念性建筑物或建筑群相连。不断演变的景观指源自宗教、社会、经济和管理的需要的景观，通过调整以适应自然环境发展成现在的模式。与人文相关的景观——这种类型的景观已列入世界文化遗产名单，主要以自然元素、宗教、艺术和文化而不是文化的物证为特点。庐山风景名胜区是以人文景观的名义列入世界遗产的唯一景点。

非物质文化遗产是指无形的或非物质的遗产，它是相对于有形遗产这一可继承的物质遗产而言的。非物质文化遗产是一代又一代传承下来的传统文化多元化的呈现和多样化的展现，它紧贴人们的生活，如民俗、表演艺术、传统技术和精湛的工艺以及器物、实物和手工艺品等。

Cultural Landscape：the intentionally designed architectural landscape—gardens and parks built on the basis of certain aesthetic standard usually connect to religion and other commemorative buildings or building complexes. Organic evolutive landscape—originated from the need of religion, society, economy and administration, it develops to the current modality through adjusting to natural environment. Relevant cultural landscape—this type written into World Heritage List is chiefly characterized with natural elements, religion, art and culture rather than the material evidence of culture. Lushan Mountain Scenic Area is the only site listed into World Heritage in the name of cultural landscape.

Intangible Cultural Heritage also regarded as invisible or immaterial heritage, is relative to the tangible heritage, which is heritable material heritage. Intangible cultural heritage is the diversified presentations and multiple exhibitions of traditional culture passed down from generation to generation and related closely to people's life such as folk custom, performing art, traditional techniques and craftsmanship as well as the associated utensils, real objects and handicrafts and so on.

中国于 1985 年 9 月 12 日加入《关于保护世界文化遗产和自然遗产公约》，并于 1999 年 10 月 29 日被选为世界文化遗产委员会成员。中国于 1986 年开始申请联合国教科文组织世界遗产项目。1987 年到 2011 年，中国共有 41 个遗产景区进入世界文化遗产名单，中国一大批非物质文化遗产也列入世界非物质文化遗产名单。今天，中国拥有世界遗产的数量居世界第三。

中国地大物博，领土规模世界第三。中国也是一个有着辉煌文明和永恒魅力的古老国度。多样的中国景点在许多方面体现了它的魅力。

中国最具魅力的景观在结构上是由自然景观、人文景观、文化和历史呈现、国家遗址以及博物馆和教育服务机构组成的。

China joined *Convention Concerning the Protection of the World Cultural and Natural Heritage* on September 12, 1985 and was selected as member of the World Heritage Committee on October 29, 1999. China began to apply for the items of world heritage in UNESCO in 1986. From 1987 to 2011, there were in total 41 heritage sites of China written into World Heritage List and a large batch of intangible heritage sites of China also written into World Intangible Heritage List. Today, China has the third largest number of World Heritage Sites around the world.

China is a vast country with the third-largest territory around the world and an ancient country with the glorious civilization and sempiternal charm. China's diversity of attractions embodies its fascination in many aspects.

Chinese Top Attraction structurally is made up of natural landscapes, humanistic landscapes, cultural and historical performances, national heritage sites as well as museums and educational services.

人文景观以强调文化和历史为目的。有许多宝贵的文化景点和历史文物的人文景观，如中国北方长城、北京紫禁城、沈阳故宫、杭州故宫、西安故宫、南京故宫、兵马俑、始皇陵、汉高祖陵墓、汉文帝陵墓、汉景帝陵墓、汉武帝陵墓和明清时期帝王陵墓、曲阜的孔庙、泰山、少林寺、三峡区、苏州园林、杭州西湖、徽州古城、黄山、龙虎山、武当山和终南山等。

Humanistic landscape emphasizes the cultural and historical destinations. There are many valuable cultural spots and historical relics like Northern Great Wall in Northern China, Forbidden City in Beijing, Imperial Palace in Shenyang, Imperial Palace in Hangzhou, Imperial Palace in

Xi'an, Imperial Palace in Nanjing, Terracotta Army, Emperor Shihuang's Mausoleum, Emperor Gaozu's Mausoleum, Emperor Wendi's Mausoleum, Emperor Jingdi's Mausoleum, Emperor Wudi's Mausoleum and Imperial Mausoleums of Emperors in Ming and Qing dynasties, Confucius Mansion in Qu Fu, Mount Taishan, Shaolin Temple, Three Gorges Area, Suzhou Classic Gardens, Hangzhou West Lake, Huizhou Ancient Town, Huangshan Mountain, Longhu Mountain, Wudang Mountain and Zhongnan Mountain and so on.

文化和历史呈现的特点是室内和户外文化呈现多样化，如功夫表演、印象西湖、印象刘三姐、印象丽江、宋朝传奇故事和唐朝歌舞。

国家遗址主要强调以国家遗产的名义保护国家级的重要的自然景区和文化景区。它们大部分都是中国旅游和休闲的最佳资源。其中一些已由联合国教科文组织列入世界文化遗产。

Cultural and historical performances are characterized by a variety of cultural shows indoors and outdoors like Kungfu Show, Impression West Lake, Impression Liu Sanjie, Impression Lijiang, The Romance of Song Dynasty and Singing and Dancing Show of Tang Dynasty and so on.

National Heritage Sites mainly stress the introduction of many important natural and cultural destinations under the nation-level protection in the name of National Heritage. Majority of them are the best resources for tourism and leisure in China. Some of them have been listed into World Heritage Sites by UNESCO.

第二节　中国十大名胜

Section 2　Ten Chinese Famous Scenic Spots

1. 故宫——中国的永恒宝藏

鸟瞰北京，最引人注目的是阳光照耀下闪烁着金光的一大片屋顶，紫墙隐现其中，繁茂的树叶左右两侧相拥。这就是故宫。明清时期二十四个皇帝住在故宫统治中国近500年——即1420年到1911年。目前，故宫成了精美的博物馆，有最大和最完整的传统建筑群和90多万件各个朝代的宫廷珍宝。故宫于1987年由联合国教科文组织列为世界文化遗产，现在成了全世界最受欢迎的旅游景点之一。

1. Imperial Palace—Eternal Treasure of China

What strikes one first in a bird's-eye view of Beijing is a vast tract of golden roofs flashing brilliantly in the sun with purple walls occasionally emerging amid them, and a stretch of luxuriant tree leaves flanking on each side. That is the Imperial Palace, in which twenty-four emperors of the Ming and Qing dynasties ruled China for some 500 years—from 1420 to 1911. At present, the Palace is an elaborate museum that presents the largest and most complete ensemble of traditional architecture complex and more than 900,000 pieces of court treasures in all dynasties in China. Listed by UNESCO as a World Cultural Heritage Site in 1987, the Imperial Palace is now one of the most popular tourist attractions world-wide.

故宫坐落于北京市中心，是明清期间的皇家宫殿。形状为矩形，是世界上最大的宫殿建筑群，占地 74 公顷。这座历经五个世纪的皇家宫殿藏有无数稀世珍宝。宫殿的建造始于 1407 年，也就是明代第三个皇帝永乐统治的第五年，十四年后于 1420 年完成的。据说 100 万工人包括 10 万工匠付出了长期的辛勤劳动才建成故宫。他们要从北京郊区房山开采石头，沿路每 50 米挖一口井以便冬天能把水泼在路上结成冰，把巨石滑入北京城。

Lying at the center of Beijing, the Palace was the imperial palace during the Ming and Qing dynasties. Rectangular in shape, it is the world's largest palace complex and covers 74 hectares. Having been the imperial palace for some five centuries, it houses numerous rare treasures and curiosities. Construction of the palace began in 1407, the 5th year of the Yongle reign of the third emperor of the Ming Dynasty. It was completed fourteen years later in 1420. It was said that a million workers including one hundred thousand artisans were driven into the long-term hard labor. Stone needed was quarried from Fangshan, a suburb of Beijing and it was said a well was dug every fifty meters along the road in order to pour water onto the road in winter to slide huge stones on ice into the city.

收藏品

故宫博物院的收藏品是基于清代皇家收藏之上的，有陶瓷、书画、青铜器、钟表、玉、宫殿用具、古籍和历史文献。经过十多年的艰苦努力，找回了大约 710 000 件来自清宫的物品。同时，通过国家拨款、请购和私人捐款，增加了 220 000 多件有文化重要性的物品，如石器时代的彩色陶瓷、商周时期的青铜器和玉器，汉代的陶俑，南北朝时期的石雕及唐三彩等，弥补了原有清收藏品的遗漏。收集的古代绘画、卷轴和书法作品，特别壮观，所有作品无一例外。

Collections

The collections of the Palace Museum are based on the Qing imperial collection—ceramics, paintings and calligraphy, bronze ware, timepieces, jade, palace paraphernalia, ancient books and historical documents. After more than a decade of painstaking efforts, some 710,000 objects from the Qing palace were retrieved. At the same time, through national allocations, requisitions and private donations, more than 220,000 additional pieces of cultural significance were added, making up for such omissions from the original Qing collections as colored earthenware from the Stone Age, bronzes and jades from the Shang and Zhou dynasties, pottery tomb figurines from the Han Dynasty, stone sculpture from the Northern and Southern Dynasties, and tri-color pottery from the Tang Dynasty. The ancient paintings, scrolls and calligraphy added to the collections were particularly spectacular—all masterpieces without exception.

2. 漓江——天然画廊

几千年来，漓江吸引了无数游客，受到无数作家和诗人的称赞。这些作家和诗人留下了许多记录漓江的文学作品，喟叹漓江之美。作为最大、最美的岩溶地形景区，漓江很早就有了声望。漓江是嵌入中国古丝绸之路的一颗璀璨明珠，也是桂林风光的精髓。

蓝天映衬下的每一条清澈河流的尽头，美丽的溶岩山峰总让人惊喜不已。水牛在田野里吃草，农民在田野里收割，上学的孩子和渔夫坐着竹筏在江上飘过。以其惊人的美景和远离水泥丛林的大都市的生活气息，漓江风光成为中国顶级的旅游胜地之一。从桂林到阳朔83公里长的航道就像一位艺术家的杰作。起伏的群山，陡峭的悬崖，神奇的洞穴，悠闲的小船和竹筏，构筑起美丽的景观。有诗云："江作青罗带，山如碧玉簪。"

2. Li River—Natural Gallery

For thousands of years, Li River has attracted countless people and has been praised by large amounts of writers and poets. They left numerous literary works to record and marveled at the beauty of Li River. Being the largest and most beautiful scenery spot of Karst terrain, Li River was prestigious in very early periods. It is a pearl embedded on the vast silk ribbon of China, and it is also the spirit of Guilin.

Gorgeous Karst peaks give you surprises at each end of the limpid river under the blue sky. Water buffalo patrol the fields, peasants reap rice paddies, school kids and fisherman float by on bamboo rafts. With its breathtaking scenery and taste of a life far removed from the concrete metropolis, the scenery along the Li River becomes one of China's top tourist destinations. The 83-km-long waterway from Guilin to Yangshuo is like an artist's masterpiece. The landscape is decorated with rolling hills, steep cliffs, fantastic caves, leisurely boats and bamboo rafts. A poem says, "The river is a green silk ribbon, and the hills are jade hair-pins".

漓江位于广西壮族自治区，起源于兴安县猫儿山，流经桂林、阳朔、平乐，下入梧州珠江西部支流西江，沿路437公里两侧是绿色的群山。漓江往往会让人联想起鸬鹚捕鱼。

漓江所在的城市有2 000多年的悠久历史。古代属于楚国。之后，秦始皇在湖南湘江和漓江之间挖了一条人工河，使桂林成为一个重要城市。宋朝以后，桂林成为广西政治、经济和文化中心。在漫长的历史发展中，漓江吸引了众多著名作家和学者。目前，游客可以看到风景区的许多雕刻艺术。1985年，漓江成为中国的主要旅游景点。

Situated in Guangxi, China, Li River originates in the Mao'er Mountains in Xing'an County and flows through Guilin, Yangshuo and Pingle, down into the Xi Jiang, the western tributary of the Pearl River in Wuzhou, and its course of 437 kilometers is flanked by green hills. Cormorant fishing is often associated with the Li River.

The city where Li River situated is a place with a long history of more than 2,000 years. In ancient times, it belonged to the Chu Country. Afterwards, Qin Shi Huang dug an artificial river between Xiang River of Hunan and Li River, and making Guilin became an important city. Since Song Dynasty, Guilin is the political, economical and cultural center of Guangxi. In the long history of development, Li River has attracted numerous famous writers and scholars. At present, travelers can see many carvings in the scenery areas. In 1985, Li River was enrolled as the key tourist attractions of China.

象鼻山

象鼻山雄伟地屹立在漓江西岸，就像大象用长鼻子在河里吸水。它已成为桂林风景的地标，出现在旅游手册或书籍上。令人印象最深刻的据说是当月光洒在这条河上的时候，水上出现月亮一样的洞的倒影，因此有"水上月亮"的美称。

塔山

从象鼻山西岸走几分钟就可以看到一座小山，山顶矗立着一座宝塔。这座六角形宝塔叫寿佛塔，是明朝建的。据说二楼陈列着很多石佛像。小山依偎着船山公园。秋天，小山上红色的枫树使小山看起来很美。

Elephant Trunk Hill

Situated majestically on the western bank of Li River, the hill resembles an elephant sucking water from the river with its long trunk. It is supposed to be the landmark of Guilin landscape, which you can find on travel brochures or books. The most impressive is said to be the water reflection of a moon-like cave when the moonlight sprinkles over the river, hence the name "Moon over the Water".

Pagoda Hill

A few minutes down from the Elephant Trunk Hill on the west bank is a small hill topped with a pagoda. The hexagonal pagoda is called Longevity Buddha Pagoda (Shoufo Ta) dating from the Ming Dynasty. It is said the second floor has stone Buddha figurines on display and the hill is compassed in Chuanshan Park. In autumn, the hill illuminated with red maples is very charming.

大圩镇

大圩镇位于漓江北岸，古老的小镇从明代以来一直保持着它的古朴美。石板街两边排列着旧住宅、商店和小摊，沿河两公里穿越镇中心。当人们偶尔光顾那些商店的时候，临街大门背后藏着的那些完好的住宅让人惊喜。那些住宅曾是商人的住处。尝一尝沿街摊位或兜售汽车上卖的各种小吃，其味道和低廉的价格让人惊喜。镇上的人们对游客非常友好。再往南有座名为寿桥的单拱桥。

Daxu Town

Perching on the northern bank of Li River, the ancient town keeps in its antique style from the Ming Dynasty. A flagging street, lined with old residences, shops and stalls, runs two kilometers along the river bank through the town. Some well-preserved residences hidden behind the street door may surprise you when you occasionally explore further into a shop. These are quarters for businessmen in the past times. Have a try on various dumping snacks on the stalls or peddle cars along the street. Some will surprise you with both its taste and cheap price. People in the town are very kind to tourists. Further to south, there is a single-arched bridge in the town named Longevity Bridge.

3. 泰山——神圣，令人敬畏

自古以来，有无数作家和学者高度赞扬过泰山。杜甫有"会当凌绝顶，一览众山小"的诗句。雄伟气派的大山吸引了来自世界各地各行各业的人们。因为泰山海拔高、风景壮美，它曾是中国古代帝王继位仪式的神圣之地。皇帝们都愿意在这最崇高和最值得敬仰的地方接受授权。目前还留有很多各个朝代皇帝、学者和诗人建下的寺庙或写下的题字。美丽的自然风景和丰富的文化古迹使泰山于 1987 年被列入世界文化遗产和世界自然遗产。泰山将吸引越来越多的来自世界各地的游客。

3. Mount Taishan—Sacred and Awesome

Since ancient China, there had been countless writers and scholars expressed their highly praises of Mount Taishan. Du Fu wrote the poetry that "Once climbed onto the top of Mount Taishan, all other mountains are outweighed into hills". The grand and magnificent mountain attracted people from all walks of life throughout the world. Because its high altitude and magnificence, Mount Taishan was the sacred place for imperial succession ceremony in ancient China. All emperors would accept the symbol of power on the most exalted and honorable place. At present, there are many temples and inscriptions on Mount Taishan, which were built and left by emperors, scholars and poets of various dynasties. Grand natural sceneries and abundant cultural remains also enabled Mount Taishan enrolled in the list of World Cultural Heritage and World Natural Heritage as early as in 1987. Mount Taishan is attracting and will attract more and more tourists from all over the world.

泰山位于山东省中部泰安市，屹立在华北高原区，占地总面积 426 平方公里。泰山形成于远古时代，是中国最古老的地层。泰山东临大海，西靠黄河，数千年以来这片地区一直是中国东部政治、经济和文化中心，有 20 多个古建筑和 2 000 个文化遗址。它是中华民族的真正象征和中国人民的骄傲。

Mount Taishan is located in Tai'an City, the central of Shandong Province. It occupies a total area of 426 square kilometers, and erected on the Northern China Plateau. Mount Taishan is formed in immemorial times, and it is the most ancient stratum in China. Mount Taishan faces the sea in the east, and back on the Yellow River to the west, hence it was the center of politics, economics and culture of eastern China for thousands of years. There are more than 20 ancient buildings and 2,000 cultural remains. It is really the symbol and pride of Chinese people.

黎明旭日

泰山日出非常绚丽，成为泰山之巅的奇妙景观，也是泰山的重要标志。当第一缕阳光撕破黎明前最后的黑暗时，东方的天空由灰色变成淡黄色，再变成橘红色，直到彩霞布满并照亮整片天空。突然间，一个火球跳出云海，照亮山顶。整个过程如此完美，就像崇高的魔术师变出数以千计的彩色图画。

日落彩霞

雨后，当太阳西沉时，如果你在泰山山顶上缓行并仰望天空，你可以看到金色的光芒透过云层把云染成金玫瑰红，山顶闪闪发光。山的所有轮廓都在闪烁着金色的镶边，绽放着珍贵珠宝般的光环。

The Rising Sun at Dawn

The sunrise on Mount Taishan is splendid and engaging as one of the marvelous spectacles on summit of Mount Taishan and is also the important symbol of Mount Taishan. While the first beam of sunlight tears the last duck before dawn, the east sky turns gray to pale yellow, then to orange red as rosy clouds suffuse and brighten the whole sky. Then suddenly, one fireball jumps out of sea of cloud to light up the peaks. The whole process is so claimed as a peak of perfection that it is like thousands of polychrome pictures brought by a lofty magician.

The Rosy Clouds at Sunset

After rain, when the sun falls down to the west, if you amble on the peak of Mount Taishan and look up to the sky, you could see the golden rays penetrate layers of clouds and dye the clouds into golden rosy and shape like gleaming apex. And all the contour of mountain is beset shining golden selvage and flickers blaze of precious jewellery.

泰山上的光环

泰山顶上的光环是奇观之一。当清晨或黄昏云雾弥散时，如果游客往光的相同方向看，就能看到光环出现在高山顶上。光环是多彩的，里边是蓝色的，外面是红色的，照在人的头上就像光环绕着佛像的头，所以有了"佛光"或"宝光"之说。泰山上的光环是一种光的衍射，只有当天气晴朗有雾，6月到8月阳光斜照的时候才会出现。

云海玉盘

云海玉盘景观是泰山顶上另一个美丽奇观。夏天，雨后太阳出来，大量的水蒸气蒸发到天空，海洋吹来的暖气约1 500米高。如果没有风，从泰山山顶看，你便能看到白云平铺数千平方米，就像白玉盘悬挂在天地之间。远处的小山淹没在云中，只有少数几座露出云端；游客像在云中踏步，似乎都来到了天堂。微风吹起，云就会像海水一样翻滚，小山若隐若现，像神秘的仙女岛；风变大时，云簇拥着像条巨龙上下飞舞，搅动着云海。

The Aura on Mount Taishan

The aura on top of Mount Taishan is one of wonders. When cloud and mist is diffusing in the early morning or nightfall, the aura emerges on the higher summit if tourists look in the same direction of the light. The aura is one colorful halo with blue color inside and red color outside and reflects an image of one person just like the aura surrounds the head of Buddha. That's why it is called "Fo Guang" (aura) or "Bao Guang" (jewellery light). The aura on Mount Taishan is one kind of light diffraction and appears only under the whether condition of sunny with fog and the sunlight slanting in June to August.

Unfurling Endlessly Sea of Cloud and Jade Like Cloud Surrounding the Summits

The view of unfurling endlessly sea of cloud and jade like cloud surrounding the summits is another gorgeous wonder on top of Mount Taishan. In summer, when sun comes out just after the rain, mass vapor vaporized to the sky, the warm air from sea is lofty above about 1,500 meters high. If there is no wind, looking from the summit of Mount Taishan, you could see white clouds tile to thousands of square meters as white jade plate suspending between earth and heaven. All forane hills are engulfed in the clouds and only few of them reveal; tourists are like stepping on the cloud as if they have come to heaven. While breeze blowing, the cloud waved like sea water and the hills conceal and emerge as mysterious faery islands; while the wind becomes strong, clusters of clouds turn into gigantic dragon flying up and down and agitate the sea of cloud.

4. 兵马俑——地下大军

兵马俑博物馆于 1979 年向市民开放。它是建在兵马俑景点的世界著名博物馆。兵马俑博物馆的主要展品是黏土士兵和马的三个裸露的坑以及有两个青铜战车和马的大厅。坑中大约有 8 000 个黏土士兵和马，10 000 多件青铜武器。博物馆像一座秦王朝军事、科技、艺术和文化的宝库。它已被世界教科文组织列为"世界文化遗产"。今天，"世界第八大奇迹"已成为众所周知的兵马俑同义词。

4. Terracotta Army—The Gigantic Army Underground

The Museum of the Terracotta Army was opened to the public in 1979. It is the world-famous museum that is constructed on the site of its findings. The main exhibits of the Museum of the Terracotta Army are three exposed pits with clay warriors and horses as well as the hall of the two bronze chariots and horses. Approximately 8,000 clay warriors and horses, more than 10,000 bronze weapons have been found in the pits. The museum is like a treasure house of Qin Dynasty's military affairs, science and technology, art and culture. It has been listed as an UNESCO "World Heritage Site". Today the "Eighth Wonder of the world" has become a synonym for the well known Terracotta Army.

兵马俑位于临潼区东部，南部是骊山，北部是渭水，距离西安 37 公里。目前，它是国家重要的文物保护单位。兵马俑是秦始皇葬礼的一种艺术形式（他于公元前 247 年到公元前 221 年统治秦国，于公元前 221 年到公元前 210 年统一中国），其目的是让兵马俑帮助秦始皇死后统治另一个帝国。

据史学家司马迁所说，这个陵墓始建于公元前246年，700 000名工人参与建设。建完一个世纪以后，司马迁在史书中写道，与秦始皇葬在一起的有宫殿、观光塔、官员、宝物和"精美的物品"。

The Terracotta Army Museum is located in the east of Lintong County—37 kilometers away from Xi'an, with Lishan Mountain in the south and Weishui in the north. At present, it is the national key unit of preservation of cultural relics. The Terracotta Army is a form of funerary art buried with the Emperor of Qin (Qin Shi Huang) (his reign over Qin was from 247 BC to 221 BC and unified China from 221 BC to 210 BC). Their purpose was to help rule another empire with Qin Shi Huang in the afterlife.

According to the historian Sima Qian, construction of this mausoleum began in 246 BC and involved 700,000 workers. Sima Qian, writing a century after its completion, wrote that the First Emperor (Qin Shi Huang) was buried with palaces, scenic towers, officials, valuable utensils and "wonderful objects".

兵马俑是1974年3月由当地农民在骊山以东钻井时发现的。骊山有做兵马俑的原材料。除了士兵之外，整个人造秦始皇墓地都已出土。

The Terracotta Army was discovered in March 1974 by local farmers drilling a water well to the east of Lishan (Mount Li). Mount Li is also where the material to make the terracotta warriors originated. In addition to the warriors, an entire man-made necropolis for Qin Shi Huang has been excavated.

士兵

兵马俑1号坑呈长方形，东西向230米，南北向62米，深五米，洞穴状土木结构。从东到西有五个有坡度的入口可到达底部。十扇墙把地下士兵分成不同的列。墙上有很粗的横梁加固，还盖上了芦苇和土。地板是用黑砖铺成的。1号坑有6 000多个兵马俑和马排列成古战阵形状。有3列士兵朝东当先锋，每列是70个士兵，共210人。他们从南北向包抄左右两侧。后面的守卫在西边，手持着弩。

青铜战车

两个大型的青铜战车于1980年12月出土，在秦始皇陵墓以东约20米处，分别标记为1号和2号战车。两千多年前这些战车被装在体积为6.8×2.1×2立方米的木箱中。木箱被埋入8米深的沟槽中。沟东西向长7米，宽2.3米。这些战车是实际大小的一半，是皇帝死后视察用的车辆。彩色方形车厢装饰着几何图案和云的图案。配着剑的马车夫在两边保卫着战车。

Warriors

Terracotta Pit No. 1 is oblong: 230 meters east to west, and 62 meters north to south. At a depth of five meters, it is cavern-like and constructed from earth and wood. Five sloping entrances reach down to it from the east and west. Ten partitioning walls separate the underground army into different columns. The walls are reinforced by stout beams, which are covered by reeds and earth. The floor is paved with black bricks. There are more than 6,000 terracotta warriors and horses in Pit No. 1, marshaled into battle line formation. Three columns facing out on the east act as vanguard. Each squad is 70 strong warriors, making it 210 troopers altogether. They flank out left and right on the south and the north. The rear guard is on the west. They are armed with crossbows.

Bronze Chariots

Two large scale-models of bronze chariots came unearthed in December, 1980, about 20 meters east of Emperor Qin's mausoleum. They were tagged Chariot No. 1 and No. 2 respectively. These were encased in a wooden box measuring 6.8 × 2.1 × 2 meters for over two thousand years. And the box was buried 8 meters down in a trench. The trench runs 7 meters east to west, with a width of 2.3 meters. They were thought to be half the actual size and were supposed to serve as the vehicle for the emperor's inspection tours in his afterlife. The colorful square carriages are decorated with geometric and cloud patterns. Coachmen armed with swords guard the chariots on both sides.

5. 布达拉宫

望着高耸的拉萨玛布日山，你会被布达拉宫极其绚丽的色彩和宏大规模所震惊。在藏族人心里，它是圣地和拉萨的象征。

布达拉宫结构巨大，室内空间 130 000 多平方米。白宫是达赖喇嘛和他的下属最主要的住处。此外，它还是西藏政府所在地，所有政府仪式活动都在此举行，僧侣和管理员在此接受宗教培训。红宫因为过去是达赖喇嘛的陵墓而成为西藏主要朝圣的目的地之一。白宫内有两个小教堂，这些教堂可以追溯到公元 7 世纪，是山上幸存的最神圣最古老的建筑。布达拉宫最令人崇拜的雕像就在主殿内，它每天吸引着成千上万来西藏的朝圣者。

5. Potala Palace

Looking up to the towering Marpo Ri Hill in Lhasa, you will be stunned by the extremely splendid colors and extensive lay-out of the Potala Palace. It is a sacred place in the minds of Tibetans, as well as the symbol of Lhasa.

The Potala Palace is an immense structure, its interior space being in excess of 130,000 square meters. The White Palace is first and foremost residence of the Dalai Lama and his staff. In addition, it was the seat of Tibetan government, where all ceremonies of state were held; it housed a school for religious training of monks and administrators. Red Palace is one of Tibet's major pilgrimage destinations because of the tombs of past Dalai Lamas. Within the White Palace are two small chapels; dating from the seventh century, these chapels are the oldest surviving structures on the hill and also the most sacred. The Potala's most venerated statue is housed inside the Phapka Lhakhang, and it draws thousands of Tibetan pilgrims each day.

布达拉宫坐落于玛布日山，高出拉萨河谷 130 米。布达拉宫本身高 170 米，成为全西藏最大的建筑结构。早期的传说认为布达拉宫所矗立的山是菩萨的栖息之地，公元 7 世纪皇帝松赞干布把它用作禅修营。637 年松赞干布在山上建起一座宫殿。这座宫殿于 17 世纪时被融入另一座今天仍在的更大的建筑物。这座宫殿的建筑开始于 1645 年五世达赖喇嘛统治期间，1648 年建成（即白宫）。红宫建于 1690 年到 1694 年之间，其建设花了 7 000 个工人和 1 500 个艺术家和工匠的劳动力。1922 年十三世达赖喇嘛重新装修了白宫的许多教堂和会堂，红宫也多建了两层。作为西藏的政治和宗教中心及西藏的象征，布达拉宫每年吸引了来自世界各地的无数朝圣者和游客。1961 年，布达拉宫被列入全国重点文物保护单位。1994 年，它被列入世界文化遗产。

Perched upon Marpo Ri Hill, 130 meters above the Lhasa valley, the Potala Palace rises a further 170 meters and is the greatest monumental structure in all of Tibet. Early legends considered the hill on which Potala Palace erected to be the dwelling place of the Bodhisattva, which was used as a meditation retreat by Emperor Songtsen Gampo in the seventh century AD. In 637 Songtsen Gampo built a palace on the hill. This structure stood until the seventeenth century, when it was incorporated into the foundations of the greater buildings still standing today. Construction of the present palace began in 1645 during the reign of the fifth Dalai Lama, and by 1648 the White Palace was completed. The Red Palace was added between 1690 and 1694; its construction required the labors of more than 7,000 workers and 1,500 artists and craftsman. In 1922 the 13th Dalai Lama renovated many chapels and assembly halls in the White Palace and added two stories to the Red Palace. Being the symbol and political and religious center of Tibet, Potala Palace attracts countless pilgrims and tourists from all over the world every year. In 1961, Potala Palace was listed in key national heritage conservation units. In 1994, it was enrolled in World Cultural Heritage.

西大殿

红宫的主要宫殿是西大殿，由四个灵塔殿组成，是布达拉宫建造者五世达赖喇嘛宣布荣耀和权力的地方。西大殿以波斯精美缩图壁画著称，描绘了五世达赖喇嘛的生活场景。他在北京拜访顺治皇帝的著名场景就在入口外边的东墙上。西大殿的许多支柱都用不丹进口的特殊布料包裹着。

The Great West Hall

The main central hall of the Red Palace is the Great West Hall which consists of four great chapels that proclaim the glory and power of the builder of the Potala, the Fifth Dalai Lama. The hall is noted for its fine murals reminiscent of Persian miniatures, depicting events in the fifth Dalai Lama's life. The famous scene of his visit to Emperor Shun Zhi in Beijing is located on the east wall outside the entrance. Special cloth from Bhutan wraps the Hall's numerous columns and pillars.

6. 清新公主——颐和园

颐和园因面积大而精致，使其尽显贵族气质。事实上，它不是一个真正的宫殿，而是清代的行宫或御花园。颐和园由昆明湖和万寿山组成。它占地近3平方公里，其中三分之二的面积是水。各类景点分散在园中，包括大厦、亭台楼阁和其他不同风格的古代建筑。在这些风景点中最著名的是佛香塔、长廊、石舫、十七孔桥和谐趣园。整个花园的建筑物与自然风景相融，将大自然的美与人类的创造物合为一体。它是中国园林的杰作，享誉全世界。

6. Grazioso Princess—Summer Palace

With extensive and exquisite arrangement, the Summer Palace carries an air of nobility. Indeed, it was not a real palace but the Xanadu or imperial garden in Qing Dynasty. The garden is composed of two major items, the Kunming Lake and Wanshou Mountain. It occupies nearly 3 square kilometers, among which two thirds of the area is water. Various scenery spots scatter in the garden, including mansions, pavilions, and other ancient buildings in different styles. In these numerous sceneries, the most famous ones are Foxiang Pavilion, Long Corridor, Marble Boat, Seventeen-Arch Bridge and Xiequ Garden. The whole garden integrates buildings with natural sceneries, and combines the beauty of nature into the human creations. It is the masterpiece of Chinese gardens, and enjoys high reputation in the world.

历史和文化

颐和园是清代的皇家园林，现在已成为中国重要的景点。花园基于杭州西湖结构和布局之上，吸收了江南地区花园的设计和风格。由于面积大，重要性不可替代，颐和园被认为是皇家园林博物馆。乾隆王朝之前，北京西郊地区有四个大的皇家园林。然而，它们没有彼此相连，而是被"望山湖"隔开。1750年清朝乾隆皇帝利用望山湖，将四个花园合成一个大花园，命名为"清漪园"，这就是颐和园的前身。1860年战争期间，清漪园被烧成废墟。28年后，慈禧重建清漪园，并将它命名为颐和园。后来，颐和园两次遭到破坏。新中国成立后，颐和园一直保存完好。1961年，它被列为全国重点文物保护单位；1998年，它被列入世界文化遗产。

History and Culture

Summer Palace was the imperial garden in Qing Dynasty, and now is a key scenery spot of China. The garden based on the arrangement and lay-out of West Lake in Hangzhou, and absorbed designs and styles of gardens in South of Yangtze River. Because of the enormous scope and irreplaceable significance, the Summer Palace was regarded the museum of imperial gardens. Before the Qianlong Kingdom, there were four big imperial gardens in the western suburb area of Beijing. However, they were not connected to each other and there was a lake called "Wangshan Lake" between them. In 1750 of Qing Dynasty, Emperor Qianlong made use of the Wangshan Lake and combined the four gardens into a larger one, named "Qingyi Garden", which was the predecessor of the Summer Palace. In 1860, the Qingyi Garden was burned into ruins during the war. 28 years later, the Empress Dowager rebuilt and named it Summer Palace. In flowing years, the Summer Palace encountered devastation for twice. After the establishment of New China, Summer Palace had been well-preserved. In 1961, it was listed as the key national heritage conservation units; in 1998, it was enrolled in the World Cultural Heritage.

十七孔桥

建于乾隆皇帝统治第十五年，这座长 150 米的桥连接东岸和南湖岛。它是中国所有御花园中最长的桥，因其十七个拱门而得名。在桥的栏杆的柱子上雕刻着姿态各异的五百多头石狮。桥的两头刻有四个怪兽。它们是著名的清代石雕。

Seventeen-Arch Bridge

Built in the 15th year of Emperor Qianlong's reign, this 150-meter bridge links the east bank and the South Lake Island. It is the longest bridge in any Chinese imperial garden and was named for its seventeen arches. Over 500 stone lions in different poses are carved on the posts of the bridge's railings. At both ends of the bridge are carved four strange animals. They are outstanding evidence of Qing stone carving.

西堤

西堤是仿照杭州西湖苏堤建的。从北到南，西堤由六座桥连接，每座桥风格独特：湖桥、豳风桥、玉带桥、镜桥、练桥、柳桥。柳桥和练桥之间是根据范仲淹《岳阳楼记》中"春和景明，波澜不惊"之名句命名的景明楼。沿堤遍植桃柳，春来柳绿桃红，有"北国江南"之称。

West Causeway

The West Causeway is modeled on the Su Causeway of the West Lake in Hangzhou. From north to south, the causeway is connected by six bridges, each unique in style: the Lake-Dividing Bridge, the Bridge of Pastoral Poems, the Jade Belt Bridge, the Mirror Bridge, the Silk Bridge and the Willow Bridge. Between the Silk Bridge and the Willow Bridge is the Pavilion of Bright Scenery. It was named after the essay, *On the Yueyang Tower*, a famous piece by Fan Zhongyan, a well-known writer of the Song Dynasty. He wrote, "The spring is peaceful and the scenery bright; the waves are asleep". Peach and willow trees were planted on the causeway so that when spring came, the green of the willow trees and the red of the peach blossoms would combine to recreate the scenery of south China.

佛香阁

佛香阁最初建于乾隆皇帝统治时期，1860 年被英法联军烧毁，光绪皇帝统治时期重建佛香阁，恢复它的原貌。八面塔有三层楼四层檐，共 36.44 米高，直立于 20 米高的石基上，构成了颐和园景观中心，突出其雄伟壮丽的一面。千手观音菩萨佛像是用青铜铸成，镀有黄金，矗立于塔中。这座佛像高五米，重五吨，是明代万历年间铸造的。佛像由八个气势磅礴的撑塔支柱支起，发出美丽、壮观和辉煌的光芒。其历史、文化和艺术价值不言而喻。

Tower of the Fragrance of the Buddha

Originally built during the reign of Emperor Qianlong and burned down by the Anglo-French Allied Forces in 1860, Tower of the Fragrance of the Buddha was rebuilt in its original style during Emperor Guangxu's reign. The octahedral tower has three stories with four-layered eaves, altogether 36.44 meters high. Standing upright on a 20-meter-high stone foundation, it constitutes the center of the Summer Palace landscape and serves to accentuate its magnificence. A statue of the thousand-handed Guanshiyin Buddha, cast in bronze and gilded with gold, stands inside the tower. The statue, five meters high and five tons in weight, was cast during the reign of Emperor Wanli of the Ming Dynasty. Set off by the eight imposing pillars which support the tower, it glows with beauty, grandeur and brilliance. Its historical, cultural and artistic value can hardly be overstated.

苏州街

苏州街最初叫商人街，于乾隆皇帝统治时期建成，是华南地区城镇建设风格。皇帝和后妃可以扮成老百姓到这条街购物。1860 年它被英法联军烧成灰烬，1990 年恢复修建。这条 300 米长的街建在水上，商店和货摊立在两旁。有 60 多个行当，包括茶馆、餐厅、药店、银行、帽子店、首饰店和杂货店等。

Suzhou Street

Originally called Merchants Street, Suzhou Street was built in the style of South China towns during Emperor Qianlong's reign. A street where emperors and empresses could pretend to go shopping as ordinary people, it was burned to the ground by the Anglo-French Allied Forces in 1860 and restored in 1990. The 300-meter street is built over water with shops and stands on the bank. There are more than 60 businesses, including a teahouse, a restaurant, a pharmacy, a bank, a hat store, a jewelry store and a grocery store.

7. 黄山

黄山，"中国最美的山"，在中国大部分历史中，黄山被人们通过艺术和文学等形式赞誉过。今天它同样吸引着来这一迷人景点朝圣的游客、诗人、画家和摄影师。它有四个著名的特点：奇松，怪石，云海和温泉。风景区占地面积 154 平方公里，海拔 1 800 米以上。它曾被称为黟山，是轩辕皇帝几千年前用草药炼丹的地方。唐朝天宝六年即 747 年更名为黄山。

7. Mt. Huangshan

Known as "the loveliest mountain of China", Mt. Huangshan was acclaimed through art and literature during a good part of Chinese history. Today it holds the same fascination for visitors, poets, painters and photographers, who come in pilgrimage to this enchanting site. Famous for its four magnificent features: Oddly shaped pines, grotesque rock formations, sea of clouds and hot springs, the scenic area occupies 154 square kilometers and reaches an altitude of over 1,800 meters. Once known as Mt. Yishan, this is where Emperor Xuanyuan is said to have prepared herbal medicines several thousand years ago. The mountain was renamed Huangshan in 747, the sixth year of Emperor Tianbao of the Tang Dynasty.

垂直平板花岗岩经过数千年来的侵蚀和裂隙，已成为高耸的石柱和深谷。云雾不断缭绕，然后露出锯齿状的岩石表面。山上本地松树生长在细小的缝隙里，根比它的树干长几倍，其顶部被风刮断，树枝向一个方向生长（同风向或朝着太阳）。因此，中国人认为松是决心和毅力的象征。

1985 年，黄山当选为中国十大风景名胜景点之一。1990 年黄山被世界教科文组织列为"世界文化和自然遗产"。2002 年，黄山与瑞士的另一个世界遗产少女峰结成姊妹山。

Vertical slabs of granite, eroded and fractured over thousands of years, have created soaring pillars of rock and deep ravines. Swirling mists constantly envelop and then reveal the jagged rock faces. The native pine on the mount makes its home in tiny crevices in the rock, with roots several times longer than its trunk, its top flattened by wind and its branches growing in one direction (with the wind or towards the sun). Therefore, Chinese people regard it as a symbol of determination and persistence.

In 1985, the mountain was elected as one of China's Top Ten Scenic Spots. In 1990, Mt. Huangshan was listed as a "World Cultural and Natural Heritage" by UNESCO. In 2002, Mt. Huangshan established the sister-mountain relationship with Mt. Jungfraujoch, another world heritage site located in Switzerland.

8. 承德避暑山庄

承德避暑山庄是清代皇帝夏天处理政务的地方。这座古代著名中国皇家宫殿始建于康熙四年，成于乾隆五十年，历时 87 年。避暑山庄占地面积 5 640 000 平方米，有蜿蜒跌宕起伏 10 000 米的墙围着，是存留下来的最大的古典皇家园林，有颐和园两倍大。

8. Chengde Summer Mountain Resort

Summer Mountain Resort is the place where emperors of Qing Dynasty dealt with administrative affairs in summer. The famous ancient Chinese imperial palace, built in four years of Kangxi, was completed in Qianlong 50 years, lasted 87 years. Summer Mountain Resort covers an area of 5,640,000 square meters, a wall around the Villa winding ups and downs over 10,000 meters, is the largest remaining classical imperial garden. The equivalent is twice of the Summer Palace.

9. 杭州西湖

中国有一句老话："上有天堂，下有苏杭。"西湖著名风景名胜区包括：苏堤和白堤，把西湖分为内湖、外湖和后湖。孤山，小瀛洲（小仙女岛），湖心亭，阮公墩等，与周围的群山和溪流一起构成了西湖的美丽风光。繁茂的植被间，点缀着无数的会堂、楼塔、露台、亭子、宝塔、石窟、寺庙等，在树林浓密的枝叶间依稀可见。西湖被覆盖着茂密森林的翡翠山包围着，山上有奇形怪状的岩石、沟渠和耐人寻味的溪流。它们是如此多彩，如诗如画！

9. West Lake of Hangzhou

An old Chinese saying declares, "There is heaven above, Suzhou and Hangzhou below." The famous scenic spots of West Lake include: Su Causeway, and Bai Causeway, which have partitioned the Lake into inner, outer and back lakes. Gushan (The Solitary Hill), Xiaoyingzhou (Small Fairy Island), Huxin Ting (Mid-lake Pavilion), Ruangong Dun (A mount after a provincial governor Ruangong), etc. in combination with the surrounding hills and streams, they make up the West Lake beautiful scenery. It is also covered in luxuriant vegetation, dotted with myriad of halls, towers, terraces, pavilions, pagodas, grottoes and temples, which are barely visible under the dense foliage of surrounding woods. The lake is embraced by emerald hills covered with lush forests, grotesque rocks, gullies and intriguing streams. They are so colorful and picturesque!

10. 云冈石窟

2001 年云冈石窟由世界教科文组织录入世界文化遗产。云冈石窟代表着中国古代佛教雕塑艺术的杰出成就，在中国四个最著名的古代石窟群中规模最大。云冈石窟有 252 个洞穴和 51 000 尊佛像，是 5 世纪和 6 世纪中国佛教艺术的典范。整个石窟群雕刻细腻，非常华丽。所有雕像栩栩如生，珍贵无比，呈现了当时艺术、建筑、音乐和宗教的发展状况。

10. Yungang Grottoes

Enrolled as a World Cultural Heritage Site by the UNESCO in 2001, Yungang Grottoes represent the excellent achievement of Buddhist sculptural art of ancient China, and are the largest among the four most famous ancient grotto complexes in China. Yungang Grottoes with 252 caves and 51,000 Buddhist statues are the classical masterpieces of Chinese Buddhist art in the 5th and 6th centuries. The whole grotto complex is magnificent with delicate carvings. All the statues are precious and vivid, representing the development of art, architecture, music and religion at that time.

口述题

1. 从全球视野角度来看，你觉得我们应对世界遗产抱以什么样的态度呢？
2. 你去过我国有名的旅游景点吗？有什么感受？

Questions

1. From a global perspective, what attitude do you think we should take towards the world heritage?

2. Have you ever been to famous tourist attractions in China? How do you feel?

学习网站

1. 故宫博物院（https://www.dpm.org.cn/Home.html）

2. CHINA HIGHLIGHTS（https://www.chinahighlights.com/travelguide/special-report/china-top-tourist-cities/）

第十三章　中国武术文化

Chapter 13　Chinese Martial Arts Culture

第一节　中国武术文化的起源和类属

Section 1　The Origin and Types of Chinese Martial Arts

中国武术，也就是中国功夫，是中国几个世纪以来形成的各种样式的格斗。这些格斗样式按共性可以分为"家"、"派"或"门"。这些共性包括模仿动物或受中国哲学、宗教和传说启发的训练法等体育锻炼。强调运气的样式称为内家拳，而专注于提高肌肉和心血管健身的称为外家拳。按区域可分为北拳和南拳，是另一种流行的分类方法。

Chinese Martial Arts, also referred to by the Mandarin Chinese term wushu and popularly as kung fu, are a number of fighting styles that have developed over the centuries in China. These fighting styles are often classified according to common traits, identified as "families" (jia), "sects" (pai) or "schools" (men) of martial arts. Examples of such traits include physical exercises involving animal mimicry, or training methods inspired by Chinese philosophies, religions and legends. Styles which focus on qi manipulation are labeled as internal (neijiaquan), while others concentrate on improving muscle and cardiovascular fitness are labeled external (waijiaquan). Geographical association, as in northern (beiquan) and southern (nanquan), is another popular method of categorization.

中国武术有两个核心流派：少林派和道教（武当）派，这两个流派经历了很多世纪的发展过程，把武术的理念当作以精神上的自我发展为主要目标的一种手段。少林派起源于印度和尚菩提达摩，而武当派是从古代中国萨满教僧对鸟类和兽类特征的研究和冥想后形成、创建和发展的。

There are two core schools of Chinese Martial Art: the Shaolin School, and the Daoist (Wudang) School, both of which were created and over the course of many, many centuries, been governed by setting the concept of martial arts as a means to spiritual self-development as their principal objective. The Shaolin School began with the Indian Buddhist monk, Bodhidharma, whilst the Daoism one derives ultimately from still more ancient Chinese shamanic origins in which study of meditation upon the characteristics of birds and animals formed principal elements in its creation and development.

有关起源的传说

据传说，中国武术 4 000 多年前起源于半虚构的夏朝。据说最早是黄帝把格斗法引入中国。黄帝在成为首领之前，是一位著名的将领，写了关于医学、占星术和武术的长篇著作。他的主要对手蚩尤是角抵的创造者，也是中国现代摔跤艺术的先行者。

Legendary Origins

According to legend, Chinese Martial Arts originated during the semi-mythical Xia Dynasty more than 4,000 years ago. It is said the Yellow Emperor introduced the earliest fighting systems to China. The Yellow Emperor is described as a famous general who, before becoming China's leader, wrote lengthy treatises on medicine, astrology and the martial arts. One of his main opponents was Chi You who was credited as the creator of Jue Di, a forerunner to the modern art of Chinese Wrestling.

早期历史

最早提到武术是在春秋时期，提到了空手搏斗理论，包括"硬"和"柔"技术的概念结合。《礼记》中提到过一种名为"角力"的搏斗法。这种搏斗法包括攻击、投掷、控制关节和压点进攻等技巧。秦王朝时期角抵成为一项运动。前汉时期的史书记载，手搏这种无拘束的无武器搏斗与角力这种运动式摔跤之间有明显的区别。摔跤由司马迁记录在《史记》里。

唐代对剑舞的描述在李白的诗中名垂千古。宋元时期，朝廷举办过相扑比赛。现代武术概念在明清时期得到充分开发。

Early History

The earliest references to Chinese Martial Arts are found in the Spring and Autumn Period, where a hand to hand combat theory, including the integration of notions of "hard" and "soft" techniques, is mentioned. A combat wrestling system called jueli is mentioned in the *Classic of Rites*. This combat system included techniques such as strikes, throws, joint manipulation, and pressure point attacks. Jue Di became a sport during the Qin Dynasty. The Han History Bibliographies record that, by the Former Han, there was a distinction between no-holds-barred weaponless fighting, which it calls shoubo, for which training manuals had already been written, and sportive wrestling, then known as jueli. Wrestling is also documented in the *Shǐ Jì*, *Records of the Grand Historian*, written by Sima Qian.

In the Tang Dynasty, descriptions of sword dances were immortalized in poems by Li Bai. In the Song and Yuan dynasties, xiangpu contests were sponsored by the imperial courts. The modern concepts of wushu were fully developed by the Ming and Qing dynasties.

分类

中国功夫经过几百年的发展，已成为包括了各个流派或教派的一大体系。据记录，全国现有 300 多种不同类型的拳击。中国北部和南部的风格完全不同。因此很难简单地归类。

有些流派是根据地理位置来分类的，例如，南拳普遍存在于中国南方，而少林派基地在河南省少林寺。有些是根据创建者和师祖命名的，如陈式太极和杨式太极。有些则是根据不同的训练方法命名的，如内家拳主要关注身体内的运气和循环，而外家拳主要关注改善肌肉和四肢等。

Classification

Over the centuries of development in China, Kung Fu has become a large system containing various schools or sects. It is recorded that there are over 300 distinct types of boxing existing around the country. The styles in northern and southern China are quite different. Therefore, it is hard to be simply classified.

Some of the schools are classified by geographical locations, for example, the Southern Fist (Nanquan) prevailing in south China, and Shaolin School based at Shaolin Temple in Henan Province. Some are named after the creator and master, like the Chen Style Tai Chi and Yang Style Tai Chi. Some are identified by different training methods, such as the Internal Boxing Arts (Neijiaquan) that concentrate on the manipulation of the inner breath and circulation of the body, and the External Boxing Arts (Waijiaquan) that concentrate on improving the muscles and the limbs.

最优秀和最有影响力的流派有：

（1）少林武术：起源于河南省少林寺，是中国最早的武术风格，已广泛传播到世界各地。其身体锻炼和心理训练都是基于佛教哲学之上的。少林拳、南拳、北腿和咏春拳是这一流派的代表。

The most outstanding and influential schools are listed as follows：

（1）Shaolin Martial Arts：Originated in the Shaolin Temple in Henan, this is considered the premier style in China and is widely spread all over the world. Both of its physical exercise and mental training are based upon Buddhist philosophy. The Shaolin Boxing, Southern Fist (Nanquan), Northern Legs (Beitui) and Wing Chun are the representatives of this school.

（2）武当武术：这个流派与少林武术享有几乎相同的美誉。基地在湖北省武当山。武当武术在道教理论的指导下得以发展。太极拳、形意拳、八卦掌是武当武术的代表。

（2）Wudang Martial Arts：This sect has almost the same fame as the Shaolin. Based at the Mt. Wudang in Hubei Province, it is developed under the guidance of Taoist theories. Tai Chi Chuan, Form/Intention Boxing (Xingyiquan), Eight-Diagram Palm (Baguazhang) are essentials of Wudang.

（3）峨眉武术：以四川峨眉山为阵营，这是个温和流派，融入了少林和武当的优点。这一流派有很多分支，包括青城、铁佛、青牛、点易、黄陵等。

（4）太极：比较缓慢，风格典雅，融入了道教、辩证法思想、传统医学和体育锻炼的思想。其特点是积累力量、以柔克刚和以静制动。

（5）形意拳：它是内家拳艺术的代表，其特点是直拳快击，很适合和敌人搏斗。其拳路包括五行拳、十二式动物拳等。

（6）八卦掌：由董海川创建，八卦掌的特点是连续变化掌式，稳步于圈内。此派别有很多分支。

（3）E'mei Martial Arts：Taking Mt. E'mei in Sichuan Province as its camp, this sect is moderate and blends the merits of Shaolin and Wudang. Many sub-branches derive under this sect, including Qingcheng, Tiefo, Qingniu, Dianyi, Huangling, etc.

（4）Tai Chi：This is a comparatively slow and elegant style originated from the combination of Taoism, dialectic ideology, traditional medicine and physical exercise. It features attack by accumulating the strength, conquering the rigidity with the flexibility, and beating action by inaction.

（5）Form/Intention Boxing (Xingyiquan)：It is a representative of Internal Boxing Arts characterized by its straightforward fist and quick attack which are well suitable for fighting against the enemy. Its boxing routines include Five Elements Boxing, Twelve Animals Boxing and so on.

（6）Eight-Diagram Palm (Baguazhang)：Created by the master Dong Haichuan, the Eight-Diagram Palm features continuous changes in palm styles and steady steps in circle. Many sub-sects derive from this school.

（7）南拳：这一传统流派在华南地区流行了400多年。以广东省和福建省为中心，其特点是套路短小精悍，结构紧凑，动作朴实，手法多变，短手连打，步法稳健，攻击勇猛。大师黄飞鸿擅长南拳。

（8）气功：气功不仅是一种武术流派，也是一种体力和脑力锻炼方法，有益于身心健康。气功主要有两种类型：通过活动身体的动态气功和通过调整呼吸和冥想的静态气功。

（7）Southern Fist (Nanquan)：This traditional school prevailed over 400 years in South China. Centered in Guangdong and Fujian Provinces, it features short and tight movements, various skills, steady steps and vigorous attacks. The grand master Wong Fei-hung is good at the Southern Fist.

（8）Qigong：It is not only a school of martial arts but also a physical and mental exercise method, which is beneficial to health and body-building. There are mainly two types—Dynamic Qigong practiced by specific body movements, and Static Qigong practiced by adjusting the breath and mind.

中国武术装备：中国武术除了大量的单个系统、形式、拳击技术和格斗技术外，武术装备也是多样的，包括少林十八种武器、铲、耙、长矛和关刀等。

Chinese Martial Arts Weapons: In addition to having the greatest variety and number of individual systems, forms, and sparring/fighting techniques, Chinese martial arts weapons are enormous in range and diversity. They include amongst many others, the 18 weapons of Shaolin, 'monk-spades', rakes, the Spear and the 'Guan Dao'.

中国功夫（功夫或武术）是一系列的搏斗形式，在中国经历了漫长的历史发展时期。如今，中国功夫被视为一项传统的运动，赢得了越来越多的声望，甚至成为中国文化的代表。形式包括少林、太极、气功，追随者遍及世界各地。一些西方人以为所有中国人都是功夫大师。事实并非如此，但这一独特传统至今仍在，对当地人的生活方式造成很大影响。

中国功夫虽然是搏斗形式，它倡导美德与和平，不侵略，不暴力。这一直是一代接一代武士坚持的共同价值观。功夫有很多动作套路、拳击样式、武器技能和搏斗特技，保留了原始的自卫功能，其健身健体的价值也被高度赞赏。

Chinese Kung Fu (Martial Arts or as popularly referred to as Gongfu or Wushu) is a series of fighting styles which has developed over a long historical period in China. Nowadays, it is regarded as a traditional sport gaining more and more popularity and even stands as a representative for Chinese culture. Styles including Shaolin, Tai Chi and Qigong have many followers worldwide. Some westerners think that all Chinese people are Kung Fu masters. That's not true, but this traditional heritage has its unique existence in modern times and has left much influence on the locals' lifestyle.

Although being fighting styles, Kung Fu advocates virtue and peace, not aggression or violence. This has been the common value upheld by martial artists from generation to generation. With a number of movement sets, boxing styles, weapon skills and some fighting stunts, Kung Fu keeps its original function of self-defense. Now its value in body-building and fitness is also highly appreciated.

第二节 中国武术文化的发展和影响

Section 2 The Development and Influence of Chinese Martial Arts

哲学影响

与武术相关的观念随着时间的推移和中国社会的演变而改变，从而获得一些哲学基础：道家作品《庄子》中涉及习武的心理学和实践。同名作者庄子生活在公元前4世纪。另一部由老子所写的《道德经》中的一些理论也适用于武术。根据儒家思想的经典文之一《周礼》记载，周朝的射、御是六艺的一部分（"六艺"还包括礼、乐、书、数）。公元前6世纪孙子写的《孙子兵法》直接涉及军事战役，但也包含中国武术思想。

Philosophical Influences

The ideas associated with Chinese Martial Arts changed with the evolution of Chinese society and over time acquired some philosophical bases: Passages in the *Zhuang Zi*, a Daoist text, pertain to the psychology and practice of martial arts. Zhuang Zi, its eponymous author, is believed to have lived in the 4th century BC. *Dao De Jing*, often credited to Lao Zi, is another Daoist text that contains principles applicable to martial arts. According to one of the classic texts of Confucianism, *Zhou Li*, archery and charioteering were part of the "six arts" (liuyi, including rites, music, calligraphy and mathematics) of the Zhou Dynasty. *The Art of War*, written during the 6th century BC by Sun Zi, deals directly with military warfare but contains ideas that are used in the Chinese Martial Arts.

早在公元前 500 年，道教徒就练习过一种类似于太极拳的气功。公元 39—92 年，"《手搏》六篇"，由作者班固列入《汉书》（前汉史）。此外，著名医师华佗大约在公元前 220 年写了《五禽戏》——虎、鹿、猴、熊、鸟。道家哲学和他们的健康运动法在一定程度上对中国武术产生过影响。"八仙"使用的打斗技巧直接参考了道教理念，其风格体现了每个神仙不同的性格特点。

显然，中国功夫不仅仅用于个人防身，而且是不同领域中的光辉艺术。

Daoist practitioners have been practicing physical exercises similar to Qigong from as early as 500 BC. In 39 – 92 AD, Six Chapters of *Hand Fighting*, were included in the *Han Shu* (history of the Former Han Dynasty) written by Ban Gu. Also, the noted physician, Hua Tuo, composed the *Five Animals Play*—tiger, deer, monkey, bear, and bird, around 220 BC. Daoist philosophy and their approach to health and exercise have influenced the Chinese martial arts to a certain extent. Direct reference to Daoist concepts can be found in such styles as the "Eight Immortals" who use fighting techniques that are attributed to the characteristics of each immortal.

Obviously, Chinese Kung Fu is not merely the personal defense skill any more, but a shining art in different fields.

在日常生活中，人们，尤其是老年人练习功夫，如击剑和太极拳等，以保持身体健康、陶冶情操。这是公园中常见的场景。

在体育界，中国功夫已于 1999 年成为奥林匹克赛事之一，越来越多的外籍人士对中国功夫感兴趣。

In our daily life, people, especially the aged, practice Kung Fu, such as fencing and Tai Chi Quan—Chinese shadow boxing, to keep fit and cultivate the soul. This is a common scene in the park.

In the sportsdom, Chinese Kung Fu became one of the Olympic events in 1999, and there is a growing number of foreigners who are interested in Chinese Kung Fu.

在电影界，中国功夫越来越受到世界各地观众的喜爱。很多国际大导演把中国功夫引入电影，与一些著名的中国功夫演员如成龙、李连杰和杨紫琼等合作。这类影片更广泛介绍了中国文化、历史、军事经典之作、道家哲学、风水、英雄人物（其中一些传统上被公认为"神"）和少林寺等的重要方面。当代中华武术（中国武术）现象很大程度上归因于这方面的成功，归因于他们精心编排的体育竞技技巧和视觉娱乐目的。

In the filmdom, Chinese Kung Fu is growingly appreciated by the audience all over the world, and more leading international directors introduce the Chinese Kung Fu to their films and corporate with some famous Chinese Kung Fu actors, such as Jackie Chan, Jet Li and Michelle Yeoh. Such films have introduced key aspects of broader Chinese culture, history, military classics, esoteric Daoist philosophies, Feng Shui, hero-figures (some of whom have traditionally been recognized as deities), and the Shaolin Temple. The phenomena of contemporary Chinese Martial Arts—Zhonguo Wushu (China's national performance sport)—has been largely responsible for this success, blending as they do brilliant carefully choreographed techniques for competitive sport, and for visual entertainment purposes.

受传统功夫王李小龙和成龙等影响，20 世纪 70 年代的"功夫"热是传统武术和当代武术之间的桥梁。

就中国习武者而言，一个鲜为人知但更重要的现象是中国传统武术已经传播到更广阔的世界。大约在 20 世纪 70 年代后，一些有远见的最高水平宗师在特定情况下有史以来第一次在国外挑选弟子教一些传统的甚至罕见的高级别武术。

The 'Kung Fu' craze of the 1970's—led by the influence of adept traditional martial arts exponents such as Bruce Lee and Jackie Chan—was a bridge between the traditional arts and those of contemporary Wushu.

There was, however, a less well known but much more—as far as Chinese Martial Arts practitioners were concerned—important phenomenon regarding the spread of traditional Chinese Martial Arts to the broader world. Circa the 1970's, certain of the highest level Chinese grandmasters and great grandmasters—through foresight—in certain rare and special circumstances selected Inner Chamber disciples to teach some of the traditional and even rare high-level arts and systems outside of China for the first time ever.

两个流派：道教和少林有共同的重要因素。罕见的无极拳（道教）（太极之母）就是一个例子，它通过少林武术（佛教）传统代代相传。它包括 36 式：18 式为自然和气候现象拳诀，18 式为运气拳诀。

The two Schools: Daoist and Shaolin have significant elements in common. The rare (Daoist) art of Wujiquan (mother art of Tai Chi) is an example, being handed down for generations through the (Buddhist) Shaolin martial arts tradition. This system comprises 36 Characters: 18 of natural and climatic phenomena and 18 of qi（martial）applications.

中国传统武术有两个目的：保护或剥夺生命和锻炼心智，以学习致命搏斗术。因此河南省少林寺习武的特殊作用是以实现精神启迪为目标，学习道教神秘的宇宙论教学理念，学习相关内部武术和系统概念之间的相互联系。

擂台（正式的传统武术比赛）：直到在 20 世纪中期的近代中国才出现擂台，通常是两个武林高手一决高低。

Traditional Chinese martial arts had two purposes: teaching deadly fighting techniques for preserving or taking life, and for spiritual and character development. Hence the special role of martial arts training is as a method for realizing the goals of spiritual enlightenment taught at the famous Henan province Shaolin Temple, and the interconnection of esoteric Daoist cosmological teachings and concepts with related internal martial arts techniques and systems.

The Lei Tai（formal traditional martial arts contest）was until the birth of modern China in the mid-20th Century a formal institution in which rival martial arts exponents would meet and fight for supremacy.

中国武术的现状

中国武术是中国文化的精髓，已在全国得以推广。它有益于身心健康，越来越多的人习武。甚至有些学校要求学生习武。作为中国人，我们感到自豪，也应该承担继承和推广这一财富的责任。

The Current Situation of Chinese Martial Arts

Since it is the quintessence of Chinese culture, it has been largely promoted in the whole country. More and more people are learning it as it can benefit our health and help build our body. Also some schools require students to learn the martial arts. As Chinese people, we may feel proud and also should take the responsibility to inherit and promote this treasure.

口述题

1. 你知道中国武术的两大核心流派吗？
2. 在你的了解中，中国人对武术持怎样的态度？

Questions

1. Do you know the two core schools of Chinese martial arts?
2. What attitudes do you know about Chinese people towards Chinese martial arts?

学习网站

1. 中国武术协会（http://www.wushu.com.cn/）
2. CHINA HIGHLIGHTS（https://www.chinahighlights.com/travelguide/kungfu/）

第十四章　中国节日文化

Chapter 14　Chinese Festival Culture

第一节　传统节日

Section 1　Traditional Festivals

农历新年（1 月/2 月）

农历新年通常在每年的冬季。确切的日期是按农历日历算的。临近新年时，每个家庭都会把他们房子的里里外外清洁干净，并在房门旁贴上红红的春联，人们还要准备新年食物，其中"年糕"当然是必不可少的，它象征家人年年高升。房子周围也会粘贴春联。所有家人一直要忙到除夕夜，直到准备好团圆饭迎接新的一年开始。儿童和未婚的成年人很喜欢过新年，因为已婚夫妻和老一代人会给他们派发红包。传统上农历正月的前几天人们会去拜访亲人和朋友。

Chinese New Year/Lunar New Year（January/February）

It is usually in the winter of a year. The exact date would follow the one in Lunar Calendar. Entering the New Year month, every family would clean and tidy both the inside and the outside of their houses. New Year couplets would be displayed around house. New Year food would also be prepared. 'Nian Gao', the Chinese cake symbolizing the rise of family every year, would be a must. All families would be busy until the New Year's Eve and a big New Year Eve's dinner would be served for the gathering to welcome the beginning of a New Year. Children and unmarried adults would love the occasion because red packets would be given to them from all married couples and older generations. As a tradition, on the first few days of the first lunar month, people would spend their time visiting relatives and friends.

元宵节（1 月/2 月）

元宵节也称中国情人节，它标志着新年的结束。年轻夫妇也会借此机会好好庆祝一下。这一天到处会挂满各种不同的灯笼。

清明节（3 月/4 月）

清明节是人们去祖先墓地祭拜的日子。人们通过点香烛、烧纸钱祭奠逝去的亲人。祭品包括烤仔猪、蒸鸡、水果和酒等，也有些人只用菊花。据说死去的亲人会在这一天从墓穴出来四处游荡，所以有时人们手里携带柳枝或把柳枝插在门上吓跑鬼魂。

Spring Lantern Festival/Yuen Siu Festival（January/February）

It is also known as the Chinese Valentine's Day and it marks the end of the Chinese New

Year. Young couples would celebrate on this day. Lanterns of different designs would be hung in different places.

Qingming Festival（March/April）

It is a day when people pay their visits to the graves of their ancestors. Joss sticks, incense and paper offerings would be burnt for the dead people. Roasted piglets, steamed chicken, fruit and wine would be offered to the dead too. Some people tend to bring chrysanthemum instead of those mentioned above. It is said that it is also a day when the dead wander about above ground and so sometimes people carry willow branches or hang them outside their doors on this day to scare away the ghosts.

端午节（6 月）

端午节是纪念爱国学者屈原的节日，他因无法身谏楚王，愤然投水而死。过节时最受欢迎的粽子，是由糯米、盐腌咸蛋黄和肉用粽叶包裹制成。端午节又称龙舟节，人们通常会在这天通过划龙舟比赛来纪念屈原。龙舟有龙头龙尾。因为龙是水神，龙舟入水后，水得神佑。传统上人们习惯用这神佑的水来洗头洗澡以便来年得到神的保佑。

Dragon Boat Festival（June）

It is a festival to show respect to a patriotic scholar—Qu Yuan, who drowned himself to protest against his emperor. Rice dumpling, which is popular during the festival, is made of glutinous rice, salted meat with a salty egg yolk and wrapped with bamboo leaves. On Dragon Boat Festival, people may commemorate Qu Yuan by holding dragon boat races. The dragon boat has the head and a tail of a dragon. Since the dragon is the god of the water world, after the dragon boats sail in the water, the water will be blessed. It is also a tradition for people to wash their hair and body with the blessed water on the day so as to be blessed for the coming year.

七巧节

七巧节是中国情人节，适逢农历七月初七这天，也称"七夕节"。对古代女士们来说它是一个充满浪漫的重要节日，虽然七巧节在当今不如其他传统节日知名，也并没有很多人过七巧节，但人们却都熟悉其背后的故事。

The Double Seventh Festival

The Double Seventh Festival known in China as Chinese Valentine's Day, falls on the 7th day of the 7th lunar month. Also called "Qi Xi Jie", it is a traditional festival full of romance and important to ancient ladies, but not as well-known as other traditional festivals. Not so many Chinese people take it as a festival as before but are all familiar with the story behind it.

中秋节（9 月/10 月）

中秋节时人们一般会送月饼给朋友和亲戚当礼物。此外，腌制香肠和新鲜杨桃也是很受欢迎的礼物。孩子们在这天会提着灯笼在街道上行走。当然，人们也会抓住良机在自己阳台上或在家里赏月。传统月饼是由甜莲蓉与一个或多个咸鸭蛋黄做成的。现代月饼样式却十分丰富，有绿茶、红豆、火腿和坚果月饼，甚至还有冰皮月饼，应有尽有。

Mid-Autumn Festival（September/October）

Moon cake is the gift people give to their friends and relatives at the festival. Apart from that, salted sausages and star fruit are other popular gifts. It is the happiest for the children because they would enjoy walking in the streets with their lanterns. Of course, people would make use of the chance to look at the full moon on the day on their balconies or just at home. Traditional moon cakes are made with sweet lotus seed paste with one or more egg yolks. Modern moon cakes come in various styles. Tastes like green tea, red beans, hams and nuts, or even moon cake ice-cream are all available. Just name it and you may find it.

重阳节（9 月/10 月）

东汉时期有一个传说。有人告诉一名男子，要他们全家去山顶避难，说他们家会有血光之灾。他与他的家人离开家，沿途喝些菊花酒。回来时他发现所有的牲畜被杀。从那以后过去大约 2 000 年，传说人们会在重阳节这一天离开家去祭拜祖先。

Double Ninth Festival（September/October）

There has been a legend from the East Han Dynasty. A man was told to leave home and go to a hill top to avoid a disaster which would kill all lives there. So he left home with his family and drank chrysanthemum wine as he had been told. When he came back after the day, he found that all livestock were killed. Since then, after almost 2,000 years, it is believed that it is a day when people should leave home and show their respect to their ancestors on the day.

冬至节

冬至节起源于阴阳概念，象征着人们对生活的平衡与和谐的向往。冬至阴寒之气隆盛，是北半球一年中白昼最短的一天，阴气盛极而转衰，阳气开始回升。因此，冬至节时人们精神畅达乐观。

北方的人们会在冬至这一天吃饺子，南方部分地区庆祝活动则更隆重，仅次于新年。农民及渔夫得在这一时间开始储存食物以度过严寒的冬天。

Chinese Winter Solstice Festival

The Winter Solstice Festival has its origins in the Chinese concept of yin and yang, which represents balance and harmony in life. It's believed that the yin qualities of darkness and cold are at their most powerful on the shortest day of the year, but also at their turning point to give way to the light and warmth of yang. For this reason, the Winter Solstice Festival is a time for optimism.

Today, people mark the occasion in Northern China by eating Chinese dumplings, while the southern part of the country puts on a much bigger celebration, second only to Chinese New Year for many families. This is because this was traditionally the time by which farmers and fishermen had to prepare for the coming colder months.

第二节　节日文化和习俗

Section 2　Festival Culture and Customs

新年的起源

农历新年的起源可以追溯到数千年前，涉及一系列精彩的传说。著名的传说中有一种极其残酷和凶猛的野兽——年，古人认为年在除夕夜会吃人，为了把年赶走，人们把红纸对联粘贴在门边，在黑夜里点燃火把和爆竹，因为据说年怕红色、火光和大响声。

第二天清早，全村的人聚在一起，为驱逐凶兽获得的胜利互相祝贺道喜。最常用的问候语是"恭喜"或"祝贺"。

准备

通常新年的准备工作在新的一年到来之前的一个月就开始了。准备工作包括彻底清洗、装饰房子、买新衣服和准备至少能吃两个星期的食物。

The Origin of Chinese New Year

The origin of the lunar New Year Festival can be traced back thousands of years, involving a series of colorful legends. One of the famous legends is Nian, an extremely cruel and ferocious beast that the ancients believed would devour people on New Year's Eve. To keep Nian away, red-paper couplets are pasted on doors, torches are lit and firecrackers are set off through the night, because Nain is said to fear the color red, the light of fire, and loud noises.

Early the next morning, as feelings of triumph and renewal fill the air at successfully keeping Nain away for another year, the most popular greeting heard is "gong xi", or "congratulations".

Preparation

Usually the preparation starts a month before the New Year. The preparation includes thoroughly cleaning and decorating the house, buying new clothes, and preparing enough food for at least two weeks.

传统

中国人认为，进入新的一年人们应该把过去的事情置于脑后。他们要清理房屋，购买新衣服，理发，为门窗重新刷漆。

红包

在喜庆场合，如婚宴、生日和新年，人们都会送钱作贺礼。它们的主要任务是授礼，第二个任务是祝愿收礼人好运、快乐和成功。礼钱通常放在红包里，红包上会装饰些符号、问候语或幸运标志。

Traditions

The Chinese believe that as they enter a New Year they should put behind them all things of the past. They clean their houses, purchase new clothes, get haircuts and paint their doors and window panes.

Chinese Red Envelopes

Monetary gifts are usually presented in red envelopes during festive occasions, like weddings, birthdays, and the New Year. While their main task is to bear gifts, their second duty is to shower

the recipient with luck, joy, and prosperity. The money is usually placed in a red packet/envelope decorated with an appropriate symbol, greeting or lucky sign.

如果花在新年这一天开，则是好运的象征。新年还是还清债务的时候，如果不还清债务，欠债人和他的家人会觉得很丢面子。

新年之前，人们会在室内用花瓶装满漂亮花朵，用盘装满橙子和橘子，用八果盘装满糖和干果。墙壁和门用红纸写上诗楹联和幸福祝愿。

楹联

春联是写着祝福语与吉祥话的红色大条幅，如"好运气"和"春"。正方形春联通常倒着贴，因为普通话中的"倒"与"到达"一词的中的"到"谐音。因此，倒着的方形纸代表春天"到达"和财运"来了"。

装饰

人们用鲜花和纸饰品装饰家，以祝愿好运、繁荣、幸福、好运气、富有和长寿。装饰品上通常画有生肖动物的图片。其中红色和金色是饰品上最受欢迎的颜色。红色也表示力量、快乐、活力，能吓走野兽。金色代表财富和好运。

If flowers open on New Year's Day, it is believed to be a symbol of good luck. The New Year is also a time to settle debts—if not, both the debtor and his family will face shame.

Prior to New Year's Day, Chinese families decorate their living rooms with vases of pretty blossoms, platters of oranges and tangerines and a candy tray with eight varieties of dried sweet fruit. On walls and doors are poetic couplets, happy wishes written on red paper.

Couplets

Spring couplets are paper scrolls and squares inscribed with blessings and auspicious words, such as "good fortune" and "springtime". The paper squares are usually pasted upside down, because the Mandarin word for "upside down", *dao*, is a homonym of the word "arrival". Thus, the paper squares represent the "arrival" of spring and the "coming" of prosperous times.

Decorations

Flowers and paper decorations adorn homes with wishes of luck, prosperity, happiness, good fortune, wealth, and longevity. Decorations include pictures of the incoming Zodiac animal. Red and gold are popular colors. Red represents power, happiness, vitality, and scares away the beasts. Gold represents wealth and good fortune.

禁忌

所有锋利的工具（如刀等）都要藏起来，因为他们可能会切断家里的好运气。不能说脏话或不吉利的话，因为这会给家庭带来坏运气。

新年前五天扫地是不吉利的，因为可能把好运和财富扫出房子。不可谈及死亡。

如果打碎了碗碟，要说"岁岁（碎）平安"，意味着年年安然无恙。

Taboos

All sharp tools (knives, etc.) are hidden away since they may sever good fortune from the family. No foul language or unlucky words because it will bring bad luck to the family.

It's unlucky to sweep the floor during the first five days of the Lunar New Year, because one might accidentally sweep one's good luck and wealth out of the house. Talk of death is severely frowned upon.

If a dish is broken, it's vital to say "sui sui ping an", means every year will be safe and secure.

除夕夜

除夕夜是家人团圆的时候。除夕晚餐很像美国的感恩节晚餐，是一年当中最丰盛的一餐。这顿晚餐有很多象征意义，例如，饺子象征着财富，因为他们的形状像古时的金元宝或银元宝。

除夕必吃鱼大餐。鱼被认为是吉祥物。这是因为汉语中的这个词听起来像"剩余"的"余"。主人认为"鱼"象征着家中富余。人们希望这些做法能给未来一年带来额外的财富。

爆竹

新年一到放鞭炮。新年你可以听到到处是鞭炮声，通常要持续几个小时。传统上放鞭炮有辞旧迎新的意思。

新年的问候

新年也是人们社交的时候。通常人们在新年会穿上新衣服，出去拜访或迎接他们的亲属和朋友，所以街头充满了欢乐的人群。问候和拜访常持续几天。

New Year's Eve

The New Year's Eve is the time for families. The New Year Eve's dinner is the biggest dinner of the year, much like Thanksgiving dinner in the United States. The dinner is full of symbolic meaning, such as Chinese dumplings implying wealth since they have the shape of ancient Chinese gold or silver ingots.

Big dinner on New Year's Eve—fish. Fish are considered lucky creatures. This is because the word "fish" in Chinese also sounds like the word meaning "surplus" or "something left over." The owners believe it will help to bring in a surplus of money. People hope these practices will bring extra wealth in the coming year.

Firecrackers

Firecrackers are set off as soon as the New Year arrives. You can hear or see firecrackers everywhere and this usually lasts for a few hours. Traditionally fireworks are the sign of getting rid of the old and welcoming the new.

New Year Greetings

Chinese New Year is also the time for socializing. People usually wear new clothes and go out to visit and greet their relatives and friends, so the streets are filled with a lot of cheerful people. The greeting and visiting can go on for a few days.

舞龙和舞狮

农历新年期间的最壮观的场面要数舞龙和舞狮。据说这些可怕怪兽的头能辟邪，舞者的灵活动作让人们欣赏到令人愉悦的盛大场面。

"龙"通常有几米到一百多米长,主要是由竹、木、藤、布和纸等做的。

糖果盒

圆形或八角形的糖果盒象征着"团结互助",琳琅满目的糖果象征新年甜蜜。

The Dragon and The Lion Dance

One of the most spectacular sights during the Lunar New Year Festival is the dragon and lion dance. The heads of these fearsome beasts are supposed to ward off evil, and the nimble movements of the dancers provide a grand spectacle enjoyable to everyone.

The dragons, usually ranging from several meters to more than 100 meters long, are mainly made of bamboo, wood, rattan, cloth and paper, etc.

Candy Tray

The candy tray arranged in either a circle or octagon is called "The Tray of Togetherness" and has a dazzling array of candy to start the New Year sweetly.

人们在除夕晚宴上会为祖先奉上饭菜。祖先的灵魂和活着的人一大家子,一起共同庆祝新的一年的开始。这顿宴席称为"围炉",象征着家人团聚和各代人的荣耀。

新年第一天全家都吃素,也称"吃斋"。尽管斋饭的各种成分是根菜或叶菜,很多人对斋饭的象征意义深信不疑,如:

* 莲子——表示有很多男性后代;
* 银杏果——表示银锭;
* 发菜——与"发财"谐音;
* 豆腐干——与"多福"谐音;
* 竹笋——听起来像"祝愿一切顺利";
* 不包括新鲜豆腐,因为它是白色的,而白色象征着死亡和不幸。

The presence of the ancestors is acknowledged on New Year's Eve with a dinner arranged for them at the family banquet table. The spirits of the ancestors, together with the living, celebrate the onset of the New Year as one great community. The communal feast is called "surrounding the stove" or weilu. It symbolizes family unity and honors of the past and present generations.

On New Year's Day, the Chinese family will eat a vegetarian dish called zhai. Although the various ingredients in zhai are root vegetables or fibrous vegetables, many people attribute various superstitious aspects to them.

* Lotus seed—signifies having many male offspring;
* Ginkgo nut—represents silver ingots;
* Black moss seaweed—is a homonym for exceeding in wealth;
* Dried bean curd—is another homonym for fulfillment of wealth and happiness;
* Bamboo shoots—is a term which sounds like "wishing that everything would be well";
* Fresh bean curd or tofu is not included as it is white and unlucky for New Year as the color signifies death and misfortune.

好运气

打开门或窗意味着新年好运气。晚上开灯可以"吓走"带来灾祸的鬼魂，给新的一年带来好运和财气。吃糖果意味着来年"甜蜜"。新年前把房子彻头彻尾打扫干净是非常重要的，意味着来年好运。有些人认为新年第一天发生什么是来年的预兆。要穿年前买的新拖鞋，因为这表示要踩说你闲话的人。新年前一天晚上用柚叶洗澡能保来年健康。

Good Luck

Opening windows and/or doors is considered to bring in the good luck of the New Year. Switching on the lights for the night is considered to 'scare away' ghosts and spirits of misfortune and bring in good luck and fortune of the New Year. Sweets are eaten to ensure the consumer a "sweet" year. It is important to have the house completely clean from top to bottom before New Year's Day for good luck in the coming year. Some believe that what happens on the first day of the New Year reflects the rest of the year to come. Wear a new pair of slippers that are bought before the New Year, because it means to step on the people who gossip about you. The night before the New Year, bathe yourself in pomelo leaves and some say that you will be healthy for the rest of the New Year.

坏运气

人们认为买鞋会带来坏运气。因为"鞋"与普通话中"邪恶"的"邪"同音。买裤也会带来坏运气，因为"裤"与"苦"谐音。不宜洗头，洗头可能洗去自己的好运气。新年第一天不能扫地，因为它将扫除财富和运气。新年前几天谈论死亡也被视为不吉利。买书也会运气不好，因为"书"与"输"谐音。避免穿黑色和白色的衣服，因为黑色是坏运气的象征，而白色则是传统葬礼的颜色。

Bad Luck

Buying a pair of shoes is considered bad luck amongst some Chinese. The word "shoes" is a homophone for the word for "rough" in Cantonese, or "evil" in Mandarin. Buying a pair of pants is considered bad luck. The word "pants" (kù) is a homophone for the word for "bitter" in Chinese. Washing your hair is also considered to be washing away one's own luck. Sweeping the floor is usually forbidden on the first day, as it will sweep away the good fortune and luck for the New Year. Talking about death is inappropriate for the first few days of Chinese New Year, as it is considered inauspicious as well. Buying books is bad luck because the word for "book" is a homonym to the word "lose". Avoid clothes in black and white, as black is a symbol of bad luck, and white is a traditional funeral color.

15 天的庆祝活动

农历新年的第一天是接天神和地神的日子。很多人新年第一天戒肉，因为人们认为这将保佑他们永远幸福地生活。

第二天是祭拜祖先和众神的日子。这天人们对狗特别友善，会让狗吃得好好的，因为这天是狗的生日。

第三和第四天是女婿拜见岳父岳母的日子。

第五天人们待在家里接财神。这一天不拜访家人和朋友，因为会使双方运气不好。

第六到第十天，可以自由拜访亲戚朋友，也可以去寺庙祈求好运和健康。

15 Days of Celebration

The first day of the Lunar New Year is "the welcoming of the gods of the heavens and earth". Many people abstain from meat on the first day of the New Year because it is believed that this will ensure long and happy lives for them.

On the second day, the Chinese pray to their ancestors as well as to all the gods. They are extra kind to dogs and feed them well as it is believed that the second day is the birthday of all dogs.

The third and fourth days are for the sons-in-laws to pay respect to their parents-in-law.

On the fifth day, people stay home to welcome the God of Wealth. No one visits families and friends on the fifth day because it will bring both parties bad luck.

On the sixth to the 10th day, the Chinese visit their relatives and friends freely. They also visit the temples to pray for good fortune and health.

新年第七天是农民展示他们的农产品的日子。农民用七种蔬菜酿酒来喝酒庆贺。第七天也是人们庆生的日子。吃面意味着长寿，吃生鱼意味着成功。

第八天人们会再吃一顿团圆饭，午夜向天公祈祷。

第九天是供奉玉皇大帝的日子。

第十天到第十二天，朋友和亲戚应邀共进晚餐。

吃了那么多丰盛的饭菜以后，第十三天人们只吃些简单的米粥和芥菜来清理肠胃系统。

第十四天为庆祝第十五天的元宵节作筹备工作。

The seventh day of the New Year is the day for farmers to display their produce. These farmers make a drink from seven types of vegetables to celebrate the occasion. The seventh day is also considered the birthday of human beings. Noodles are eaten to promote longevity and raw fish for success.

On the eighth day people have another family reunion dinner, and at midnight they pray to Tian Gong, the God of Heaven.

The ninth day is to make offerings to the Jade Emperor.

The 10th through the 12th are days that friends and relatives should be invited for dinner.

After so much rich food, on the 13th day you should have simple rice congee and mustard greens to cleanse the system.

The 14th day should be for preparations to celebrate the Lantern Festival which is to be held on the 15th night.

花灯节

农历一月的第十五天是花灯节。由于正月叫元月，古人称夜为宵，正月十五这天是新年第一次看到满月，所以正月十五这天也被称为元宵节。

根据中国传统，新年开始有皎洁的月亮挂在天空时，就会有数以千计的七彩灯笼挂出来供人欣赏。此时，人们会猜灯谜和吃元宵（糯米球），在欢乐的气氛中与家人团聚。

6世纪隋炀帝邀请来中国的大使看彩灯和节日表演。

7世纪唐朝初期，彩灯展持续三天。皇帝取消了宵禁令，允许人们日夜赏灯。中国很多诗歌都描述过这一幸福场景。

Lantern Festival

The 15th day of the 1st lunar month is the Chinese Lantern Festival because the first lunar month is called yuan-month and in the ancient times people called night Xiao. The 15th day is the first night to see a full moon. So the day is also called Yuan Xiao Festival in China.

According to the Chinese tradition, at the very beginning of a New Year, when there is a bright full moon hanging in the sky, there should be thousands of colorful lanterns hung out for people to appreciate. At this time, people will try to solve the puzzles on the lanterns and eat yuanxiao (glutinous rice ball) and get all their families united in the joyful atmosphere.

Until the Sui Dynasty in the sixth century, Emperor Yang invited envoys from other countries to China to see the colorful lighted lanterns and enjoy the gala performances.

By the beginning of the Tang Dynasty in the seventh century, the lantern displays would last three days. The emperor also lifted the curfew, allowing the people to enjoy the festive lanterns day and night. It is not difficult to find Chinese poems which describe this happy scene.

在宋代，节日当天，全国各大城市都开展庆祝活动，共持续五天。用多彩玻璃甚至玉石来做灯笼，并在灯笼上绘出民间故事中的人物。

然而，最盛大的元宵节庆祝活动发生在15世纪的早期，持续了十天。皇帝明成祖特此留出市区作为灯笼中心展区。因此今天的北京市仍然有个叫灯市口的地方。汉语中，灯意味着灯笼，市就是市场。这个地方成了白天售卖灯笼的市场和晚上漂亮灯展的舞台。

元宵节期间的公园简直就是灯笼的海洋！许多新设计的灯笼吸引着无数游客。最引人注目的灯笼是龙杆，它是一个金龙形状的灯笼，盘旋在一根27米高的杆上，从它的嘴里喷出烟花的场景是多么令人印象深刻！

In the Song Dynasty, the festival was celebrated for five days and the activities began to spread in many of the big cities in China. Colorful glass and even jade were used to make lanterns, with figures from folk tales painted on the lanterns.

However, the largest Lantern Festival celebration took place in the early part of the 15th century. The festivities continued for ten days. Emperor Chengzu had the downtown area set aside as a center for displaying the lanterns. Even today, there is a place in Beijing called Dengshikou. In Chinese, Deng means lantern and Shi is market. The area became a market where lanterns were sold during the day and a stage where beautiful lighted lanterns on display in the evening.

During the Lantern Festival, the park is literally an ocean of lanterns! Many new designs attract countless visitors. The most eye-catching lantern is the Dragon Pole. This is a lantern in the shape of a golden dragon, spiraling up a 27-meter-high pole, spewing fireworks from its mouth. It is quite an impressive sight!

除了娱乐和看灯笼，元宵节的另一个重要内容是吃一种由糯米粉制成的米球——元宵或汤圆。很明显，元宵因节日本身而得名。据说吃元宵的习俗起源于4世纪的东晋，并于唐、宋时期开始流行开来。

元宵的馅料或甜或咸。甜馅料有糖、胡桃、芝麻、桂花、玫瑰花瓣、甜的陈皮、豆沙或枣泥，可用一种或多种馅料来做。咸馅料往往用剁碎的肉和蔬菜。

中国北部和南部做元宵的方法也各不相同。南方各省的通常做法是把米团做成球形、打洞、加入馅料，然后用手滚动、封洞，使元宵平滑。在华北地区，有甜或不甜两种馅料。先把填料变成硬芯，在水中蘸一下，然后放入有干糯米粉的平底篮中，馅料就会粘上一层米粉，然后在水中蘸一下，再在米粉中滚一次，就像滚雪球一样，直到滚成所需的汤圆大小。

Besides entertainment and beautiful lanterns, another important part of the Lantern Festival, or Yuanxiao Festival is eating small dumpling balls made of glutinous rice flour. We call these balls Yuanxiao or Tangyuan. Obviously, they get the name from the festival itself. It is said that the custom of eating Yuanxiao originated during the Eastern Jin Dynasty in the fourth century, then became popular during the Tang and Song periods.

The fillings inside the dumplings or Yuanxiao are either sweet or salty. Sweet fillings are made of sugar, walnuts, sesame, osmanthus flowers, rose petals, sweetened tangerine peel, bean paste, or jujube paste. A single ingredient or any combination can be used as the filling. The salty variety is filled with minced meat, vegetables or a mixture.

The way to make Yuanxiao also varies between northern and southern China. The usual method followed in southern provinces is to shape the dough of rice flour into balls, make a hole, insert the filling, then close the hole and smooth out the dumpling by rolling it between your hands. In North China, sweet or non-sweet stuffing is the usual ingredient. The fillings are pressed into hardened cores, dipped lightly in water and rolled in a flat basket containing dry glutinous rice flour. A layer of the flour sticks to the filling, which is then again dipped in water and rolled a second time in the rice flour. And so it goes, like rolling a snowball, until the dumpling is the desired size.

清明节

清明节也称扫墓节，是在公历每年四月初四或初五，是中国二十四个节气之一。自该日起气温开始上升，降雨量增加，表明春天播种的黄金时刻到了，因此清明节与农业有密切关系。然而，它不只是一个季节的象征，同时也是人们祭拜死去的人、进行春游和其他活动的节日。

起源

据说清明节最初是为纪念春秋战国时期一个名为介子推的忠诚之士而成立的。介子推从他自己身上砍一块腿肉，烤了给当时被流放落魄避难、饥寒交迫的晋文公重耳吃。十九年后，晋文公复国了，把有过救命之恩的介子推忘了。有人提醒他后，他深感惭愧，并决定奖励介子推。然而，介子推和他的母亲躲进了绵山。为了找到介子推，晋文公下令大火烧山。后来发现介子推和他的母亲，紧紧搂住一棵大柳树，已经被活活烧死。为了纪念介子推，晋文公下令把介子推去世的这天（清明前一天）定为寒食节。第二年，晋文公上山祭拜介子推，发现山上那颗烧死的柳树复活成荫。于是下令寒食节后的那天为清明节。后来这两个节日合并成一个节日——清明节。

Qingming Festival

Qingming Festival, also known as Tomb-sweeping Day, which falls on either April 4th or 5th of the gregorian calendar, is one of the Chinese Twenty-four Solar Terms. From that date temperatures begin to rise and rainfall increases, indicating that it is the crucial time for plowing and sowing in the spring. Qingming Festival therefore has a close relationship with agriculture. However, it is not only a seasonal symbol; it is also a festival of paying respect to the dead, a spring outing, and other activities.

Origin

It is said that the Qingming Festival was originally held to commemorate a loyal man living in the Spring and Autumn Period, named Jie Zitui. Jie cut a piece of meat from his own leg in order to save his hungry lord who was forced to go into exile when the crown was in jeopardy. The lord came back to his position nineteen years later, and forgot Jie Zitui but later felt ashamed and decided to reward him. However, Jie had blocked himself up in a mountain with his mother. In order to find Jie, the lord ordered that the mountain should be set on fire. Later Jie was found burnt to death with his mother, holding tightly to a willow tree. In order to commemorate Jie, the lord ordered that the day Jie died was Hanshi (Cold Food) Festival—the day that only cold food could be eaten. The second year, when the lord went to the mountain to pray to Jie, he found willows revived, so he gave instructions that the day after Hanshi Festival was to be Qingming Festival. Later, the two festivals were combined as one—Qingming Festival.

传统习俗

清明节时，人们会开展许多不同的活动，其中最主要的是扫墓、春游和放风筝。这一天还有一些习俗如头上戴柳树枝圈和荡秋千，给人们增添了无穷的乐趣。

扫墓

扫墓从扫墓节得名那天起一直是最重要的习俗。扫墓和祭拜是怀念亲人的两个重要环节。人们以清除坟墓周围的杂草，添加新土的方式来表示对死去的人的关心。带上死去的人最喜欢的食物、酒和纸钱供奉他们。烧掉这些纸钱，希望逝者不缺钱用，并在逝者灵牌前叩头。

Traditional Customs

Qingming Festival is a time of many different activities, among which the main ones are tomb sweeping, taking a spring outing, and flying kites. Some other customs like wearing willow branches on the head and riding on swings have added infinite joy in past days.

Tomb Sweeping

Tomb sweeping is regarded as the most important custom in the Qingming Festival from which the name of Tomb-sweeping Day is got. Cleaning the tomb and paying respect to the dead person with offerings are the two important parts of remembering the past relatives. Weeds around the tomb are cleared away and fresh soil is added to show care of the dead. The dead person's favourite food and wine are taken to sacrifice to them, along with paper resembling money. This is all burned in the hope that the deceased are not lacking money. Kowtow before the tablets set up for the dead are made.

今天，由于火葬代替了土葬，城市的这些习俗已简化了。只送花给死去的亲戚和革命烈士。不管人们用何种方式表示对逝者的敬重，他们总会为逝者送上最真挚的祈祷。

Today, with cremation taking over from burying, the custom has been extremely simplified in cities. Only flowers are presented to the dead relatives and revolutionary martyrs. No matter how respect is shown, good prayers for the deceased are expressed.

春游

清明节不只是纪念死去的人的节日，同时也是适合人们出游的节日。3 月，大自然中的一切面貌全新，树木变绿，鲜花盛开，阳光明媚，是出游欣赏大自然美景的好时候。春游习俗的起源可以追溯到唐朝，随后历朝历代直至今日都有这一习俗。所以清明节期间到处可以看到游客。春游不仅能给人们带来生命的快乐，也能促进身心健康。

Spring Outing

Not only is it a day for commemorating the dead, it is also a festival for people to enjoy outing. During March, everything in nature takes on a new look, as trees turn green, flowers blossom, and the sun shines brightly. It is a fine time to go out and to appreciate the beautiful scenes of nature during the festival. This custom can be traced back to the Tang Dynasty and followed by each dynasty later till today. So visitors can be seen everywhere during the month of the festival. Spring outings not only add joy to life but also promote a healthy body and mind.

放风筝

放风筝是清明节期间为许多人所喜爱的活动。不仅白天有人放风筝，傍晚也有人放风筝。人们把小灯笼绑在风筝上或拉风筝的线上。风筝在天空中飞舞时，灯笼就像闪烁的星星，给夜间的天空添加一道独特的风景。节日放风筝最特别的一点是剪断拉风筝的绳，而让风筝在天空自由地飞翔。据说这样做可以消灭疾病，带来好运气。

总之，清明节是个独特的节日，伴随着人们祭拜逝者悲伤的眼泪和人们外出春游喜悦的笑声。

Flying Kites

Flying kites is an activity favored by many people during the Qingming Festival. Kites are not only flown during the day time but also in the evening. Little lanterns are tied to the kite or to the string that holds the kite. And when the kite is flying in the sky, the lanterns look like twinkling stars that add unique scenery to the sky during the night. What makes flying kites during this festival special is that people cut the string while the kite is in the sky to let it fly free. It is said this brings good luck and that diseases can be eliminated by doing this.

All in all, the Qingming Festival is an occasion of unique characteristics, integrating sorrowful tears to the dead with the continuous laughter from the spring outing.

龙舟节

龙舟节和龙舟赛正值农历五月第五天。夏至在6月21日左右，所以龙舟节就是指"端午节"。人们认为太阳和龙是阳性（月球和凤是阴性）。太阳和龙在这一天是一年中最有力的时候，于是便有了端午节赛龙舟的活动，农民也是从这一天开始忙于在水稻田里插秧。

Dragon Boat Festival

Dragon Boat Festival and Dragon boat racing traditionally coincide with the 5th day of the 5th Chinese lunar month. The Summer Solstice occurs around June 21 and is the reason why Chinese refer to their festival as "Duan Wu". Both the sun and the dragon are considered to be male (The moon and the mythical phoenix are considered to be female). The sun and the dragon are at their most potent during this time of the year, so cause for observing this through ritual celebrations such as dragon boat racing. It is also the time of farming year when rice seedlings must be transplanted in their paddy fields.

这个时节常有瘟疫和疾病发生，因为原始社会缺乏现代制冷设备和其他卫生设施，夏天高温易导致食物腐烂和疾病恶化。有一种习俗就是用红纸剪出五种有毒动物的形状的东西来防治这些瘟疫疾病。纸蛇、蜈蚣、蝎子、蜥蜴和蟾蜍，能引诱"妖魔鬼怪"，有时人们还把它们放在雕花木龙的嘴里。

人们崇拜龙的神性是为了避免不幸和灾难，并祈求降雨，因为农作物的生长和地里的生物成长都需要水，而神龙掌控着雨、季风和云。皇帝是"龙"或"天子"，中国人也称自己为"龙"，因为他们希望有龙一样的力量和生命力。与欧洲神话中龙被认为是邪恶和恶魔所不同的是，亚洲龙是有益的，仁慈的，因而值得崇拜而不是攻杀。

This season is also associated with pestilence and disease, due to the high summer temperatures which can lead to rot and deterioration for in primitive societies lacking modern refrigeration and sanitation facilities. One custom involves cutting shapes of the five poisonous or venomous animals out of red paper, so as to ward off these evils. The paper snakes, centipedes, scorpions, lizards and toads—those that supposedly lured "evil spirits"—where sometimes placed in the mouths of the carved wooden dragons.

Venerating the Dragon deity was meant to avert misfortune and calamity and encourage rainfall which is needed for the fertility of the crops and thus for the prosperity of an agrarian way of life. Celestial dragons were the controllers of the rain, the monsoon winds and the clouds. The Emperor was "The Dragon" or the "Son of Heaven", and Chinese people refer to themselves as "dragons" because of its spirit of strength and vitality. Unlike the dragons in European mythology which are considered to be evil and demonic, Asian dragons are regarded as wholesome and beneficent, and thus worthy of veneration, not slaying.

屈原

与龙舟节有关的是著名中国爱国诗人屈原凄凉的传奇故事。据说他是战国时期人，中国被划分为七个主要国家，这些国家彼此争夺霸权，军事阴谋达到空前程度。当时处在周朝即将结束的孔子生活的年代。据说，孙子的著名军事战略经典《孙子兵法》也是在这一时期所写。

屈原是战国时期南部楚国的大臣，政治上忠诚义胆，一心维护楚国的霸权，然而，一些小人嫉妒屈原的才能，视屈原为"眼中钉，肉中刺"，造谣诽谤屈原。最终楚王流放了最忠诚的谋士屈原。

Qu Yuan

The other main legend of Dragon Boat Festival concerns the poignant saga of a famous Chinese patriot poet named Qu Yuan. It is said that he lived in the pre-imperial Warring States Period. During this time the area today known as central China was divided into seven main states or kingdoms battling among themselves for supremacy with unprecedented heights of military intrigue. This was at the conclusion of the Zhou Dynasty period, which is regarded as China's classical age during which Kong Zi (Confucius) lived. Also, the author Sun Zi (Sun Tzu) is said to have written his famous classic on military strategy *The Art of War* during this era.

Qu Yuan is popularly regarded as a minister in one of the Warring State governments, the southern state of Chu, a champion of political loyalty and integrity, and eager to maintain the Chu state's autonomy and hegemony. The Chu king, however, fell under the influence of other corrupt, jealous ministers who slandered Qu Yuan as 'a sting in flesh'. So the fooled king banished Qu Yuan, his most loyal counselor.

据传说，屈原流放以后，开始了中国文学史上早期的诗歌创作，在作品中洋溢着对楚地楚风的眷恋和对其未来的担忧。他的知名诗歌集为《楚辞》，其中最广为人知的是《离骚》和《天问》。

公元前278年，当获知楚国即将被邻国（特别是秦国）毁灭之后，屈原背着一块大岩石涉水到今天的湖南省汨罗江自杀以抗议腐败的王朝。秦朝最终征服了其他六国，第一次统一了全国。"中国"一词起源于秦朝。

In Qu's exile, so goes the legend, he supposedly produced some of the greatest early poetry in

Chinese literature expressing his fervent love for his state and his deepest concern for its future. The collection of odes is known as the *Chuci* or *Songs of the South* (*Chu*). His most well known verses are the rhapsodic *Li Sao* or *Lament* and the fantastic *Tian Wen* or *Heavenly Questions*.

In the year 278 BC, upon learning of the upcoming devastation of his state from invasion by a neighboring Warring State (Qin in particular), Qu is said to have waded into the Miluo River in today's Hunan Province holding a great rock in order to commit ritual suicide as a form of protest against the corruption of the era. The Qin Dynasty or Chin Dynasty eventually conquered all of the other states and unified them into the first Chinese empire. The word "China" derives from Qin.

老百姓听说屈原自杀，赶紧乘渔船冲进河中拼命救屈原。他们击鼓，用桨泼水是为了使鱼和邪恶的灵魂远离他的身体（因而称为龙舟节）。后来人们在河里撒些米饭以防屈原饥饿。也有人说老百姓撒些米来喂鱼，以阻止鱼吞食诗人的身体。

然而，一天深夜，屈原的灵魂出现在他的朋友们面前，告诉他们撒给他的米饭被巨大的河龙截获。他要他的朋友们用丝绸把米饭包成三角形以避开河龙。这一传统食物就是大家熟知的粽子，是用树叶包糯米而成，而不是用丝绸包成。据说，为了纪念屈原，人们每年于他的死亡之日举行龙舟赛。

The common people, upon learning of Qu Yuan's suicide, rushed out on the water in their fishing boats to the middle of the river and tried desperately to save Qu Yuan. They beat drums and splashed the water with their paddles in order to keep the fish and evil spirits from his body (thus called Dragon Boat Festival). Later on, they scattered rice into the water to prevent him from suffering hunger. Another belief is that the people scattered rice to feed the fish, in order to prevent the fish from devouring the poet's body.

However, late one night, the spirit of Qu Yuan appeared before his friends and told them that the rice meant for him was being intercepted by a huge river dragon. He asked his friends to wrap their rice into three-cornered silk packages to ward off the dragon. This has been a traditional food ever since known as zongzi or sticky rice wrapped in leaves, although they are wrapped in leaves instead of silk. In commemoration of Qu Yuan it is said, people hold dragon boat races annually on the day of his death.

今天，世界各地在龙舟节这一天仍然举行龙舟赛来庆祝节日，但这一赛事至今仍然与香港和中国内地中南部地区的传统端午节有文化上的关联。

Today, dragon boat festivals continue to be celebrated around the world with dragon boat racing, although such events are still culturally associated with the traditional Chinese Tuen Ng Festival in Hong Kong (Cantonese Chinese dialect) or Duan Wu festival in south central mainland China (Mandarin Chinese dialect).

双七节

双七节是每年农历七月初七，是充满了浪漫的传统节日，经常在公历 8 月到来。

这个节日是在盛夏天气暖和、草木茂盛的时候。夜晚，当天空点缀着星星，人们可以看到银河系跨越南北。银河的两边各有一颗明亮的星星，从远处与对方相视。他们是牛郎和织女，关于他们，有一个代代相传的美丽的爱情故事。

很久很久以前，有个诚实、善良名叫牛郎的小伙。他还很小的时候他的父母就去世了。后来他被嫂嫂赶出了家。所以他独自一个人住，以放牧和耕作为生。一天，天上的织女爱上了他，偷偷下凡与他结婚。牛郎在地里耕种，织女在家织布。他们过着幸福的生活，并生了一男一女。不幸的是，天神发现了这件事，并下令要西宫的王母娘娘把织女带回来。

The Double Seventh Festival

The Double Seventh Festival, on the 7th day of the 7th lunar month, is a traditional festival full of romance. It often goes into August in the Gregorian calendar.

This festival is in mid-summer when the weather is warm and the grass and trees reveal their luxurious greens. At night when the sky is dotted with stars, people can see the Milky Way spanning from the north to the south. On each bank of it is a bright star, which sees each other from afar. They are the Cowherd and Weaver Maid, and about them there is a beautiful love story passed down from generation to generation.

Long, long ago, there was an honest and kind-hearted fellow named Niu Lang (Cowherd). His parents died when he was a child. Later he was driven out of his home by his sister-in-law. So he lived by himself herding cattle and farming. One day, a fairy from heaven Zhi Nv (Weaver Maid) fell in love with him and came down secretly to earth and married him. The cowherd farmed in the field and the Weaver Maid wove at home. They lived a happy life and gave birth to a boy and a girl. Unfortunately, the God of Heaven soon found out the fact and ordered the Queen Mother of the Western Heavens to bring the Weaver Maid back.

在天牛的帮助下，牛郎带着他的儿子和女儿飞上了天宫。在他正要赶上他的妻子时，王母取下了她的金簪在空中划了一下。一条汹涌的河流顿时出现在牛郎面前。牛郎织女被永远分隔在银河两岸，只能流泪而视。他们真诚的爱情感动了喜鹊，数以万计的喜鹊飞来搭成桥梁，使牛郎织女得以相见。最终也感动了王母娘娘，允许他们每年农历七月初七相见。因此他们的会见日称为"七夕"（双七）。

有学者认为双七节起源于汉代。东晋的历史文献中提到了这个节日，记录和描述了当天唐太宗和他的嫔妃盛大晚宴的情况。到宋朝和元朝时期，京城市场上出售七夕的物件，繁华的集市表明节日的特别含义。

With the help of celestial cattle, the Cowherd flew to heaven with his son and daughter. At the time when he was about to catch up with his wife, the Queen Mother took off one of her gold hairpins and made a stroke. One billowy river appeared in front of the Cowherd. The Cowherd and Weaver Maid were separated on the two banks forever and could only feel their tears. Their loyalty to love touched magpies, so tens of thousands of magpies came to build a bridge for the Cowherd and Weaver Maid to meet each other. The Queen Mother was eventually moved and allowed them to meet each year on the 7th of the 7th lunar month. Hence their meeting date has been called "Qi

Xi" (Double Seventh).

Scholars have shown the Double Seventh Festival originated from the Han Dynasty. Historical documents from the Eastern Jin Dynasty mention the festival, while records from the Tang Dynasty depict the grand evening banquet of Emperor Taizong and his concubines. By the Song and Yuan dynasties, special articles for the "Qi Xi" were seen being sold on markets in the capital. The bustling markets demonstrated the significance of the festival.

今天，中国农村地区仍然有一些七夕节的传统习俗，但城市的习俗已减弱或消失。然而，关于牛郎织女的传说已经在人们心中扎根。近年来，城市青年甚至把七夕节作为情人节来庆祝。因此，花店、酒吧和小商店店主很高兴，因为他们可以卖出更多的商品。

Today some traditional customs are still observed in rural areas of China, but have been weakened or diluted in urban cities. However, the legend of the Cowherd and Weaver Maid has taken root in the hearts of the people. In recent years, in particular, urban youths have celebrated it as Valentine's Day in China. As a result, owners of flower shops, bars and stores are full of joy as they sell more commodities for love.

中秋节

中秋节适逢农历八月十五日，通常在公历10月。

这一节日具有悠久的历史。在中国古代，皇帝在春天举行祭日，在秋天举行祭月仪式活动。周代的史书中已有"中秋"一词。后来贵族和文人在老百姓中开展这些仪式活动。当晚，他们在月下欣赏皎洁的满月，借月亮寄予相思和情感。唐朝时期，中秋节已定下来，到宋代成为更盛大的节日。到明朝和清朝时期，中秋节成了中国的一个重大节日。

有关节日的起源，传说是这样的：远古时候，天上的十个太阳晒焦了所有作物，人们的生活极其贫困。一个名叫后羿的人很担忧，他登上昆仑山顶，使出全身超人的力量，拉满弓，把九个多余的太阳一个又一个射下来。他命令最后一个太阳依照时间来升落。为此，他深受人们的爱戴，很多有理想的正直之人前来拜师习武。彭蒙就是其中的一个。

The Mid-Autumn Festival

The Mid-Autumn Festival falls on the 15th day of the 8th lunar month, usually in October in Gregorian calendar.

The festival has a long history. In ancient China, emperors followed the rite of offering sacrifices to the sun in spring and to the moon in autumn. Historical books of the Zhou Dynasty had had the word "Mid-Autumn". Later aristocrats and literary figures helped expand the ceremony to common people. They enjoyed the full, bright moon on that day, worshipped it and expressed their thoughts and feelings under it. By the Tang Dynasty, the Mid-Autumn Festival had been fixed, which became even grander in the Song Dynasty. In the Ming and Qing dynasties, it grew to be a major festival of China.

Folklore about the origin of the festival goes like this: In remote antiquity, there were ten suns rising in the sky, which scorched all crops and drove people into dire poverty. A hero named Hou Yi was much worried about this, he ascended to the top of the Kunlun Mountain, directing his superhuman strength to full extent, drew his extraordinary bow and shot down the nine superfluous suns one after another. He also ordered the last sun to rise and set according to time. For this reason, he was respected and loved by the people and lots of people of ideals and integrity came to him to learn martial arts from him. A person named Peng Meng lurked in them.

后羿有个美丽善良的妻子，叫嫦娥。一天，后羿到昆仑山访友求道，巧遇由此经过的西王母，便向西王母求得一包不死药。据说，服下此药，能即刻升天成仙。然而，后羿舍不得撇下妻子，只好暂时把不死药交给嫦娥珍藏，嫦娥将药藏进梳妆台的百宝盒里，不料被彭孟看到了。

有一天，当后羿带领众人出去打猎，他走后不久，彭孟手持宝剑闯入内宅后院，威逼嫦娥交出不死药。嫦娥知道自己不是彭孟的对手，危急之时她当机立断，转身打开百宝盒，拿出不死药一口吞了下去。嫦娥吞下药，身子立刻飘离地面，冲出窗外，向天上飞去。彭孟则逃跑了。

Hou Yi had a beautiful and kindhearted wife named Chang E. One day on his way to the Kunlun Mountain to call on friends, he ran upon the Empress of Heaven Wangmu who was passing by. Empress Wangmu presented to him a parcel of elixir, by taking which, it was said, one would ascend immediately to heaven and become a celestial being. Hou Yi, however, hated to part with his wife. So he gave the elixir to Chang E to treasure for the time being. Chang E hid the parcel in a treasure box at her dressing table when, unexpectedly, it was seen by Peng Meng.

One day when Hou Yi led his disciples to go hunting, Peng Meng, with sword in hand, rushed into the inner chamber and forced Chang E to hand over the elixir. Aware that she was unable to defeat Peng Meng, Chang E made a prompt decision at that critical moment. She turned round to open her treasure box, took up the elixir and swallowed it in one gulp. As soon as she swallowed the elixir her body floated off the ground, dashed out of the window and flew towards heaven. Peng Meng escaped.

当后羿天黑回到家中时，从女仆那里知道发生了什么事。他忍住悲伤，抬头看着夜晚的天空，叫唤着他心爱的妻子的名字。令他吃惊的是，他发现月亮特别清晰明亮，有一个摇曳的影子像是他的妻子。他尽全力去追月亮，但他向前跑，月亮则向后退；他向后退，月亮也折了回来。后羿始终追不到月亮。

后羿日夜想念着他的妻子，他在嫦娥喜爱的后花园搭起了一个香坛。他把嫦娥最爱吃的糖果和新鲜水果放在香坛上。他眷恋着月宫中的嫦娥，隔空举行纪念仪式。

人们听说嫦娥变成了仙女后，他们在月光下搭起香坛，祈求善良的嫦娥好运平安。从那时起人们便有了拜月的习俗。

When Hou Yi returned home at dark, he knew from the maidservants what had happened. Overcome with grief, Hou Yi looked up into the night sky and called out the name of his beloved wife when, to his surprise, he found that the moon was especially clear and bright and on it there was a swaying shadow that was exactly like his wife. He tried his best to chase after the moon. But as he ran, the moon retreated; as he withdrew, the moon came back. He could not get to the moon at all.

Thinking of his wife day and night, Hou Yi then had an incense table arranged in the back garden that Chang E loved. Putting on the table sweetmeats and fresh fruits Chang E enjoyed most, Hou Yi held at a distance a memorial ceremony for Chang E who was sentimentally attached to him in the palace of the moon.

When people heard of the story that Chang E had turned into a celestial being, they arranged the incense table in the moonlight one after another and prayed kindhearted Chang E for good fortune and peace. From then on the custom of worshiping the moon spread among the people.

不同的地方习俗不同，但都是对美好生活的热爱和渴望。人们在这一天赏月和吃月饼。每年农历 15 日这天，月亮看上去又圆又大又明亮。人们选择八月十五日庆祝是因为这季节农作物和水果都成熟了，天气宜人。中秋节这天，所有的家人或朋友来到户外，把食物放在桌子上，仰望天空，探讨人生。这是多么美妙的时刻！

People in different places follow various customs, but all show their love and longing for a better life. Today people will enjoy the full moon and eat moon cakes on that day. The moon looks extremely round, big and bright on the 15th day of each lunar month. People selected the August 15 to celebrate because it is a season when crops and fruits are all ripe and the weather is pleasant. On the Mid-Autumn Festival, all family members or friends meet outside, putting food on tables and looking up at the sky while talking about life. How splendid a moment it is!

重阳节

重阳节在每年农历九月初九。在中国，数字"9"属阳（男性属阳，女性属阴）。九月份的第九天有两个属阳的数字，"重"在汉语中是"双"的意思，重阳节因此而得名。节日期间，人们吃重阳糕、喝菊花酒、登山和欣赏菊花等。

关于重阳节的传说：

与其他节日一样，重阳节也有自己的传奇故事。据说，东汉时期，一个栖居在汝河的恶魔传播疾病、蹂躏百姓。一个名为恒景的年轻人的父亲死于恶魔的魔法。为了消灭恶魔，恒景长途跋涉找到一位仙人教他降妖剑术以驱逐恶魔。

Chongyang (Double Ninth) Festival

Held on the 9th day of the 9th lunar month, Chongyang Festival is also called Double Ninth Festival. In Chinese, nine is regarded as the number of Yang (which means masculine as opposed to Yin which is feminine). The ninth day of the ninth month is the day that has two Yang numbers, and 'chong' in Chinese means double which is how the name Chongyang was created. It is a festival during which people eat Chongyang cake, drink chrysanthemum wine, climb mountains, and pay homage to chrysanthemums.

Legend about the Festival:

Just as other Chinese festivals have their own unique story, so does the Chongyang Festival. It is said that, during the Eastern Han Dynasty, a devil inhabited the Ru River which caused disease in the neighbouring people. The parent of a young man, named Hengjing, died because of the devil's magic. In order to rid the people of the devil, Hengjing went through extraordinary lengths to find an immortal to teach him swordsmanship in order to expel the devil.

阴历 9 月初八这天，神仙告诉恒景第二天魔鬼会出现，他可以回去驱除恶魔，祛除疾病了。于是恒景拿着一袋茱萸和一些菊花酒，回到他的家乡。农历九月初九的早上，恒景带领所有的村民来到了附近的一座山上，发给每人一片茱萸叶，一盅菊花酒，做好了降魔的准备。中午，瘟魔冲出汝河，但是瘟魔刚扑到山下，突然闻到阵阵茱萸奇香和菊花酒气，便戛然止步，脸色突变。这时恒景手持降妖宝剑追下山来，几个回合就把瘟魔刺死剑下。

从此，九月初九登高、喝菊花酒、插茱萸避疫的风俗流传下来。

On the eighth day of the ninth lunar month, the immortal told Hengjing that the next day the devil would appear and he was to go back to get rid of the devil and the disease. Taking a bag of dogwood and some chrysanthemum wine, Hengjing returned to his hometown. In the morning of the ninth day of the ninth lunar month, Hengjing led all the villagers who were each holding a piece of dogwood leaf and a cup of Chrysanthemum to the nearest mountain. At noon, when the devil came out from the Ru River, the devil suddenly stopped because of the fragrance emitted from the dogwood and the chrysanthemum wine. At that moment Hengjing used the sword to battle the devil for a few rounds and won.

Since then the customs of climbing mountains, drinking chrysanthemum wine and holding onto dogwood on the ninth day of the ninth month have become popular.

习俗：

重阳节有吃重阳糕和喝菊花酒的传统。欣赏美丽的菊花和登山为节日增添了欢乐的气氛。

重阳糕是一种有上下两层，中间夹有坚果和枣的糕点。由于汉语中"高"和"糕"谐音，人们认为登高与吃重阳糕相同，吃重阳糕后个人事业有所进展，因为"高"意味着取得进步，上升到更高层次。

喝菊花酒是重阳节的不可或缺的一个环节。人们认为菊花是一种有抗毒素作用的花，可以驱邪。人们常常认为喝菊花酒后可以治愈各种疾病，还可以预防各种灾害。

Customs:

During the Chongyang Festival, Chongyang cake and chrysanthemum wine is the traditional cuisine. Climbing mountains and admiring beautiful chrysanthemums are interesting events that add to the festival creating a joyous atmosphere.

Chongyang Cake is a kind of steamed cake having two layers with nuts and jujube sandwiched between them. Since cake in Chinese is pronounced 'gao' meaning high, people consider climbing a high mountain to be the same as eating Chongyang cake. Also personal progress is thought to be made in the following days after eating the cake, for 'high' means that one makes improvements moving to a higher level.

Drinking Chrysanthemum wine is an indispensable part of Chongyang Festival. Chrysanthemums are regarded as a kind of flower having the function of an antitoxin and can drive the evil away. People often think that by drinking chrysanthemum wine, all kinds of diseases and disasters can be cured and prevented.

据说登高山可以预防疾病。唐代很多诗人的著名诗歌中描述了登山的情景和登山的感觉。现在，家人、亲戚或好朋友聚在一起爬山，欣赏美丽的风景，彼此分享节日的快乐。

重阳节是菊花盛开的时节，在公园内欣赏各种菊花能令人赏心悦目。公园举行盛大的菊花展览吸引着无数游客。

以前人们还有佩戴茱萸的习俗。人们认为茱萸是一种可以消除灾难的植物。以前，妇女和儿童喜欢在身上戴一个茱萸香囊。然而，这种习俗目前不是很受欢迎。

It is said that by ascending to a high mountain, diseases could be prevented. Many widely-known poems were created by poets in the Tang Dynasty describing the scene and feeling of mountain climbing. Now, family, relatives or good friends gather to climb mountains to enjoy the beautiful scenery and share happiness of the holiday with each other.

As chrysanthemums blossom during the Chongyang Festival, it is a pleasure to admire the various chrysanthemums in parks. Grand chrysanthemum exhibitions are held in big parks that attract numerous visitors.

The custom as wear dogwood—a kind of plant that can dispel the disaster in people's values—was popular in the old days. Women and children like to wear a fragrant pouch with dogwood sewed in. However, this custom is currently not very popular at all.

重阳节的新含义：

由于数字"9"与"久"谐音，意味着长久，所以人们赋予了长寿之意。1989 年，重阳节被指定为老人节，要尊重长者，让老年人开心。很多公司组织退休的老人到户外去爬山或郊游。家人也会陪伴着他们的长辈，在自然美景中放松心情，同时希望他们健康和幸福。

New Meaning of Chongyang Festival：

As nine is pronounced 'jiu' meaning long in Chinese, so people endow the word jiu with the meaning of longevity with a person's life. In the year of 1989, Chongyang Festival was designated as Senior's Day—a day to respect the elderly and to let them enjoy themselves. Many companies organize groups where retired people can go out to climb mountains or on other outings. Members of a family also accompany their elders to have a relaxing day in a natural setting while wishing health and happiness upon them.

冬至节

早在 2 500 年前，大约是春秋战国时期，中国人用日晷观测太阳的运动确定了冬至日。它是国内最早的二十四节气，时间是每年公历 12 月 21 或 22 日。

这一天，北半球白天最短和夜间最长。冬至后，白天将变得越来越长。古人认为，冬至日后阳性变得越来越强，所以应该庆祝。

冬至在汉代成为节日。在唐宋时期蓬勃发展。汉族人把冬至当作"冬节"，官方会组织庆祝活动。这一天，官员和老百姓放假，驻扎在边塞的军队也休息，商务和旅行活动停止。亲戚和朋友相互赠送美味的食物。唐宋两代，冬至这一天，人们会祭天祭祖，皇帝会去郊区祭天；老百姓祭祀他们已故的父母或其他亲属。清朝甚至有"冬至与春节一样正式"的记录，表明了对这一天的高度重视。

Chinese Winter Solstice Festival

As early as 2, 500 years ago, about the Spring and Autumn Period, China had determined the point of Winter Solstice by observing movements of the sun with a sundial. It is the earliest of the 24 seasonal division points. The time will be each December 21 or 22 according to the Gregorian calendar.

The Northern hemisphere on this day experiences the shortest daytime and longest nighttime. After the Winter Solstice, days will become longer and longer. As ancient Chinese thought, the yang, or muscular, positive things will become stronger and stronger after this day, so it should be celebrated.

The Winter Solstice became a festival during the Han Dynasty and thrived in the Tang and Song dynasties. The Han people regarded Winter Solstice as a "Winter Festival", so officials would organize celebrating activities. On this day, both officials and common people would have a rest. The army was stationed in, frontier fortresses closed and business and traveling stopped. Relatives and friends presented to each other delicious food. In the Tang and Song dynasties, the Winter Solstice was a day to offer sacrifices to Heaven and ancestors. Emperors would go to suburbs to worship the Heaven; while common people offered sacrifices to their deceased parents or other relatives. The Qing Dynasty even had the record that "Winter Solstice is as formal as the Spring Festival", showing the great importance attached to this day.

在中国北方的一些地区，人们在这一天要喝饺子汤，而其他一些地方的居民则吃饺子，据说这样做会使他们在即将到来的冬天不会挨冻。但在中国南方一些地区，全家人会坐在一起吃红豆沙和糯米饭以驱走魔鬼和其他邪恶的东西。有些地方，人们吃汤圆，这是一种糯米粉做的有馅料的小面球。冬至汤圆可以用作祭祀祖先或给朋友和亲戚的礼物。台湾人甚至保持用九层糕点祭祀祖先的习俗。他们用糯米粉把糕点做成鸡、鸭、龟、猪、牛或羊的形状，放入九层锅上蒸。中国传统中所有这些动物都象征着吉祥。同姓氏或同宗族的人们聚在祖庙里按年龄顺序祭祀祖先。祭祀仪式后会举行一场盛大的宴会。

In some parts of Northern China, people eat dumpling soup on this day; while residents of some other places eat dumplings, saying doing so will keep them from frost in the upcoming winter. But in parts of South China, the whole family will get together to have a meal made of red-bean and glutinous rice to drive away ghosts and other evil things. In other places, people also eat *tangyuan*, a kind of stuffed small dumpling ball made of glutinous rice flour. The Winter Solstice rice dumplings could be used as sacrifices to ancestors, or gifts for friends and relatives. The Taiwan people even keep the custom of offering nine-layer cakes to their ancestors. They make cakes in the shape of chicken, duck, tortoise, pig, cow or sheep with glutinous rice flour and steam them on nine different layers of a pot. These animals all signify auspiciousness in Chinese tradition. People of the same surname or family clan gather at their ancestral temples to worship their ancestors in age order. After the sacrificial ceremony, there is always a grand banquet.

口述题

1. 你最喜欢的节日是什么？有什么特殊的习俗？
2. 你了解这个节日的由来吗？

Questions

1. What's your favorite festival? What are the special customs?
2. Do you know the origin of the festival?

学习网站

1. 中国民俗网（http://www.chinesefolklore.com/）
2. CHINA CULTURE TOUR （https://www.chinaculturetour.com/culture/chinese-festivals.htm）

第十五章 四大发明和万里长城

Chapter 15 Four Great Inventions and the Great Wall

第一节 四大发明

Section 1 Four Great Inventions

我们都知道，中国是一个伟大的东方国家。它是世界上历史最源远流长的文明古国之一。中国拥有世界上连续使用最久的书面语言系统，同时也是许多重大发明的起源地，如"中国古代四大发明"。

中国悠久的历史已见证了极其重要的发明的出现，最著名的有火药、造纸术、活字印刷术和指南针。用罗杰·培根的话说，它们改变了世界一切事物的原貌和状态。

As we all know, China is a great oriental nation. It has one of the world's longest history and continuous civilizations. China also has the world's longest continuously used written language system, and is the source of many major inventions, such as the "four great inventions of Ancient China".

China's long history has seen some extremely important inventions emerge, most noticeably gunpowder, paper making, movable type and the compass, which, in the words of Roger Bacon, changed the whole appearance and status of things in the world.

造纸术

中国是世界第一个正式造纸的国家。已在甘肃省、陕西省西安市等地和新疆发现了西汉时期的造纸。东汉蔡伦改进了造纸术。他用植物纤维如树皮、绳索、破布和废旧渔网作为造纸原料。105 年，蔡伦把他监制的第一批纸呈献给汉皇帝，汉武帝非常高兴，当即把纸命名为"蔡侯纸"。1974 年甘肃省武威县发现了东汉时期纸张，上面的文字还清晰可辨。这种纸薄、软、光滑、纹理紧，是迄今所发现的最精致、最古老的纸。

Papermaking

China was the first country in the world to make proper paper. Paper made during the Western Han Dynasty has been found in Gansu Province, Xi'an and other places in Shanxi

Province as well as Xinjiang. A further development of paper is credited to Cai Lun of the Eastern Han. He used plant fiber such as tree bark, bits of rope, rags and worn-out fishing nets as raw materials. In 105, Cai presented the first batch of paper made under his supervision to the Han emperor, who was so delighted that he named the material "Marquis Cai's paper". Eastern Han Dynasty paper found in Wuwei, Gansu, in 1974 carried words which were still clearly decipherable. Thin, soft, and with a smooth finish and tight texture, this paper is the most refined and oldest paper discovered to date.

纸发明以前，古人把文字刻在陶器、兽骨、石头、青铜器上，或把它们写在竹条或木条和丝绸织物上。但是这些材料要么太重，要么太昂贵不宜广泛使用。纸的发明和使用使书写材料发生了革命，为日后印刷术的发明铺平了道路。

Before paper was invented, the ancient Chinese carved characters on pottery, animal bones and stones, cast them on bronzes, or wrote them on bamboo or wooden strips and silk fabric. These materials, however, were either too heavy or too expensive for widespread use. The invention and use of paper brought about a revolution in writing materials, paving the way for the invention of printing technology in the years to come.

火药

自秦汉时期开始，炼金术士用硫黄、硝石和其他材料来炼丹，他们从意外爆炸的现象中得到了启示。之后经过反复实践，他们发现了火药的配方。三国时期，魏国一个名叫马钧的聪明技师把火药用纸包扎做成爆竹以娱乐，为火药应用打开了大门。

火药的发明无疑是中世纪中国最重要的成就之一。9世纪发现用硝石、硫黄和碳制造火药的配方。事实上，3世纪葛洪的书中记录了制作一种可以燃烧的混合物的过程。唐朝以后，火药发展很快，人们已经能使用火药制成简单的手榴弹用弹射器弹射。1126年，兵部侍郎李刚记录了他是如何下令开封的防卫队向入侵的女真部落"发射大炮"的，使入侵者造成重大伤亡。

火药的发明与冶炼业的先进工艺有密切关系。

Gunpowder

Since the Qin and Han dynasties, alchemists have ever used sulfur, saltpeter and other items to make pills of immortality and got inspiration from the phenomenon of the accidental explosion. Then after repeated practice, they found the formula of gunpowder. During the Three Kingdoms Period, there was a smart technician named Ma Jun in the state of Wei, who made firecrackers for entertainment with gunpowder wrapped in paper, and opened the door to the gunpowder application.

The invention of gunpowder was no doubt one of the most significant achievements of the Middle Ages in China. The correct prescription for making gunpowder with saltpeter, sulphur and carbon was probably discovered in the ninth century. In fact, in his book, Ge Hong in the third century records the procedures for making a kind of mixture that could be ignited. After the Tang Dynasty, things took a much faster course as gunpowder was already used in simple hand-grenades which were thrown by a catapult. In 1126, Li Gang, a local official, recorded how he ordered the defenders of the city of Kaifeng to "fire cannons" at the invading Nvzhen tribal people, inflicting heavy casualties on the invaders.

The invention of gunpowder had a close relationship with the advanced ancient workmanship of smelting industry.

活字印刷术

在 11 世纪 40 年代，北宋毕昇基于印刷术，利用唐朝的雕版发明了活字印刷术，迎来了印刷史上的一次重大革命。

毕昇的活字印刷术包括四个过程：做活字、排版、上墨印刷和拆板。根据《梦溪笔谈》记载，毕昇在方形的黏土上雕刻单个汉字，然后在火上烤干。排版一篇文章时，他将大铁框放在一块大铁板上，并在框内排字。可以边印一版，边排另一版。

印完一版以后，把活字取下来存储以备将来使用。活字印刷在印刷史上有非常重要的位置，因为后来的木活字、铜活字和铅活字都是在黏土活字印刷的基础上发展起来的。毕昇发明的活字印刷术比欧洲早四百多年。

Movable Type

On the basis of printing, using carved blocks in the Tang Dynasty, Bi Sheng of the Northern Song Dynasty invented movable type printing in the 1040s, which ushered in a major revolution in the history of printing.

Bi Sheng's printing consisted of four processes: making the types, composing the text, printing and retrieving the movable types. According to *Dream Stream Essays*, Bi Sheng carved individual characters on squares of sticky clay, then baked them to make clay type pieces. When composing a text, he put a large iron frame on a piece of iron board and arranged the words within the frame. While one plate was being printed, another plate could be composed.

After printing, the movable types were taken away and stored for future use. Movable type printing has a very important position in the history of printing, for all later printing methods such as wooden type, copper type and lead type printing invariably developed on the basis of movable clay types. Bi Sheng created movable type printing more than four hundred years earlier than it was invented in Europe.

指南针

最早的指南针非常复杂。南宋时期有三或四层方向的指南针，后来出现了七或八层方向的指南针。方向的读数因古时地球磁场的变化或十天干和十二地支不同的记法而不同，

也与风水大师的神秘性相关。后来，人们发明了船用罗盘以满足海上航行时寻找方向的需要。

指南鱼

北宋时期的文献中有关于"指南鱼"的记载。这种方向指向设备是把薄钢板切成鱼的形状在地磁场中加以磁化。鱼尾磁化成地理北极，因而尾巴指向地磁南极而鱼头指向地磁北极。把鱼放入水中，它的头指向南方。

The Compass

The earliest compass was very complicated. In the Southern Song Dynasty, there were compasses with three or four layers of directions and later appeared compasses with seven or eight layers of directions. The accumulation of directions was due to the change of the Earth's magnetic filed in ancient times or the different accounts of the ten Heavenly Stems and the Twelve Earthly Branches. It also had something to do with the mysterious nature of Fengshui master's trade. Later, the simple and clear mariner's compass was created to meet the direction-finding need of marine navigation.

The South-Pointing Fish

"The south-pointing fish" was recorded in the documents of the Northern Song Dynasty. Such direction-pointing device is a thin steel plate cut into the shape of a fish magnetized in the geomagnetic field. The tail of the fish is magnetized in the geological direction of the North Pole, thus the tail has the south magnetic pole and the head of the fish has the north magnetic pole. When put into the water, the floating fish has its head pointing to the south.

指南龟

"指南龟"是南宋陈元靓设计的。它是一只木头雕刻的乌龟，肚子里插上一小块磁铁。从尾部插入一根钢针与磁铁相连。乌龟用竹钉支撑着。受磁场的影响，乌龟指向南方。

司南

司南是春秋战国时期发明的中国最早的指向南北方向的设备。"司"一词意味着"指向"，"南"是指"南方"。早在两千多年前，中国人发现山上有一种石头有磁性，他们把它叫做"磁石"。他们把石头抛光，凿成长柄勺形状，放在刻有图案表明方向的光滑青铜板镜上。板镜上的磁性长柄勺停止转动时，长柄勺的柄将指向正北方，另一端则指向正南方。

The South-Pointing Turtle

"The south-pointing turtle" was designed by Chen Yuanliang of the Southern Song Dynasty. It is a turtle carved out of wood that has a small slip of magnet inside its stomach. A steel needle is inserted from the tail and connects with the magnet. The turtle is supported by bamboo nails. Under the influence of a magnetic field, the turtle points to the south.

Si Nan

Si Nan is China's earliest south-north direction-pointing device invented in the Spring and

Autumn and Warring States Period. The word "Si" means "pointing to" and "Nan" means "the South". As early as more than 2,000 years ago, the Chinese discovered that a type of mountain stone was magnetic and they called it "magnetic stone". The stone was polished and chiseled into the shape of a dipper, which was placed on a mirror-smooth bronze board carved with patterns indicating directions. When the magnetic dipper on the board stops turning, the handle of the dipper will point to the exact south, with the other end pointing to the exact north.

指南针结构简单，后来逐渐变复杂，最后又被简化，应用于海上导航。在它的帮助下，人类终于征服了大海，指南针随着海浪踏遍全世界，促进了中国和世界航海业的发展。

The compass body was first made simple, then complicated and finally simple enough for application in navigation. With the help of it, human beings finally made their first stride in conquering the sea, while the compass itself was brought to all over the world along with the sea waves, significantly driving the development of navigation in both China and the world.

中国古代的四大发明无论对中国还是对世界都是非常重要的，因为它们标志着中国古代先进的科学和技术，对人类的文明和发展的巨大影响。

The Four Great Inventions of ancient China are very important for both China and the world, for they are the signs of ancient China's advanced science and technology and have tremendous effects on human civilization and development.

第二节　中国万里长城

Section 2　Chinese Great Wall

中国长城曾经是抵御北方游牧民族联盟入侵的防御工事。总长 10 000 多英里，所以它被冠名为万里长城。长城的修筑可追溯到春秋时期的齐国，当时是位于今天山东省东北地区最强大的国家，建了中国第一段长城，随后，秦国、赵国和燕国都建了长城以捍卫边界领土不被北方少数民族侵占。今天的长城主要属于明朝建的长城。长城最著名的部分如八达岭长城、居庸关长城、司马台长城等主要是明朝建造或重建的。因此明朝长城就是我们今天谈论的长城。长城从中国西部的嘉峪关开始，到中国东北辽宁省的虎山。长共 8 851.8 公里，平均高度为 6~7 米，宽度为 4~5 米。中国长城、西安兵马俑和北京紫禁城是中国的象征和中国古代历史的见证。中国长城也被视为世界上人类第八大奇迹，与埃及金字塔齐名。今天，中国长城已经被写入世界文化遗产名录。

Chinese Great Wall used to be the military defense project specially constructed for turning against the invasion of northern horde nationality alliance. The total length is over 10,000 miles, so it is famously called Wan Li Chang Cheng. Great Wall Construction traces back to the period of Spring and Autumn when Qi State, a most powerful state located in today's northeast area of Shandong Province, built China's first section of Great Wall, subsequently, Great Wall of Qin

State, Great Wall of Zhao State and Great Wall of Yan State were built mainly for defending their areas from exterior invasion from northern minorities. Today, the remainders of Great Wall chiefly belong to Great Wall built in Ming Dynasty. The world-famous sections of Great Wall available today such as Badaling Great Wall, Juyongguan Great Wall, Simatai Great Wall are mostly constructed or rebuilt in Ming Dynasty. Hence Ming Dynasty Great Wall is no other than what we talk about at present. Great Wall starts from Jiayuguan Pass in western China to Hushan Mountain in Liaoning Province, Northeast China. The Great Wall in total is 8,851.8 kilometers long and the average height is 6 or 7 meters and its width is 4 or 5 meter. Chinese Great Wall together with Xi'an Terracotta Army and Beijing Forbidden City has been accepted as the symbol of China as well as the witness of Chinese Ancient History. In the world, Chinese Great Wall is also regarded as the Eighth Miracle of Humankind and as famous as Egyptian Pyramid. Today, Chinese Great Wall has been written into the World Cultural Heritage List.

从历史上看，中国的长城发挥着防御的作用，这作用在秦朝和明朝更为突出。今天，长城已成为展现中国古代历史的博物馆。此外，中国长城与许多感人故事也密切相关，如孟姜女哭长城和秦始皇鞭打灵山的故事。在某种程度上今天中国长城在防止森林砍伐和抵御沙尘暴上仍然发挥着重要作用，同时它无疑也是重要的旅游资源。今天，爬长城已成为一种时尚，能否爬完全程甚至成为检验你是不是真正好汉的标准。因为毛主席曾说过：不到长城非好汉。由于世界变迁和全球和平，中国长城从防御工事戏剧性地转变为文化景点。

Historically, Great Wall of China played the role of defense, which was more vivid in Qin Dynasty and Ming Dynasty. Today, Great Wall has been the museum displaying the ancient history of China. Also, Chinese Great Wall is also closely connected with many touching stories such as Meng Jiang Nv's Heartbreaking Story and Emperor Qin Shi Huang's Whip of Driving Mountains. Chinese Great Wall today is also playing the important role in defending the deforestation and sandstorm to some extent. It is undoubtedly also the important tourist resources. Today, Climbing up Great Wall becomes a fashion, even a spirit to check whether you are a true hero or not. Because Chairman Mao used to say: You're not a true hero if you haven't got up to the Great Wall. From the defensive role to today's cultural part, Chinese Great Wall has a dramatic change thanks to the change of the world and the peaceful globe.

八达岭长城的历史

传统上，八达岭长城是重要的军事战略基地。春秋战国时期修建长城以防御北方民族南侵。今天，八达岭长城仍有城墙和堡垒残余。八达岭山是有重要战略地位的山关，高峰星罗棋布于军都山。"八达岭"意思是通过这座山，你可以到达中国的任何地方，它也是这一地区的最高峰。明代花了八十多年的时间建筑八达岭长城以加强中国北部的防御。明朝还委派戚继光将军成功带领他的军队来指挥和处理长城防御事务，击退日本军的侵略。

从历史上看，八达岭长城是居庸关的保护口。八达岭和南门之间有 20 公里长的山沟，称为"关沟"，居庸关就位于此。八达岭最高点有两个高峰，从这可以看见一条狭长的山沟。从这里往下看，地形非常险峻。所以，居庸关只是一个堡垒，虽然雄伟，但真正的长城是八达岭。

History of Badaling Great Wall

Traditionally, Badaling Great Wall is the important military strategic base. In the time of Spring and Autumn Period and Warring States Period, the Great Wall was built for fighting against the northern ethnic groups' southward invasion. Today Badaling Great Wall still has the remnants of walls and forts. Badaling Mountain is a mountain pass of the strategically important and high peaks dotted Jundoushan Mountain. Badaling, means the mountain by which you can go to everywhere in China, is also the highest in the area. In the Ming Dynasty, it took over eighty years to build the Badaling section to intensify the defensive shield of northern China. The Ming army also appointed General Qi Jiguang, who had successful led his army division to repel the invading Japanese, to command and handle the defense affairs in the Great Wall.

Historically, Badaling Great Wall has been the protecting gate of Juyongguan Pass. A 20-kilometer long gap, called "Pass' Gap" is located between Badaling and the southern gate, and Juyongguan Pass is here. At the highest point of Badaling, there are two tall peaks, with which a narrow gap is being seen. If looking down from here, the dangerous topography is truly overwhelming. So, Juyongguan Pass is only a fort, though majestic, the real Great Wall is Badaling.

八达岭长城见证了中国的很多历史事件。暴君秦始皇抵达碣石，途经八达岭和大同，到达陕西省西安附近的咸阳。成吉思汗和元代的皇帝每年两次从北京返回蒙古的家乡时，必须经过八达岭长城，那里也是明朝皇帝北伐的场所。慈禧太后哭着西逃避难，中国第一条铁路奠基仪式，孙中山先生访长城都在这留下了很多历史轶事和旧时记忆。

Badaling Great Wall has witnessed many China's historical events. The First Monarch Qin Shi Huang arrived Jie Shi Mountain, passed Badaling and went to Datong, later to Xianyang near Xi'an in Shaanxi. Genghis Khan and Yuan Dynasty's emperors had to return twice a year to their homeland in Mongolia from Beijing that they must be via Badaling Great Wall, where was also the venue for northward expedition and conquering of Ming's emperors. The tears of crying of Dowager Cixi when she was fleeing westward, the laying ceremony of the first Chinese built railway line and the great founding father of modern China, Dr. Sun Yat-sen's visit have left many and many historical anecdotes and old memories.

居庸关

居庸关位于北京昌平区，距北京市中心 50 公里。名字起自秦朝，据说秦始皇的士兵和大臣修建长城时，他们让罪犯、年轻的士兵和农民工住在那里，所以称之为"徙居庸徒"，意思是"把普通和平庸的人移居在这里"。居庸关现已成为世界最大的关塞。

居庸关由于其特殊的地理位置和险峻的地势，在历史上一直具有重要的战略意义。居庸关有一南一北两个关口，北面的关口一直被称为居庸关。我们今天看到的居庸关是在明朝开元皇帝朱元璋的一个将领徐达的监督下建成的。它是古代老北京城的西北大门。

The Juyongguan Section of Great Wall is in Changping District fifty kilometers to downtown Beijing. It got its name in the Qin Dynasty, it was said that when Qin Shi Huang's soldiers and subjects were building the Great Wall, they put the criminals, young soldiers and migrant workers to live there, so it had been called "xiju yongtu" which meant "Move the Common and Mediocre People Here", and it is also known as the Most Magnificent Pass in the World.

Historically, the Juyongguan Pass has always been strategically important because of its special geographical condition and dangerous landscape. Juyongguan has two passes, one in the south and the other in the north, which the latter has been known as Juyongguan Pass. The pass we see today is the site that has been built under the supervision of Xu Da, a general of Zhu Yuanzhang, the First Emperor of the Ming Dynasty. It was the northwestern gate of ancient Beijing City.

居庸关的两边是陡峭的高山，中间有一条18公里长的深谷。周边有许多青翠的高峰环绕着，鸟儿在这里翱翔和歌唱。所以居庸关一直被称为燕京（古代燕国都城）八景之一。

春秋时期，燕国占领过居庸关。汉代时形成了大规模的关区。南北朝时期居庸关与长城相连。唐朝以后，这一地区有了城堡和堡垒。

明代，居庸关得以重建和扩建。清末由于时局混乱而被遗弃。但是，现在它仍然是人们了解更多军事历史和古代中国文化的一个窗口。

The both sides of the Juyongguan Pass are steep mountains. In the middle, there is a deep valley of a length of 18 kilometers. It is green all round with many high verdant peaks stood. Birds are flying and singing too. So the valley has been known as one of the Eight Great Sights of Yanjing, the capital of the ancient Yan State.

During the Spring and Autumn Period, Yan State had already occupied Juyongguan Pass. In the Han Dynasty, the large scale of the pass area had been formed. Later in the Southern and Northern Dynasties, Juyongguan Pass was linked with the Great Wall. In Tang and some later feudal dynasties, this area had castles and fortresses.

The rebuilding and expansion had been made in the Ming Dynasty. And in late Qing Dynasty, it was abandoned due to chaotic situation of the time. However, now it is still being a window for people who would like to know more about the military history and culture of ancient China.

居庸关的中间，有一个称为"云台"的过街塔基座，意思是"从远处看似乎是在云端"。它修造于1342年到1345年之间，用白色大理石砌成，9.5米高，25米宽，为元代古典建筑风格。在基座中心，有让行人、马匹和马车通过的拱门。拱门上刻有动物、植物和佛的图像。

元朝末年和明朝初年分别建造了三个喇嘛宝塔和一座佛庙，但被大火严重烧毁。现在只留下地基。

南关的土城堡形状像马蹄。战斗期间，敌人因不能逃脱一个隐蔽的城垛而被俘。北部城堡设置了炮位。

在南关和北关城墙边陈列了古代五种明朝大炮。明朝时期是中国制作古代大炮的最佳时期。

In the middle of Juyongguan Pass, there is a cross-street pagoda base foundation called Yuntai, which means "it looks like staying in the clouds when you seeing from afar". It was built in 1342 to 1345, of white marble stones, 9.5 meters high and 25 meters wide and in the classical architectural style of the Yuan Dynasty. At the center of the base foundation, there is an arch doorway for pedestrians, horses and carriages to pass through. It is carved with images of animals, plants and Buddha.

Three Lama Pagodas and a Buddhist Temple had been built in late Yuan Dynasty and early Ming Dynasty respectively, but they were all destroyed by serious damage and great fire. Now just the base foundation is left.

The South Pass' Earthen Castle is shaped like a horse's hoof. During battles, the enemies will be caught inside the Earthen Castle when they are running through a hidden battlement and they can't escape. Emplacements are set up at the North Castle.

The five ancient cannons are being displayed near the walls of South and North Passes. They were from the Ming Dynasty. This period was the best era for making ancient cannons in China.

秦朝时期，有一个叫孟姜女的善良美丽的女孩。一天，她在院子里做家务，突然发现葡萄支架下藏了一个男人。她害怕得想大声叫喊，年轻男子向她挥手请求她帮助："请别喊！救我！我叫范喜良。我在这避难。"当时秦始皇在修建长城，他部署部队去抓年轻的平民男子，帮助完成这项巨大工程。许多平民都累死或饿死。孟姜女同意救他。她知道他是一个帅气博学的绅士。她感觉很爱他，他也爱她。他们相爱后，征得父母的同意，准备结婚。

In the Qin Dynasty, a good-hearted and beautiful girl named Meng Jiang Nv, one day, when she was doing housework in her courtyard, suddenly she discovered a man was hiding below the grape rack. She was so afraid and she wanted to shout aloud, but the young man waved his hands and asked for help, "Don't yell please, and save me! My name is Fan Xiliang. I am here to seek refuge." At that time Emperor Qin Shi Huang was building the Great Wall and he deployed troops to catch civilian young men to help to complete the gigantic project. Many workers were tired or starved to death. Meng Jiang Nv agreed to save him. She knew that he was a handsome and well-learnt gentleman. She had the feeling of adoration of him and he loved the girl too. So in love and they asked for their parents' consent, they were to be married.

婚礼当天，孟家挂满了红灯笼和精美的饰品。客人们高兴地挤在大厅里吃婚宴。天黑时，所有的客人都回家了。范喜良和孟姜女正要进入洞房时，他们听到鸡飞狗吠声。凶恶的士兵冲进他们的房子。士兵什么都没说，只是逮捕了范喜良，把他抓到长城建筑工地做苦工。

孟姜女的心充满无限的悲伤。她非常想念她的丈夫。她想，与其待在家里等丈夫的消息，还不如去施工现场找他。她收拾好行李，向长城出发。

On the day of wedding, red lanterns and beautiful decorations were in Meng's family. Happy guests were crowded in the dining hall. When the darkness came, all the guests returned home. When Fan Xiliang and Meng Jiang Nv wanted to get into their bridal chamber they heard the flying noise of chicken and the barking sound of dogs. The ferocious soldiers entered their house. They didn't say anything, they just arrested Fan in locks. He was transferred to the Great Wall construction site to do harsh labor work.

Heartbreaking sadness fully filled the heart of Meng Jiang Nv. She missed her husband very much. She thought that instead of staying at home to wait for the news of him, she would like to search him in the construction site. She tidied up her baggage and set out to the Great Wall.

一路上，由于地势险峻、天气恶劣，她历经了艰难险阻，但她没哭，也没感到痛苦。爱的精神力量支撑她的身体和心理。她到达了施工现场，但她得在每个小工地挨个寻找。找了很长时间也找不到他。后来，她问一名农民工："范喜良在这里吗？""是的，他在这里，是新来的。"他回答。"他现在哪里？""他已经死了，他的尸体就埋在墙脚下！"不幸的是，这竟然是最后的答案。

就像空中一声惊雷。孟姜女眼前一片黑暗！她突然放声大哭。她凄凉地哭了三天三晚。她的眼泪打动了上天。天空变暗，大风狂作。长城倒了一大段，范喜良的尸体出现了。孟姜女的眼泪淌落在她心爱的丈夫扭曲的脸上！孟姜女终于见到了范喜良，只可惜他却看不见她，因为他被秦始皇杀了。

On the road, she weathered many hardships because of dangerous landscape and harsh climate, but she didn't cry and feel pain. The spirit of love had supported her physically and psychologically. She reached the construction site. But she had still to find him in every small site. For a long time she couldn't find him. At last, she asked a migrant worker, "Is Fan Xiliang here?" "Yes, he is here and is a new comer." He answered. "Where is he now?" "He is dead, and his corpse is buried under the foot of the wall!" Unfortunately, that was the final answer.

It was like a big thunder in the sky. Meng Jiang Nv didn't see anything but darkness! She suddenly burst into tears. She cried mournfully for three whole days and nights. The Heaven was moved by her tears. The sky turned dark and the wind grew strong. A part of the Great Wall was collapsed and the body of Fan Xiliang appeared. The tears of Meng Jiang Nv dropped on the distorted face of her beloved husband! Meng had finally seen Fan Xiliang but he didn't see her, because he was killed by Qin Shi Huang.

长城的防御功能
其实长城是由城堡和堡垒组成。自原始社会后期中国就有了防御性建筑。其预防效果在封建时代得以确认。长城修建于春秋战国时期，最好的城墙是当时楚国（现在的河南省）的方墙。战国时代后期，魏国的西部地区和赵国的漳水地区修建了城墙。当时，这些防御墙在阻止敌人方面发挥了巨大作用。

长城的修建对于秦国领土的建设和扩张至关重要。显然，没有长城，秦国将不得不把庞大的军事力量部署到北部以防止匈奴军队骚扰，再去打败六国统一全国，这样会很疲惫。但有了长城，就不需要那么多士兵守卫边疆，也可以阻挡匈奴的入侵。

The Defense Function of the Great Wall

Actually the Great Wall was formed by castles and fortresses. These defensive constructions had been used since the late primitive society period in China. Their preventive effectiveness was recognized in the feudal era. The rudiment of the Great Wall was appeared in the Spring and Autumn Period, the best part was the Square Wall of Chu State in what now we called Henan Province. When later in the Warring States Period, walls were built in the western part of Wei State and Zhangshui area of Zhao State. At that time these defense walls had provided great functions to bar the enemies.

The construction of the Great Wall was vital for the building up and expansion of the Qin's territory. It isn't difficult to see that without the Great Wall, the Qin would have to deploy large military forces to the north to prevent the Hun army's harassment, and they would be so tired to beat the six states in order to unify the Chinese land. The Wall area just needed much less number of soldiers to guard and it could block the Huns' entering.

赵国的城墙是用土筑的，不是很坚固。赵国军队虽然力量很强大，往往不能驱逐匈奴。当时的赵悼襄王，于公元前 236 年至公元前 224 年在位，他的部队再次失利。李牧将军受命保卫北方。李将军尽力为战士提供最好的食物，以牛肉为主。"当匈奴人想抢劫时，所有的士兵要把所有的牛和马赶进城墙内的安全区，杀死强盗！"他吩咐道。匈奴人来时没找到任何他们想要的东西，于是他们撤回来。但他们仍然不能打败野蛮的敌军。几年后，李将军选了最好的战车、战马和最强的士兵并训练他们。最后他们打败了匈奴人和其他一些北方部落。

The Great Wall of Zhao State was built of earth but not quite strong. The Zhao's army often failed to expel the Huns though their forces were quite powerful. At the time of Zhao Dao Xiang Emperor (reigned 236 BC – 224 BC), his forces had failed again. General Li Mu was ordered to defend the north. Li provided the best possible food for the soldiers, beef was the main diet. "When the Huns want to loot, all the soldiers have to make all the cattle and horses into safe area of the Wall, and kill the looters!" He commanded. The Huns didn't find anything they wanted when they came, so they fled back. But they still couldn't defeat the barbaric army after all. A few years later, Li chose the best chariots, war horses and tough soldiers, and trained them. At last they defeated the Huns and other northern tribes.

有个著名的故事是关于西周王妃褒姒的。她很受人尊敬，但从来没有人见她笑过。周幽王尝试过很多方法想让她笑，但他一次次失败了。一位狡诈的朝廷官员虢石父前来进谏："在烽火台上点火愚弄那些诸侯，说不定这样王妃就笑了。"那天晚上，周幽王和王妃的马车到达骊山脚下，周幽王下达了命令。一瞬间，熊熊火焰照亮了天空，诸侯迅速派部队赶到骊山。果然，褒姒大笑了。后来，周幽王又重复他的笑话。公元前771年，犬戎（当时的一个少数民族）组成一支反叛军抗议西周。国王紧急下令烽火台放火，但因诸侯都没有赶来而战败。

The famous story is told about Baosi, Queen of the Western Zhou Dynasty. She was highly honored, yet she never cracked a smile. King You tried many ways to put a smile on her face, but he failed over and over again. Guo Shifu, a treacherous court official, came and offered advice: "Set the beacon tower on fire and fool your sovereign rulers." That night, the carriage of the King and Queen reached Lishan Mountain and gave the order. In a split second, the flames of the fire lit up the sky and the sovereign rulers moved their troops to Lishan Mountain. Sure enough, Queen Baosi burst into laughter. Later, King You repeated his joke. In 771 BC, Quan Rong (a then ethnic group) staged an armed rebellion against the Western Zhou Dynasty. King You urgently ordered the beacon tower set on fire, but all the sovereign rulers did not come and he was defeated.

口述题

1. 中国四大发明是什么？
2. 你去过万里长城吗？你对万里长城有什么了解？

Questions

1. What are the four great inventions of China?
2. Have you ever been to the Great Wall? What do you know about the Great Wall?

学习网站

1. 万里长城·八达岭（http://www.badaling.cn/）
2. CHINA HIGHLIGHTS（https://www.chinahighlights.com/travelguide/culture/four-great-invention.htm）